OVER THE RIM

Parley P. Pratt, 1850. Daguerreotype by Marsena Cannon. Copy photograph by
Nelson B. Wadsworth.

Over the Rim

The Parley P. Pratt Exploring Expedition

to

Southern Utah, 1849–1850

William B. Smart and Donna T. Smart, Editors

Utah State University Press
Logan, Utah

Utah State University Press
Logan, Utah 84322–7200

Typography by WolfPack
Cover design by Michelle Sellers
Front cover illustrations from Clarence E. Dutton, *Atlas to Accompany the Monograph on the Tertiary History of the Grand Cañon District* (Washington: U.S. Government Printing Office, 1882; reprint, Santa Barbara: Peregrine Smith, 1977).

Library of Congress Cataloging-in-Publication Data

Over the Rim : the Parley P. Pratt exploring expedition to Southern Utah, 1849-50 / William B. Smart and Donna T. Smart, editors.
      p. cm.
   Includes bibliographical references (p.) and index.
   ISBN 0-87421-282-0
   ISBN 0-87421-281-2 (pbk.)
   1. Utah—Discovery and exploration. 2. Mormons—Utah—History—19th cen-
   tury. 3. Pratt, Parley P. (Parley Parker), 1807-1857. I. Smart, William B.
   (William Buckwalter), 1922- II. Smart, Donna Toland, 1923-F826.O84 1997
      979.2'01—dc21
                              99-6764
                               CIP

CONTENTS

Maps

PREFACE

Among many who helped, one man is chiefly responsible for this book. He is—or was—William Henrie. A desire to know better this great-great-grandfather led to examination of the journals kept on the Southern Exploring Expedition of 1849–1850, of which he was a member. Henrie left no account of that adventure, but perhaps journals kept by others would tell something about him? They do, but not much. He is mentioned four times. The roster of the expedition lists him as a member of the Fourth Ten. The list of contributors to meet expenses tells us he gave five dollars. Isaac Haight's journal reports that on January 3, at the present site of Parowan, "camp met at 7 ocl P.M. Singing Prayer by Br Henry." And on March 17, in the south end of Juab Valley, two weeks from home, Robert Campbell's journal records, "fa Henry leaves his weak ox with the Indians, gives it to them."

That's not much. But examination of the journals in search of William Henrie led to a paper presented to the Mormon History Association in 1992 and published in the *Utah Historical Quarterly,* spring 1994. And it led to the conviction that these remarkable journals deserved to be published in full in their original spelling, punctuation, and grammar. This we have attempted to do, along with an effort to place them in context of other exploration and travel in the region, the land itself, and what has resulted from the expedition.

So, first acknowledgment and thanks must go to those who made this book possible, the journal-keepers themselves. Other reminiscences were written years later, but the contemporary journals were four. Most detailed and accurate, and therefore valuable, is that of Robert Campbell, official clerk of the expedition. Thanks to cooperation of the staff of the Archives, Historical Department of the Church of Jesus Christ of Latter-day Saints, we were privileged to work from the original holograph that resides there. The Archives also houses typescript copies of the journals of John C. Armstrong and John Brown as well as holographs of various papers of the expedition, including financial accounts, letters, and, of course, the official report to the Legislative Assembly. The original holograph of Isaac Haight's journal is in the Henry E. Huntington Library, San Marino, California. All were made fully available to us.

Special thanks to W. Randall Dixon and William W. Slaughter of the LDS Church Historical Department; Dixon for help in locating obscure materials, Slaughter for help in providing archival photographs to accompany biographies of expedition members. Cooperation was also unfailing from staffs of the Utah State Historical Society Library; Special Collections, Brigham Young University Library; Western Americana Collection, University of Utah Library; the Henry E. Huntington Library; and the small library in the Territorial Capitol Museum in Fillmore, Utah.

The Southern Exploring Expedition is treated briefly in a number of histories of Utah and the LDS Church, but the only previous examination in depth is a master's thesis by Rick J. Fish, Brigham Young University, December 1992. We found his work useful and acknowledge it with thanks.

Others helped. Lavoid Leavitt, St. George, indefatigable researcher of historic trails, guided us over the route the expedition followed from the time they crossed over the Great Basin rim into the Virgin River country until they exited it at Mountain Meadows. Alvah Matheson, nonagenarian virtual human encyclopedia of Iron County history, guided us through that region, including location of signatures carved into the rocks by the exploring company. With the late historian C. Gregory Crampton, we followed each foot of the Spanish Trail traversed by the expedition. James E. Bowns, Southern Utah University professor of biology and range ecology, was invaluable in identifying plants described by Campbell's journal, and archaeologist Mark Stuart was able to describe their use by Indians, prehistoric to the present.

John R. Alley, executive editor of the Utah State University Press, has been unfailing in his support of the project and his counsel in how to accomplish it. His close attention to detail has done much to improve the product, as has his own expertise in western history and geography. Thanks to Tyler Leary for meticulous copy editing, to J M. Heslop for generously photocopying many of the portraits and other illustrations in the book, and to Chantze Kin and Michael Spooner for preparing the maps.

Finally, though, thanks to Parley P. Pratt himself, to his officers and journal-keepers, and to the unsung members of the expedition—including William Henrie—for their fortitude, dedication, and grace under the harshest conditions. We feel honored to have known them, and to share their stories.

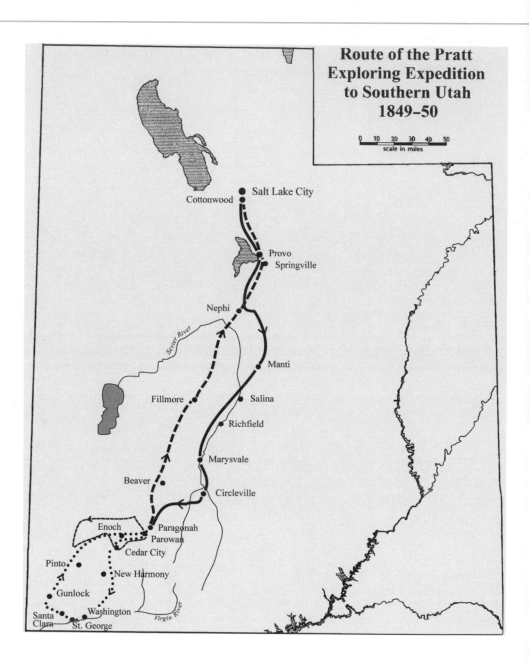

Route of the Pratt Exploring Expedition to Southern Utah 1849–50

scale in miles
0 10 20 30 40 50

Salt Lake City
Cottonwood

Provo
Springville

Nephi

Sevier River

Manti

Fillmore   Salina

Richfield

Marysvale

Beaver

Circleville

Enoch   Paragonah
               Parowan
          Cedar City

Pinto
          New Harmony

Gunlock

Santa   Washington
Clara   St. George   Virgin River

INTRODUCTION

Brigham Young's accomplishment in bringing his 1847 Mormon Pioneer Company across 1,100 miles of prairie, mountain, and desert to Salt Lake Valley without death or serious accident required leadership, planning, competence, cooperation—and sacrifice. But as a demonstration of those qualities it pales by comparison with his accomplishment in the next two decades of bringing to the valley in organized companies seventy thousand other Mormon converts from the eastern and southern United States and Europe. Even that was far from enough. There remained the challenge of finding places for all these immigrants to live, getting them there, and weaving them into the fabric of what was at one time a vast inland Mormon empire.

This book is the eyewitness account of a little-noticed but important part of the latter effort. In its pages will be found abundant evidence of the qualities demanded by Mormon pioneering, as well as the human weakness and questionable judgment that sometimes plagued it.

The land to which the nineteenth century Moses led his chosen people was harsh: little rain; thin, often-alkali soil; 95 percent of the land mountainous or desert unsuitable for habitation. With the nearest supporting civilization more than a thousand miles away to the east and nearly that far to the west, it was going to take a special kind of people to survive here.

But there were compensations. Out of those mountains came streams of clear water that, the Mormons soon found, could soften the hard-baked soil and bring forth sustenance. The land was vast: in an area that included most of the Great Basin and Colorado Plateau and stretched north in the Snake River drainage as far as the Lemhi River and south to the lower Virgin and across the desert as far as San Bernardino, there was room enough. And because the region was so harsh and remote, it contained no American or European competitors. Except for Indian tribes that the Mormons would ultimately push aside, there were no neighbors to trouble or

1

be troubled by. For a people whose peculiar beliefs, economic aggressiveness, and political cohesion had raised opposition that drove them from the church's birthplace of upper New York to Ohio and then, in turn, to Missouri, Illinois, and finally the Great Salt Lake, that was no small thing.

The heart of what would become the Mormon empire is the Great Basin. Gloria Griffen Cline in her book *Exploring the Great Basin* describes it well as "the land of interior drainage."[1] Stretching five hundred miles west from Utah's Wasatch Range and high plateaus to the Sierra Nevada and eight hundred miles north and south between latitudes 34 and 42 degrees, the Great Basin encompasses some 210,000 square miles. Geologists include it in the Basin and Range Province for its thirty-five north-to-south mountain ranges and the alluvial valleys below.[2] Near the eastern edge, the Great Salt Lake lies as a shallow, salty remnant of the vast Lake Bonneville that until some fifteen thousand years ago covered most of western Utah.

Except where high mountain ranges trap moisture, the Great Basin is arid country. Vegetation ranges from the creosote, yucca, cactus, and mesquite of southern areas to broad expanses of sagebrush and shadscale at mid-elevations, pinyon and juniper on foothills and in higher valleys, and pine, fir, and spruce on the highest mountains. Human life was hard in such country, but Native Americans had roamed the area for ten thousand years or more. When Brigham Young arrived with his Mormon band, Shoshones occupied the northern part of the basin, while Gosiutes lived in western, Pahvant Utes central, and Southern Paiutes southwestern Utah. Northern Utes and Southern Utes roamed the Colorado Plateau but spilled into the basin's eastern valleys.[3] The more fortunate clustered around such water holes as Utah, Sevier, and Little Salt Lakes in Utah and Pyramid and Humboldt Lakes in Nevada, where they supplemented their diets with fish and waterfowl. The Utes with their horses more effectively hunted large game animals— and some achieved a greater measure of prosperity by capturing and

1. Gloria Griffen Cline, *Exploring the Great Basin* (Norman: University of Oklahoma Press, 1963), 3ff.
2. William Lee Stokes, *Geology of Utah* (Salt Lake City: Utah Museum of Natural History and Utah Geological and Mineral Survey, 1986), 2.
3. Catherine S. and Don D. Fowler, "Notes on the History of the Southern Paiutes and Western Shoshonis," *Utah Historical Quarterly* 39 (spring 1971): 89.

trading slaves along the Spanish Trail. But for many, if not most, life in the Great Basin depended on rabbits and other rodents, birds, insects, pine nuts, and the great variety of plants they had learned to eat. Anthropologists and ethnographers have never been able to estimate with any precision the Indian population of the Great Basin prior to arrival of white settlers. One thing they do know—which the journals in this book confirm—is that many Indian bands had been severely decimated by white men's diseases before Brigham Young arrived.

This, then, was the place the Mormons would put down roots to stay. Samuel Brannan, who in 1846 had shepherded a shipload of Mormons around Cape Horn to California, tried to persuade Brigham that California would be a far more desirable place to settle. So did some veterans of the Mormon Battalion, recruited during the Mexican War, who had marched from Fort Leavenworth to California. Brigham paid no attention. "God has appointed this place for the gathering of His Saints," he declared. "We have been kicked out of the frying-pan into the fire, out of the fire into the middle of the floor, and here we are and here we will stay. God . . . will temper the elements for the good of His Saints; He will rebuke the frost and the sterility of the soil, and the land shall become fruitful. Brethren, go to, now, and plant out your fruit seeds. . . . We have the finest climate, the best water, and the purest air that can be found on the earth; there is no healthier climate anywhere."[4]

But for the Saints to stay in this appointed place, Brigham had to learn what was out there. Where in this vast, to him largely unknown region could be found the right combinations of water, soil, timber, grazing, building stone, and crop-producing climate that would make settlement possible?

Others had been here before, of course, but none with the same goal as Brigham's—that of building permanent homes. A few Spanish traders, slavers, or miners may have penetrated the Great Basin and/or the Colorado Plateau in the seventeenth and eighteenth centuries. Father Escalante of the 1776 Domínguez-Escalante expedition, which tried to establish a trail from Santa Fe

---

4. Sermon of February 4, 1849, as reported by James S. Brown, *Life of a Pioneer* (Salt Lake City, 1900), 121–22. Quoted in Leonard J. Arrington, *Great Basin Kingdom* (Lincoln: University of Nebraska Press, 1958), 439.

to Monterey, left a remarkable account, describing in some detail the Uintah Basin, Utah Valley, and much of the route Brigham wanted to establish to southern California. The expedition's cartographer, Bernardo de Miera y Pacheco, made the first maps of the area, reasonably accurate ones for the times, though with the major mistake of having the Green River flow into Sevier Lake. But neither the report nor the map was available to Brigham Young.

The mountain men who trapped much of the area for beaver in the two decades before the Mormon arrival in Salt Lake Valley acquired extensive knowledge of the region. But, except for the rambling, somewhat incoherent description Jim Bridger gave the Mormon Pioneer Company at his fort in southwestern Wyoming in 1847 and brief conversations along the trail with Moses Harris and Miles Goodyear, Brigham benefitted little from their knowledge. Few left contemporary written records. Peter Skene Ogden kept diaries and wrote reports back to his Hudson Bay Company employers about the region, and the redoubtable Jedediah Smith left an invaluable record of his two trips the length of the Great Basin en route to and from California in 1826 and 1827. But there is no evidence that Brigham saw either man's report.

Others who knew parts of the Great Basin well were travelers on the Spanish Trail. During the 1830s and 1840s traders from Santa Fe drove mule trains loaded with woolen goods over the trail to California and returned with huge herds of horses and mules, up to four thousand at a time. Of the trail's 1,120 miles, some 450 crossed what is now Utah, entering the area south of the La Sal Mountains and looping in a great arc as far north as Castle Valley before exiting near the Arizona-Nevada-Utah border.[5] Of the comparatively few reports written by travelers on that trail, apparently none were known to Brigham Young.

Others came. In 1833–1834, Capt B. L. E. Bonneville, on leave from the U.S. Army, led a large, military-style expedition into the region. The party split, Bonneville going north to the Snake River and Oregon. His lieutenant, Joseph Walker, led a forty-man party to explore the Great Salt Lake region, where they killed buffalo and loaded up on the meat, then struck west through the heart of the Great Basin to reach California, following the

---

5. C. Gregory Crampton and Steven K. Madsen, *In Search of the Spanish Trail* (1952; reprint, Salt Lake City: Gibbs-Smith Publishing Co., 1994).

Humboldt River that became so essential to the California Trail. Washington Irving's book, *The Adventures of Captain Bonneville*, describes the region, but the book wasn't published until 1868. In 1841, John Bidwell and John B. Bartleson, without a guide but determined to reach California, cut the first wagon tracks through the Great Basin. From Soda Springs in what is now Idaho they made their way down the Bear River, around the north end of the Great Salt Lake to the life-saving spring at the base of Pilot Peak on the present Utah-Nevada border, and on to the Humboldt. They learned much of the thirsty character of the Great Basin, but Bidwell's description of it would not see publication in time for the Mormons to use it.

One whose knowledge may have been useful was the Catholic missionary Father De Smet, who had wandered through part of the region in 1841. He wrote of a meeting with Brigham Young on November 19, 1846, at Winter Quarters on the Missouri River near Omaha, where the exiled Saints, after crossing Iowa from Nauvoo, were waiting out the winter before pushing on to the Great Salt Lake. "They asked me a thousand questions about the regions I had explored," he wrote, "and the valley [Great Salt Lake Valley] which I have just described to you pleased them greatly from the account I gave them. [He had not seen it but had learned about it from others.] *Was that what determined them? I would not dare assert it. They are there!*"[6] His advice may have been helpful but certainly didn't "determine them." The decision to settle in the Great Basin had already been made. And finally there was Lansford Hastings, the California promoter who, guided by mountain man Jim Clyman, rode east across the Salt Desert in 1846 and persuaded immigrants to take his shortcut to California, with disastrous consequences to that year's Donner party. Brigham had access to Hastings's wildly creative *Emigrants' Guide to Oregon and California*, but found it of little use.

What Brigham did have, and had carefully studied, was the report of John Charles Frémont's second expedition. In the mid-nineteenth century, the country was caught up in the conviction that its destiny was to Americanize the continent all the way to the Pacific coast and as far north as it could manage. Foremost apostle of Manifest Destiny in Congress was the powerful senator Thomas

---

6. B. H. Roberts, *A Comprehensive History of the Church of Jesus Christ of Latter-day Saints* (Salt Lake City: Deseret News Press, 1930), 3:85.

Hart Benton, who also happened to be father-in-law to a young
army officer named Frémont. Five western exploring expeditions
led by Frémont resulted, ranging from brilliant to disastrous. From
Brigham's point of view, the second expedition was most important. In 1843, guided by Kit Carson, Frémont crossed South Pass
and descended the Bear River to Great Salt Lake. There he hoped
to find the secret of the Buenaventura, the storied river that flowed
west to the Pacific. Of the Great Salt Lake he wrote: "It was generally supposed it has no visible outlet; but among the trappers,
including those in my own camp, were many who believed that
somewhere on its surface was a terrible whirlpool, through which
its waters found their way to the ocean by some subterranean communication." That Frémont himself believed in the existence of a
waterway to the Pacific is clear from subsequent entries. In southern Oregon he wrote: "In our journey across the desert, Mary's
lake, and the famous Buenaventura river, were two points on which
I relied to recruit the animals, and repose the party. Forming,
agreeably to the best maps in my possession, a connected water
line from the Rocky mountains to the Pacific Ocean, I felt no other
anxiety than to pass safely across the intervening desert to the
banks of the Buenaventura." And a few days later, at the edge of
the Black Rock Desert in northwestern Nevada: "We were evidently
on the verge of the desert which had been reported to us; and the
appearance of the country was so forbidding, that I was afraid to
enter it, and determined to bear away to the southward, keeping
close along the mountains, in the full expectation of reaching the
Buenaventura river."[7]

He didn't reach it, of course; the closest thing to the
"Buenaventura" was the muddy Humboldt River, which heads not
in the Rockies but the East Humboldt and Ruby Mountains of
northeastern Nevada and ends not at the Pacific but in the salty
marshes of the Humboldt Sink in west-central Nevada. By the time
Frémont had circled the Great Basin, traveling through southern
Oregon and western Nevada before crossing the Sierra Nevada to
California, crossing the Mojave Desert to the springs at Las Vegas,
up the Virgin, which he called "the most dreary river I have ever

---

7. See John Charles Frémont, *Report of the Exploring Expedition to the Rocky Mountains in the
    Year 1842 and to Oregon and North California in the Years 1843–44* (28th Cong. [1845], 2d
    sess., House Exec. Doc. 166), 106, 205, 214.

seen,"[8] up the Santa Clara ("prettily wooded with sweet cotton-wood trees"), to Mountain Meadows ("rich in bunch grass, and fresh with numerous springs of clear water, all refreshing and delightful to look upon"), across the mountains to the Sevier and on north to Utah Lake—by the time he had seen all that—he knew the truth. There at Utah Lake he finally acknowledged what the mountain men had long known: there was no Rio Buenaventura. Waters of the vast region between the Wasatch Mountains and the Sierra Nevada had no outlet. The region was a great basin; the map he submitted with his report so named it.

His findings were important to the Mormons. After a mob murdered Joseph Smith, the church's founder and leader, in the Carthage Jail on June 27, 1844, it became increasingly clear the Latter-day Saints had to abandon their city of Nauvoo on the banks of the Mississippi and, in fact, leave the state of Illinois. Carefully the leaders studied where to go. Frémont's report, published in 1845, was reprinted in part in the Mormon journals *Nauvoo Neighbor* and *Millenial Star*. Brigham Young and his senior advisors spent hours studying the report and its map; on December 20 Franklin D. Richards, in a meeting in the unfinished Nauvoo Temple, read it aloud to the Quorum of the Twelve Apostles.[9] Its descriptions of the area's vastness, its mountain streams and fertile soil, and particularly its emptiness confirmed a decision that had already been made. Despite speculation about going to Texas or Oregon or Vancouver Island, Joseph Smith as early as August 6, 1842, recorded in his history, "I prophesied that the Saints would continue to suffer much affliction and would be driven to the Rocky Mountains. . . . [S]ome of you will live to go and assist in making settlements and build cities and see the Saints become a mighty people in the midst of the Rocky Mountains."[10] And on June 23, 1844, when Joseph fled Nauvoo, before returning to his martyrdom in the Carthage Jail, he sent back word by Porter Rockwell to bring horses for his escape and "be ready to start for the great Basin in the Rocky Mountains."[11] Men of the Mormon Battalion were told in August 1846, before

---

8   John C. Frémont, *The Exploring Expedition to the Rocky Mountains* (1845; reprint, Washington, D.C.: Smithsonian Institution Press, 1988), 258.

9.   Roberts, *Comprehensive History*, 2:521.

10.   Joseph Smith, *History of the Church of Jesus Christ of Latter-day Saints* (Salt Lake City: Deseret News Press, 1949), 5:85.

11.   Ibid., 6:548.

beginning their two-thousand-mile march to southern California, that the Mormons would settle in the Great Basin.

So they came, 143 men, 3 women, and 2 boys in the Pioneer Company of 1847. With all they had learned from Frémont and others, they came with an attitude best expressed by William Clayton in his trail journal. After hearing a negative report about the Great Basin from mountain man Moses Harris, whom they met at South Pass, and a "very imperfect and irregular" description from Jim Bridger two days later, Clayton wrote: "We shall know more about things and have a better understanding when we have seen the country ourselves."[12] Brigham lost no time in doing just that, declaring that he intended to have "every hole and corner from the Bay of San Francisco to the Hudson Bay known to us."[13] Within weeks, explorers looking for the best combinations of soil, water, timber, grazing, and mill sites had searched out valleys to the north as far as Cache Valley, south to Utah Valley, southwest to Cedar Valley, and west to Tooele Valley. Settlement quickly followed. Within days of his arrival in the valley in September 1847, Perrigrine Sessions went a few miles north to find pasturage for the church's cattle herd and established Sessions Settlement, later to be renamed Bountiful. Provo was established in March 1849, Tooele later the same year, and Manti that fall after the Ute chief Walker (the version of Wakara, his Ute name, that the settlers usually used) invited the Mormons to settle Sanpete Valley. Brigham personally chose the site of Ogden in 1849 and sent settlers there the next year. Brigham City followed in 1851.

But Brigham was nothing if not expansionist. For the hordes of converts he knew would gather to Zion—seventy thousand of them, it turned out, by the coming of the railroad in 1869—he had to look to settlement far beyond the Wasatch Front. Pushing out settlements to far places would establish the borders of the Mormon empire and, he mistakenly hoped, keep outsiders away. And there was the matter of an outlet to the sea.

---

12.   George D. Smith, ed., *An Intimate Chronicle: The Journals of William Clayton* (Salt Lake City: Signature Books, 1995), 353.
13.   Journal History of the Church of Jesus Christ of Latter-day Saints, chronological collection of clippings and other information, typescript and microfilm, Archives of the Historical Department, Church of Jesus Christ of Latter-day Saints, Salt Lake City, July 20, 1847 (hereafter cited as Journal History).

Just when he conceived the idea of a Mormon corridor to southern California is uncertain. But almost from the time of arrival in Salt Lake Valley he was looking in that direction. In August 1847 a party of Mormon Battalion veterans, some of whom were present when gold was discovered at Sutter's Mill, had returned to the valley by way of the California Trail along the Humboldt. Among them was Jefferson Hunt. By mid-November Hunt, with a small party, was on the way to southern California, sent to bring back seeds, tree cuttings, and livestock. Relying in part on Frémont's description of the route and intercepting the Spanish Trail in central Utah, they completed the task and returned by mid-February—though with only one bull and one hundred cows of the forty bulls and two hundred cows he had obtained in California. A month later, on March 21, twenty-five Mormon Battalion veterans led by Captain H. G. Boyle left San Diego for Salt Lake Valley, bringing not only one hundred mules but also seeds and cuttings in a wagon that cut the first wheel tracks on the Spanish Trail.

The knowledge these men brought of what became the Southern Route was useful, but for settlement of the country to the south much more specific information was needed. As early as March 9, 1849, in a long letter to Orson Pratt, who was presiding over missionaries in Great Britain, Brigham declared his intentions: "We hope soon to explore the valleys three hundred miles south and also the country as far as the Gulf of California with a view to settlement and to acquiring a seaport."[14] By November of that year he was ready to act, and with his control of the Legislative Assembly events moved quickly. At his request, the assembly in its November session voted to commission Parley P. Pratt to assemble an exploring party of fifty men, outfit it with the necessary wagons and teams, raise the needed finances, and secure the provisions. All this Pratt was instructed while he sat there as a member. The expedition would be called the Southern Exploring Company. Its instructions were to explore south to the rim of the Great Basin, over the rim to the Virgin River country, and on to the springs called Las Vegas.

Pratt's account of those days says much about his own energy and enterprise as well as the effort required to put down Mormon roots in Salt Lake Valley:

_____

14. Journal History, March 9, 1849.

I devoted the fore part of the summer [of 1849] to farming; but, my crop failing, I commenced in July to work a road up the rugged canyon of Big Canyon Creek [today's Parleys Canyon]. I had the previous year explored the canyon for that purpose and also a beautiful park [now called Parleys Park], and passes from Salt Lake City to Weber River eastward, in a more southern and less rugged route than the pioneer entrance to the valley [the route followed in 1847 and subsequently over Big and Little Mountains and down Emigration Canyon].

I soon so far completed my road as to be able to obtain a large amount of fuel and timber. In November I ceased operations in the canyon and broke up my mountain camp and returned to the city.

I now received a commission from the Governor and Legislative Assembly of the State of Deseret to raise fifty men, with the necessary teams and outfit, and go at their head on an exploring tour to the southward.[15]

Selecting and recruiting that many men and accomplishing everything else requested would seem to be a formidable task. Incredibly, by November 17, barely a week after his assignment, Parley reported that except for a couple more wagons and some provisions he was ready to go.[16] That was a little premature. Of the $238.50 he raised to finance the expedition, $186.02 was donated at a meeting in the bowery the following day.[17] Two days later, Parley met with the First Presidency and received final instructions, including that they would go no farther than Las Vegas and be back in the spring. As a final act, the First Presidency blessed Parley and David Fullmer with safety for the journey.[18]

By November 23 the explorers had gathered at the recently completed adobe house of John Brown in what is now Murray. "Our company," Pratt reported, "had 12 wagons, 1 carriage, 24 yokes of cattle, 7 beeves [to be killed for food], number of

---

15. Parley P. Pratt (son), ed., *Autobiography of Parley P. Pratt* (1938; reprint, Salt Lake City: Deseret Book Co., 1985), 336–38. With fees of fifty cents for a one-animal or seventy-five cents for a two-animal wagon; ten cents per draught, pack, or saddle animal; five cents per head for loose stock; and one cent per sheep, Pratt's Golden Pass toll road was used by some six thousand emigrants the summer of 1850, earning approximately $1,500. With some of those funds, Pratt left the following March for Chile to open Mormon missionary work in South America, and for the next decade the road was used only sporadically.
16. Journal History, November 17, 1849.
17. Ibid., November 18, 1849.
18. Ibid., November 20, 1849.

[riding] horses and mules, 38. Average in flour, 150 lbs. To each man; besides crackers, bread and meal. One brass field piece; firearms; ammunition in proportion."[19] As John Brown's journal recorded, "We were all well armed and quite a quantity of Indian trade &c."

It was a diverse group of men, many selected for special skills. William W. Phelps, a surveyor and engineer, who was made topographical engineer; Ephraim Green, chief gunner, whose wagon would pull a brass cannon; Robert Campbell, an experienced secretary and clerk, whose wagon would carry the odometer; Dimick Huntington, Indian interpreter. John Brown, William Henrie, and Joseph Matthews, hunters with Brigham's Pioneer Company of 1847, would perform the same service on the Southern Expedition. Besides these three, five other members of the Southern Exploring Company—Rufus Allen, Sterling Driggs, Benjamin Stewart, William Vance, and William Wadsworth—had entered Salt Lake Valley in July 1847. The company's oldest man was Samuel Gould, seventy-one; the youngest, Alexander Lemon, eighteen; the average age about thirty-five. Pratt was forty-two.

At the November 23 meeting, the company voted to organize as had the Pioneer Company of 1847, with a captain of fifty and five captains of ten. By unanimous vote, Parley P. Pratt was named president of the expedition, with William W. Phelps and David Fullmer counselors and John Brown captain of fifty. The full roster as organized November 23 was as follows:

Parley P. Pratt, president; William W. Phelps and David Fullmer, counselors; John Brown, captain; Robert Campbell, clerk; W. W. Phelps, engineer

First Ten	Second Ten	Third Ten
Isaac Haight, captain	Joseph Matthews, captain	Joseph Horne, captain
Parley P. Pratt	John Brown	Alexander Wright
William Wadsworth	Nathan Tanner	David Fullmer
Rufus Allen	Sterling G. Driggs	William Brown
Chauncey West	Homer Duncan	George Nebeker
Dan Jones	William Matthews	Benjamin F. Stewart
Hial K. Gay	John D. Holladay	James Farrer
George B. Matson	Schuyler Jennings	Henry Heath

---

19. Pratt, *Autobiography*, 339.

Samuel Gould   John H. Bankhead   Seth B. Tanner
William P. Vance   Robert M. Smith   Alexander Lemon

Fourth Ten   *Fifth Ten*
Ephraim Green, captain   Josiah Arnold, captain
William W. Phelps   Christopher Williams
Charles Hopkins   Stephen Taylor
William S. Willis   Dimick B. Huntington
Andrew Blodgett   John C. Armstrong
William Henrie   Isaac B. Hatch
Peter Dustin   Jonathan Packer
Thomas E. Ricks
Robert Campbell
Isaac Brown

The vacancy of three men in the Fifth Ten was to be filled by recruits from the new Sanpitch settlement in Sanpete Valley. Actually, five men, Madison D. Hambleton, Gardner G. Potter, Edward Everett, John Lowry, Jr., and Sylvester Hewlitt, joined there, but two of the explorers would be sent home after reaching the Little Salt Lake, keeping the expedition at fifty men as planned.

So, outfitted, provisioned, organized, and in high spirits, they started. By the time they returned, the men with wagons, according to their amazingly accurate odometer, would have traveled 526 miles. Half the party would have ridden an additional 190 miles on horseback to explore the Virgin River region. The trip would be more arduous than they imagined—the snow deeper, the temperatures colder (as low as 30 degrees below zero), some of the terrain more rugged, the oxen less able to keep their strength on what grass they managed to find under the snow. Because of failing teams, dwindling supplies, and the unpromising character of the 120 miles of desert between what are now St. George and Las Vegas, they cut short their trip, going no farther south than the Virgin. On the return trip, dangerously low on supplies and bogged down by heavy snowstorms, half of the party remained snowbound for seven weeks at the present site of Fillmore in Pavant Valley, while the other half mounted the strongest horses and mules and pushed ahead toward Utah Valley and safety. Even that strategy almost failed. The mounted party ran out of food and were saved when Parley Pratt and Chauncey West rode ahead fifty miles the last two days to reach Fort Utah and send back a rescue party.

But despite obstacles and hardships, described matter-of-factly but compellingly in their journals, they completed their mission, bringing back to Brigham Young detailed knowledge of the country that led to much of its settlement. On his dash home Parley carried with him the expedition's official report, chiefly a summary of the journal kept by the company's clerk, Robert Campbell. During two days in the snowbound camp near present-day Fillmore, Parley dictated it to Campbell, who wrote it, as his journal reports, on a cold, snowy night in an open wagon "laying on my belly & a hundred other positions." Parley reached Salt Lake City on February 1, reported to Brigham, and submitted the official report to the Territorial Legislative Assembly February 5.

The report lists at least twenty-six desirable locations for settlement. To almost all of them, Brigham sent colonists, many within two or three years. It recommended, for example, Peteetneet Creek for a settlement that would become Payson. Yohab (Juab) Valley was "in every way calculated for a city Settlement." Nephi was settled there. Parley noted the presence of coal near the present site of Salina, the rich bottomlands on the Sevier where Richfield would be built, and reported that river was "apparently navigable, for small steamers." Those who know the Sevier must conclude he was thinking of *very* small steamers. He was less than enthusiastic about the Virgin River country, calling it "a wide expanse of chaotic matter . . . a country in ruins," but noted three thousand and four thousand acres of desirable land in the twin valleys where St. George and Washington would be built. Of the expansive meadows, good soil, cedar, and tall pines in the present area of Beaver, he wrote: "This is an excellent place for an extensive settlement." And so it went. In the official report, printed in full in the final chapter of this volume, where Parley recommended settlements we have inserted the names of cities and towns built there, together with the dates of their founding.

The most immediate and direct result of the expedition's findings was the dispatching of a mission to settle Parowan and subsequently Cedar City to exploit the iron ore in the region. Of all the places he saw, Parley was most enthusiastic about Cedar Valley. He describes its "soil mostly black loam very rich," streams running out of the mountains "nearly level with the surface of the ground" and easily used for irrigation, a delightful climate that in what must have been an unusual December was "frosty but not extreme . . . snowy but not much. But the best of all," he wrote, "remains to be told. Near this large body of good land on the southwestern borders are thousands of acres of cedar constituting an almost inexhaustible supply of fuel. . . . In the centre of these forests rises a hill of the richest Iron ore, specimens of which are herewith produced." Cedar Valley, together with Little Salt Lake Valley to the north, he wrote, "constitutes a field of rich resources capable of sustaining and employing 50,000 inhabitants at present, and 100,000 eventually. . . . Taken as a whole we were soon convinced this was the 'firstrate good' place we were sent to find as a location for our next Southern colony." Brigham was not one to delay; within the year 119 men, 310 women, and 18 children were called and on their way to the Iron Mission, arriving to establish Parowan January 13, 1851. From Parowan many moved the following year to found Cedar City, closer to the iron ore.

Another direct result was the settlement of Fillmore, intended to be the territorial capital. Based on Parley's report, Brigham had the Territorial Assembly create Millard County on October 4, 1851, and later that month led a group of lawmakers to select a site for the capitol building. The first settlers to arrive camped the first night precisely where Parley's snowbound wagon company had dug in on Chalk Creek to spend part of the winter, and by February 1852, just two years after those miserable shelters were dug, had built thirty houses and a schoolhouse, all arranged as a fort.

A third early result was the calling of missionaries to the Indians in southern Utah. Parley's report and especially Campbell's journal speak of the friendliness of the Indians, particularly along Ash Creek and the Santa Clara, where Indians pleaded with the explorers to come settle with them and teach them Mormon farming methods. Brigham responded, sending John D. Lee and others in 1852 to establish Harmony on Ash Creek, the first settlement over the rim of the Great Basin. Other missionaries arrived in 1854, built Fort Harmony, and from there Jacob Hamblin and others moved down to establish Santa Clara, where they would teach and assist the Indians. Several towns in the now-booming Virgin River basin stem from that small beginning.

But while the official report led to the practical results of the Southern Exploring Expedition, the human drama, the interplay of relations among the explorers and between them and the Indians, a sense of their immense labor and suffering and of the spiritual strength and commitment that sustained that effort, can only come from the journals. While other members of the exploration wrote reminiscences years later, the only known contemporary journals are collated here. There are four of them, by men of widely differing temperament. Most important is that of Robert Lang Campbell, twenty-four years old at the time he was elected secretary and clerk of the expedition. Meticulously, with an odometer attached to his wagon, he recorded to a quarter of a mile the distance traveled each day. He recorded daily temperatures, often both morning and night. He recorded the width and depth of streams, the nature of soil, the abundance or lack of grass or sage or timber. He wrote every day, except for one unexplained three-day gap while in the snowbound wagon camp and again when he was on a four-day exploration to find a way out of their snowbound predicament. From his journal comes much understanding of the habits and temperament of Indians encountered, as well as much understanding of the explorers themselves. The official report of the expedition, also in Campbell's handwriting, was primarily based on his journal.

The journal of John C. Armstrong, thirty-six, the company's bugler, is more eloquent and particularly valuable because of its portrayal of human emotions, especially his own. But it is less precise and, because of several lengthy lapses, less reliable. John Brown, twenty-nine, captain of the expedition, was the most experienced explorer in the group, the man who found a pass over the most difficult mountain the company encountered. His journal is less detailed than Campbell's, but clear, accurate, and particularly compelling in its dispassionate description of the difficulties they encountered and the effort required to overcome them. More than the others, his journal reflects awareness of and concern for the condition of the expedition's livestock. Isaac Chauncey Haight, thirty-six, kept the briefest journal, but he wrote it faithfully and it occasionally helps clarify questions of terrain and campsites.

What these journals describe, aside from knowledge of the land they were sent to discover, is what has to be as unusual an exploring expedition as the West ever knew. These were men sent out in winter, suffering frequent and heavy snowstorms and temperatures often below zero. In those conditions, picture individuals, sent to ride into the mountains to find a way over snow-choked passes, composing a song about what they found and singing it as they rode into camp to report. That happened twice on the expedition. Picture them writing original hymns and poetry and teaching them to the camp. Picture them, almost every night, chilled and sometimes frostbitten after a day of exhausting labor, holding camp prayers, singing, sometimes even sermonizing, before crawling into their bedrolls. They agreed from the beginning to conduct themselves as befitted Latter-day Saints and were frequently reminded, as, for example, when Isaac Haight on December 30 recorded an admonishment about "laying aside our folly and living in such a manner that we should not be ashamed to have Angles [*sic*] come into our midst and behold our acts."

Or, for a different mood, picture them preparing an elaborate banquet, 250 miles from the nearest settlement, in a celebration that included hours of speech-making. Or, in their snowbound camps, holding daily lyceums of learning. Or dancing cotillions—even appointing one of their number, Campbell, to teach others the steps.

The journals describe Indian customs and attitudes. Except for a brief and harmless skirmish on the Santa Clara, relations were friendly. While tensions were building to a point of violence and death in Utah Valley to the north, the Indians of central and southern Utah welcomed the explorers, traded with them, invited them to come and settle. Only once did a journal suggest that a missing oxen *perhaps* was stolen by Indians. By contrast, on the way home, Campbell's journal notes that "fa [William] Henry leaves his weak ox with the Indians."

What comes most clearly from the journals, though, are images of immense labor. Of struggling five days to cross the mountains between the Sevier River and Little Salt Lake Valley, shoveling head-high snow to climb precipitous ridges, hauling oxen up by ropes tied to their yokes so the oxen could then pull up the wagons. Or of the wagon company struggling homeward over Scipio Pass after six snowbound weeks: unable to move through four feet of crusted snow, they fashioned their wagons into sleds but abandoned that when the snow got too soft. The men shoveled trails and retraced their steps to drive the livestock cattle forward. They melted snow for the cattle to drink, but many died anyway. They spent fourteen days going twenty-seven miles.

But readers can discover this and much more for themselves. The journals follow.

THE JOURNALS

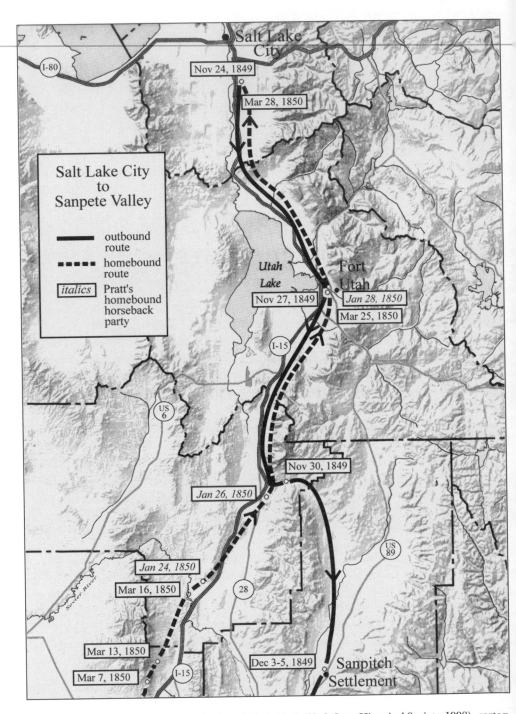

Base map from Peter H. DeLafosse, ed., *Utah Historic Trails* (Utah State Historical Society, 1998), cartography by David H. Vaughn. Used by permission.

Great Salt Lake City to Sanpete

Friday, November 9, 1849

ISAAC HAIGHT: President Young wanted I should postpone going to the mines and go with Br P.P. Pratt to explore the vallies South. Accordingly I altered my purpose and prepared to go with him.

In the fall of 1849 Brigham Young quietly sent two groups of missionaries to California to dig gold for the benefit of the Mormom Church. Haight was to have been one of these until his instructions were changed. The first "gold missionaries," twenty young men led by apostle Charles C. Rich and James M. Flake, left Salt Lake City October 11.[20] Near present-day Beaver they caught up with five hundred '49ers in 108 wagons being guided to California by Mormon Battalion veteran Jefferson Hunt. From there to near Cedar City, they helped build the wagon road the Pratt exploring expedition would follow on part of its trip. Most of the '49ers rebelled against Hunt and followed a supposed shortcut into an ordeal of thirst and starvation that gave Death Valley its name. Rich and his missionaries started on the shortcut but, after days of wandering in the waterless wastes of eastern Nevada, returned to the known route, the Spanish Trail, caught up with Hunt, and accompanied him to California.

Friday, November 23

ROBERT CAMPBELL: Left Council house at 11 A.M. Cold day. muddy. To Kanyon creek bridge 4 1/4 miles. Mill creek bridge over at Gardners mill; 6 3/4. Good road. Cotton wood crossing 8 3/4 camp at Captn John Brown's rendezvous. 10 1/2 m Parley writes letter to Brigham

JOHN BROWN: This fall a company went and settled San Pete valley and another company of men was raised to explore to the south under the direction of Parley P. Pratt. I was called to take command

---

20. Arrington, *Great Basin Kingdom*, 74.

of said company as captain of fifty. On the 23rd of November the
company was organized at my house by brother Pratt. Joseph
Mathews, Joseph Horn, Isaac Haight, Ephraim Green and Josiah
Arnold were chosen to act as captains of tens. Capt. Green chief
gunner to manage the brass field piece, Robert Campbell clerk. We
were fitted up with ox teams, having also quite a number of riding
and pack animals to enable us to explore the country where we
could not take our wagons. We were all well armed and quite a
quantity of Indian trade &c

HAIGHT: bade adieu to all on Earth that is desirable my wives children and home to go with Elder P P. Pratt and a company of fifty
men to find a vally for another settlement of the saints in the south
part of the Mountains of Israel went to Captain Brown on
Cottonwood and there organized the company by appointing a capt
of fifty and tens I was appointed capt of 1st ten. In the evening went
with Br Fielding to Utau Fort [Provo] in search of stolen horses.
Arrived there 2 oclock the next morning the weather was cold &
piercing. But the moon shone bright, which made the travelling
more acceptable. We were very hospitably received by Br Alexander
Williams. Wearied with a ride of 36 m.

The "good road" was the well-established wagon road all the way to
the settlement at Provo. It became, essentially, State Street and U.S.
Highway 89-91. In the fall of 1848, John Brown and a number of the
immigrants he had converted in Mississippi were assigned farms
between Big and Little Cottonwood Creeks in what is now Murray.
Brown built a log house there that fall and winter, and completed
the first adobe house in the summer of 1849.[21] It was at this house
that the Pratt exploring company assembled. Two of Brown's
Mississippi converts, John H. Bankhead and John D. Holladay,
joined the expedition. Brown, named captain of the Southern
Expedition, was an experienced explorer, having been with the
Pioneer Company of 1847 and, with Orson Pratt, one of the first
two Mormon pioneers to see the Salt Lake Valley, on July 19.

Minutes of the organizational meeting were kept by Campbell
and sent back to church headquarters with a short letter from
Pratt:

---

21. John Brown, *Autobiography of John Brown, 1820–1896* (Salt Lake City: Stevens and
      Wallis, 1941), 101–2. See also G. Wesley Johnson and David L. Schirer, *Between the
      Cottonwoods: Murray City in Transition* (Salt Lake City: Timpanogos Research
      Associates, 1992).

Captain Browns, Cottenwood
Saturday, Nov 24th 1849

President Young and Council

Dear Brethren, We are now about Hitched up and ready to start. All is well and I believe we lack for nothing essential.

Our Company is full except three Men and the Little dog Trip, which Br Campbell wishes to go but we cannot wait & he keeps with his [illegible] all the time Br D. Jones not yet arived but will probably overtake us today.

We found and Rec'd the Ox of Bishop Whitneys also new Oxen of the Marshal from the Stray pen, ~~a fe~~ Pair Oxen of Br Young, and a few Oxen, Waggens, etc, from Individuals not Recorded. We are well fited out and in good Spirits, and we now commend our selves to the Lord and to your Prayers and that of the Church.

God Bless you and the saints
for ever and ever

Amen
Parley P. Pratt[22]

At Capt John Brown on cottonwood
23d Nov. 1849 2 oclk. PM.

Meeting of company for exploring south—

Called to order by P. P. Pratt, who gave instructions relating to the necessity [of] peace, order, & of good feeling being preserved during the expedition—Supported in this by W. W. Phelps & David Fulmer

Voted that Parley P Pratt be president of company—That Wm W Phelps & David Fulmer be his councillors carried unanimously.

Voted that John Brown be cap of fifty carried

——— William W Phelps act as Topographical engineer

——— Ephraim Green be Chief Gunner

——— Isaac C. Haight, Joseph Mathews, Joseph Horn, Ephraim Green, Josiah Arnold be capt of tens

——— Robert Campbell be clerk for the camp

——— We support President Pratt in carrying out his instructions in the journey agreed

——— That this meeting adjourn to hitch up to morrow after breakfast

W W Phelps clk & P P. Pratt president

---

22. Robert Campbell, Southern Exploring Expedition Papers, 1849–1850, LDS Church Archives. This early part of Campbell's journal was sent with a letter to Brigham Young from the infant colony at Manti, December 5, 1849.

Sum total of receipts by subscription
[illegible] $223.50
Supplement Wm Henry   5.00
———— W. W. Phelps   10.00

                                 ――――――
                                 $238.50
Total expenditures $239.11
Receipts $238.50
Balance   .61

Enclosed I send Report of Fifty Minutes of meeting for organization
Parleys subscription list, other list &c—Phelps notes &c—I think if
Trip could be sent along, another Thermometer, & a long measur-
ing tape it would be good We are strung out 10 3/4 miles from
Council house—Good spirit prevails—liberality evinced all around,
as is common amongst a Co[mpan]y just starting
                                       Rob Campbell

                                 Cottonwood, Nov. 24, 1849

Mr Enoch Reese,—
     Please send by bearer another Thermometer the best one.
The mercury sticks in the middle. You can afford it for $1.25, seeing
it is the second one. Send also a measuring line to measure creeks.
We need these instruments.
                                 Yours, &c.
                                 W. W. Phelps
Br. Major did not send the water colored paints and brushes. Can
they be sent?

Saturday, November 24
     CAMPBELL: D Fulmer weighing out Bal of Groceries & Flour, some
60 lbs coffee to return to city. R. C. copies letter to B. Y. encloses
returns &c aggregate in camp 12 Wagons 1 Carriage 2 yokes of cattle Beeves No of horses & mules not ascertained. one Brass field
piece, on fore wheels of wagon with a tongue. guns innumerable,
ammunition in proportion. Start 11 1/2 A.M. Bishop Crosslys, where
irrigation furrow enters & road leaves Big field 11 3/4—Further
Cotton wood crossing 12 3/4 Forks of road, take the right 14 m
Pleasant but cool. Dry feed plenty. Dry creek 17 1/2 no water some
fuel good road. Camp at Willow creek. Soft & swampy, no fuel. 20
1/4. Plenty feed, kill a yearling, fat & good. Cattle tied up about 8
P.M. As the snow falls fast, gather round fire, many jokes and stories
told. Singing Songs & afterwards a hymn. PP Pratt prayed.
     HAIGHT: Remained at Utau to wait for the Com

BROWN: On Saturday the 24th of Nov we moved out and camped on Willow Creek and at evening it began snowing. Next morning the snow was eight and a half inches deep which made travelling very difficult.

Campbell's "Little dog" mentioned by Parley in his final letter before leaving apparently didn't get there on time; none of the journals mentions a dog on the trip. Instead of the three men Parley hoped to recruit in Sanpete Valley, five would volunteer. His mention of getting a "new Oxen of the Marshal from the Stray pen" is an interesting insight to the city's state of organization.

Here and frequently throughout his journal Campbell refers to himself as R.C. Camp this night on Willow Creek was about at the present site of the Utah state prison.

Sunday, November 25
CAMPBELL: T 31 Snow 2 in deep all over; Wind Start 1/2 h after noon, ceased snowing reach Hollow steep ascent 21 3/4 Hot Springs 23 m. 136 heat, by roadside. road turns left, ascend steep kanyon 24 1/2 Double teams Summit 25 m, turn to the left few hundred yds then descend long hill. No Wind reach Dry creek 6:25. Camp S side 31 1//4 miles
HAIGHT: Arose in the Morning found it Snowing and continued most of the day it fell about one foot.
BROWN: Next morning the snow was eight and a half inches deep which made travelling very difficult, we went as far as Dry Creek in Utah Valley camped after dark.

The "Hot Springs" are just south of the Utah state prison, about one-quarter mile west of I-15. They became the site of a successful business enterprise of Joseph Smith's and Brigham Young's one-time bodyguard, Porter Rockwell. In 1858, with 2,500 soldiers stationed at Camp Floyd twelve miles away in Cedar Valley and with the proscribing of liquor not yet very effective among Mormons, Rockwell saw an opportunity. With $500 he bought sixteen acres of land surrounding the hot springs, built what he called the Hot Springs Brewery Hotel, and not only served his guests home-brewed beer but also obtained a license to sell whiskey. Situated near the junction of roads to Camp Floyd and to Provo, the business proved successful.[23] In 1860 the place became the Rockwell

---

23. Harold Schindler, *Orrin Porter Rockwell: Man of God, Son of Thunder* (Salt Lake City: University of Utah Press, 1966), 291–92.

Pony Express Station, the second station south of downtown Salt Lake City.

After a snowy passage over the toe of Traverse Mountain, known today as Point of the Mountain, camp was about in the center of present-day Lehi on Dry Creek, which flows out of the Lone Peak Wilderness of the Wasatch Range to the east.

Monday, November 26
> CAMPBELL: T 25 snowing, freezing. Good water. Cotton woods on banks 10 h start. Small Winding hollow 33 m Snow 9 in deep. American Fork 34 1/2 Ft Wide 10 in deep small cotton wood near 10 in snow 38 1/4 to Swamp creek, muddy & soft for 100 yds 39 m Pond at the right of road. Sage & Greasewood abundant. Pass Cedar Groves. Cloudy Camp by 5 h P.M. at Cedar Grove 20 yds left of road 43 1/2 m.
> HAIGHT: remained there still waiting Br Pratt come in the after noon the company camped about one mile off.
> BROWN: We faced a snow storm which was very disagreeable camped in the cedars two or three miles from the fort on Provo. Bro Pratt and others went to the fort and held meeting

This was not Pratt's first visit to the area. In December 1847, he led a small party to explore fishing possibilities in Utah Lake. With a boat and net, "We sailed up and down the lake shore on its western side for many miles, but had only poor success in fishing. We, however, caught a few samples of mountain trout and other fish." Taking the long way home, he explored Cedar, Rush, and Tooele Valleys.[24]

The "Swamp creek" Campbell mentions was Battle Creek in what is now Pleasant Grove, where on February 28, 1848, thirty or forty men led by John Scott attacked a group of cattle-stealing Indians, killing four of them. Nine days after this first armed conflict between Mormons and Indians, a council meeting presided over by Brigham Young voted "that a colony of 30 men settle in Utah Valley this spring for the purpose of farming and fishing and of instructing the Indians in cultivating the earth and of teaching them civilization."[25] Just three weeks later, April 1, thirty-three colonists arrived to build a fort (Fort Utah) south of Provo River

---

24. Pratt, *Autobiography*, 401–3.
25. *Inventory of the County Archives of Utah*, no. 25 (Ogden, Utah: Utah Historical Records Survey, 1940), 10.

about where I-15 crosses the river. Their position was precarious, given the uncertain temper of the Timpanogos Utes and the settlers' shortage of armament. On April 19, Dimick Huntington wrote Brigham Young: "We marshaled ourselves yesterday and find twenty muskets in camp and no cartridges. I wish you would send by Capt Hunt twenty round apiece for each gun, if you think best. . . . We have but one keg of powder and no cartridges."[26]

On August 1, the killing of an Indian called "Old Bishop" in an argument over a shirt raised tensions to a danger point. "About September 1ˢᵗ a bastion was constructed on the mound in the fort, of heavy posts, 30 feet square, with log railings, and a six pounder iron cannon placed on the platform of the bastion, which was sufficiently elevated to protect the fort and stockyards from attack, which was considered liable to occur at any time."[27] This was the condition of the fort into which Parley Pratt rode on November 26. He described it as composed of fifty-seven log houses built on one and a half acres of ground one hundred yards from the Provo River.[28]

This difficulty with Indians was not the first in the area, nor would it be the last. In 1825 the French-Canadian trapper Etienne Provost led a band of trappers that was decoyed into a massacre by visiting Shoshones in the Narrows between Utah and Salt Lake Valleys. Most of his men were killed, but Provost and three or four others escaped. He gave his name to both Provo River and City.

Tuesday, November 27
>   CAMPBELL: T 43 reach Provo by 11 A.M. 46 m 34 yds Wide 18 in deep. E Wind, Rocky bottom Muddy Wet & soft roads 3/4 mile from Fort Utah (which is at the crossing of the Provo) cross a branch of Provo, Soft Swampy Springs 2 of them 50 1/2 miles To Slough caused by spring few yards East, bad crossings 51 3/4—Spring Creek Rocky bottom 19 yds Wide, 10 in deep—53 1/2 Hobble Creek 28 ft Wide 2 ft deep, Camp South side, Plenty cotton wood fuel (& Willows) firstrate feed T 40
>   HAIGHT: The waggons 13 in number came and proceed on our journey went 7 1/2 miles and camped on Hobble creek cold and rainy
>   BROWN: We reached Hobble Creek here it snowed on us again John Scott with a posse camped with us they were in search of stolen horses supposed to have been taken by the gold diggers

---

26. Ibid., 12.
27. George Washington Bean's journal, quoted in *Inventory of the County Archives*, 13.
28. Campbell, Southern Exploring Expedition Papers.

On Hobble Creek they were at the future site of Springville, which
Pratt's report to the legislature described as "a desirable place for a
Settlement. Good soil, and plenty water. "

Wednesday, November 28

> CAMPBELL: Beautiful morning Sun rises little after 7 T 31 9 h 22 m.
> Start bear S.W. level Prairie. Small Hollow 55 1/2 steep banks T at
> noon in the Sun 57 cool N Wind. Thawing. Wet roads snow only 2 in
> deep. Dry feed, Plenty all along. Spanish Fork 59 1/2 14 yds Wide
> 14 in deep. Rocky bottom steep banks, & steep descent 100 yds from
> Creek & steep ascent 150 yds past it, Cotton wood timber & plenty
> willows Good camping place. Sage & Greasewood studded thickly
> all over right & left. Low Swamp, 62 1/2 This Swamp continues for
> 3/4 m. Some good black soil, soft travelling—Thawing Pateatneat
> creek 64 3/4 9 ft wide 17 in deep. Col. C. [J.?] Scott & party who r
> after Purbelow the Mountainman who stole horses stay here till we
> come up, hear that Purbelow camps at the hot springs to night.
> Camp here at 3 P.M. Cotton woods & willows plenty.
>
> HAIGHT: travelled 11 3/4 miles and camped on a creek travelling
> bad snow going off thru night clear & cold the creek called
> petetenete
>
> BROWN: We reached Piasateatment Creek here Colonel Scott fell in
> with us again and called on us for some to go with him. And we let
> him have ten mounted men to be gone a few days and return to us
> again.

Peteetneet Creek became the site of Payson, settled in 1850 after
Pratt's report that "here is fine soil, beautiful grass, and desirable
place for a Settlement." Colonel Scott was John Scott, a colonel in
the Nauvoo Legion whose title had been reaffirmed in the recently
formed Utah Militia. He had led the attack on the Indians on
Battle Creek nine months earlier and had fallen into disfavor with
Brigham Young because of the killing. As a result, he took part in
no more Indian campaigns.[29] Research fails to identify Purbelow,
whom Pratt's party will encounter weeks later in southern Utah.

Thursday, November 29

> CAMPBELL: T 17 Beautiful spot. Start 9 A.M. Sun strong. Good road
> sage plentiful The Range of Mts on the East in Utah valley curve

---

29. Orson F. Whitney, *History of Utah* (Salt Lake City: George Q. Cannon & Sons Co.,
     1892), 1:423–24.

from N to South round East. We have travelled at the East foot of
the mts 2/3 of a circle round. Plenty dry feed. Up creek 68 miles,
bad descent 8 yards wide 1 ft deep Gravelly bottom best crossing at
the right Pass some beautiful fine feed. Pleasant view of Utah lake
and valley. Mts East covered with snow & studded with Fir & Cedar
Branch of Summit creek 3 ft wide. 10 in deep 70 3/4 fine rushing
stream, 200 yds further. Summit creek 30 ft Wide 1 ft deep, clear
water. Cotton wood timber steep ascent from creek, main run of
Water 3 ft wide. 1 1/4 mile from mouth of Kanyon beautiful fine
feed. Bench land S of crossing T 68 in the sun view of Utah lake
West of the Mountains. Dense cedar Groves 2 1/2 miles S.S.W. 73
1/2 m Rocky spot begin to descend into the Valley at this point a
few yards to the left of road is a lay of Cobble stones studded on the
bluff 1 mile long from 20 to 100 yards broad. rich feed, 78 m.
Pang'un Spring right of road. Within 1//4 mile 3 other Springs left
of road. 78 3/4 to Warm Spring Creek 3 1/2 P.M. Camped.
Beautiful day, Good roads all day. All ox very fat. Wolves howl, beautiful clear Moonlight evg T 28. Camp called together sing hymn,
prayers, other hymns is sung. 2 Bre are hands laid on them, one of
them Dan Jones—R.C. prophesied on his head, God would heal up
his lungs and restore him to vigor & strength & the time would
come when he would be able to roar like a lion in the congregations
of this world in preaching this Gospel, notwithstanding thro his zeal
he has injured his vitals and bodily organs. Alex Wright reports himself healed by laying on of hands last night—Sing "Ye slumbering
nations" Parley tells the origin of that hymn—the introduction of
the Gospel into New York. God's power displayed in healings,
visions &c Dimic tells about the Indians when heard preaching—
their traditions.

HAIGHT: We passed into the Yoab Valley camped at a spring that is
called Bottomless Spring come 14 mile

BROWN: We camped at a large spring in Juab valley where there was
no wood, next morning an ox was missing supposed to have been
stolen by the Indians.

The gentle pass from which they looked back at a "pleasant view
of Utah lake and valley" was noted by the Domínguez-Escalante
expedition seeking a route from Santa Fe to Monterey in 1776.
They named the pass Puerto de San Pedro—"St. Peter's Gate."[30]
I-15 crosses it at the line between Utah and Juab Counties, the

---

30. Ted J. Warner, ed., *The Domínguez-Escalante Journal* (Provo, Utah: Brigham Young
University Press, 1976), 62.

latter of which Parley reported to be "every way calculated for a
city and Settlement, rather limited in its resources." The name,
already in use by the Paiutes living there, means "flat or level
plain."[31]

Dan Jones had earlier served a mission in his native Wales,
helping to convert some two thousand persons. As Campbell
prophesied, he did again preach the gospel, serving a second mission to Wales from 1852 to 1856 and then taking charge of a company of seven hundred Mormons crossing the Atlantic and the
plains to Salt Lake Valley.[32]

Friday, November 30

CAMPBELL: Ther 6 A.M. 12 18 below Freezing. R.C. sleeps out on
the ground. Camp woke by sound of Carnopean. Beautiful moonlight night, but hard Frost. Range of high Mts on the East of us,
running N & S 3 miles distant . . . this creek tho so hard frost still as
warm as usual. No bad taste to it. Leave part of head, intrails & skin
of ox, beautiful morning. Camp start at 9 A.M. firstrate road. Third
day with scarcely one cloud in the blue ethereal sky. To Watadge
creek 82 miles—Willows muddy crossing. Vallies rich in feed to the
R & left Warm sun. Ther at 11 A.M. 71. From Mts East to the range
of hills on the West 14 miles, which would include some bench
land. light brown soil little gravel in places. Phelps peak of Mt.
Nebo highest peak to the left these Mts Rocky and r studded with
small timber near the summits. Forks of road 85 3/4 Take the left'
Leave the road make a new trail 86 m, join the old road 88 1/2—
this avoids a hill. We pass some miles of beautiful light Brown soil
loose & Mellow land. To mouth of Onappa Kanyon 90 3/4 Just
before entering the Kanyon, on the hill to the left thick grove of
cedar. Pass up the Kanyon 2 miles Camp near branch of Kanyon
which forks on the left 92 3/4 miles. but little timber in the
Kanyon, some cedar, & cotton woods. Crossed the creek 6 times 4
yards Wide 12 in deep. Some steep bad crossings. One ox left
behind this morning. Could not be found. Vance's poor horse left
behind— 4 1/2 P.M. Camped T 28. Bre with Col Scott return, they
went to the Sevier, found Purbilow had gone too far ahead—
Singing songs, afterwards hymns then prayer by Phelps. Afterwards

31. John W. Van Cott, *Utah Place Names* (Salt Lake City: University of Utah Press, 1990),
     208.
32. Andrew Jenson, ed., *Latter-day Saint Biographical Encyclopedia* (Salt Lake City: Deseret
     News Press, 1920; reprint, Salt Lake City: Western Epics, 1971), 3:658–59 (hereafter
     cited as Jenson, *Bio. Enc.*).

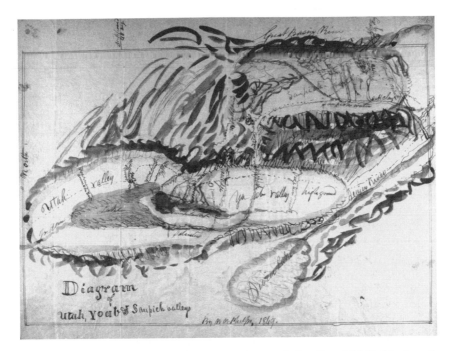

W. W. Phelps's sketch map of "Utah, Yoab & Sanpitch valleys," 1849. He drew it while on the top of Mt. Nebo, barely discernible above the Y in Yo ab. Courtesy LDS Church Archives, copy photograph by J M. Heslop.

discussion till late on Gods, Angels, Prophets &c Bro Phelps saw a Robin in the Kanyon today.

HAIGHT. travelled over a rolling prairie and passed up into the Salt Creek Canon and camped came 14 mile Some snow lost an Ox suppose the Indians killed it last night.

BROWN: We reached Salt Creek where we camped two miles up the canyon here we discovered plenty of Plaster of Paris also our men returned who went with Col Scott. They went so far as the Sevier River on the California road but to no effect.

Watadge Creek is North Creek, flowing out of the Mt. Nebo Wilderness and into the south end of what is now Mona Reservoir. Campbell's "Onappa Kanyon" is today's Salt Creek Canyon, near the mouth of which the city of Nephi sits on the "beautiful light Brown soil loose & Mellow land" Campbell describes.

The summit of Mt. Nebo, at 11,877 feet, is the highest point in the Wasatch Range. Campbell calls it "Phelps peak" because three months earlier, on August 24, W. W. Phelps had climbed it to

sketch Sanpete Valley and surrounding country.[33] Brigham Young
had sent him there to examine the country that Ute chief Walker,
in a meeting with Brigham on June 24, had invited the Mormons
to come and settle.

Saturday, December 1

CAMPBELL: moderate morning Ther 28 Parley & Dimic B.
Huntington start for the Sandpitch settlement Camp starts at 10 to
9 A.M. but few on horseback this morning, all keep close by their
wagons. To the third crossing this morning 95 1/4 we leave the
main Kanyon now which turned up to the left, 300 yards up before
you cross, there is a salt rock in a cave. It is on the left of the bluff
below ground 30 ft. It is mingled with the Red earth. at the corner
south as you turn up the mt r pillars of earth like the pillars over
Fugals [Fingals?] cave. beautiful. Of light colored earth. Brought
specimens of Salt Rock along, it is about half salt & half Red earth
Summit of ascent from Kanyon 98 1/4. You then travel on level land
for 2 miles. Then gently descend into Sandpitch valley. Snow 2 & 3
inches deep all day both in Kanyon & on the ridge. Camp on the
left of the road at the first cedars by wayside. Get water from
Pleasant creek right of road 300 yds. Ther at noon in shade 46. Pass
lots of sage & Camp right in it tonight at 3 P.M. 11 1/4 miles T 25.
Camp prayers & singing. 104 miles from city. Pleasant creek 3 ft
wide 18 in deep.

JOHN C. ARMSTRONG [the part of his journal that has been preserved begins here]: Very cold and frosty, hard traveling. Most of
the men on foot today. Went and visited a Salt cave about three hundred yards from the road. Decended about 30 feet under ground.
Crossed the Creek on the right. 75 and 3/4 miles from the city.
Ascended the canyon, camped among the cedars Pahquity Pahson
creek, eighty rods from camp. This is the San Pitch Valley, full of
sage, cedars on the mountains.

HAIGHT: Passed through the Canon up on to a high beautiful table
Snow one foot deep decend from the table and camped on a creek
called Pawquets weather quite cold and unpleasant came 11 1/4
miles

BROWN: bro. Pratt went on horseback to San Pete settlement, the
camp moved over in to the upper end of San Pete valley. The
ground was still covered with snow but not so deep.

---

33. Andrew Jenson, *Church Chronology* (Salt Lake City: Deseret News Press, 1914), 37.
    Phelps's original map is in LDS Church Archives.

Their route up Salt Creek and over the summit into Sanpete Valley is followed closely by Highway 132 today. The "main Kanyon" which turned to the left is Pole Canyon, up which the Nebo loop road now goes. On the level land Campbell describes, shortly before the summit, a Daughters of Utah Pioneers monument notes where on June 4, 1858, Indians killed four members of the Jens Terkelsen family. Pleasant or Pahquity or Pahson or Pawquets Creek is Big Hollow, and camp this night was on the future site of Fountain Green.

Sunday, December 2

CAMPBELL: Ther 25. Camp start at 9h 20m. Pass sage, cedars studded abundantly on hills right & left of Valley 110 3/4 to Springs & slough right of road. Cloudy day Ther at noon 46, snow 2 in deep but level good road strike Sandpitch Creek on the left 112 1/2 m. Greasewood thick all over reach crossing of Sandpitch 14 1/4—steep descent 25 ft wide 1 1/2 ft deep. Clear stream. Sage and greasewood abundant. Mts right & left black with cedar. Level road. Willows on the banks of the Sandpitch. The road in two miles crossed another crik supposed to rise from Springs. Sage & Greasewood all over right & left—level good road—Sun breaks thro—reach Camp by 5 P.M. on the North bank of Timpa creek—123 1/2 miles. Cloudy & dark. Singing prayers & sing. few Indians attend at our devotions. Bro Phelps tells about the angel appearing to Joseph Oliver David & Martin & about translating Hieroglyphics.

ARMSTRONG: Got along pretty well through the sage, crossed the creek After crossing a slough, I set fire to a patch of grass to burn out a wolf, I ran to the wagons, told the boys to watch the fire and see what would come out They watched the fire and presently Isaac Brown came out and they got a good laugh. Long drive today; Dark when we got into camp. Drove 19 and 1/2 miles. Visited by three SanPitch Indians, one of them joined in with us when we were singing prior to evening prayers. Evening spent well, Brother Phelps conversed freely about the coming forth of the plates of the Book of Mormon and the translating of them by the Prophet Joseph Smith, It was edifying.

HAIGHT: The Valley through which we passed is a sage plain some little grass on Sampitch creek but the Indians had burnt it off we passed over another Sage plain and camped on a creek called Timpa or stoney creek

The crossing of San Pitch River was at the present site of Moroni. Laughter over Isaac Brown's plight demonstrates a rough frontier humor not often found in the journals. Camp this night was at the present site of Ephraim. The Phelps account of the angel appearing to "Joseph Oliver David & Martin" refers to the June 1829 appearance of an angel showing to Oliver Cowdery, David Whitmer, and Martin Harris the golden plates from which the Book of Mormon was being translated by Joseph Smith. These men became known as the Three Witnesses to the validity of the Book of Mormon.[34]

Monday, December 3

CAMPBELL: Snowing nearly all night T 30, clearing up. Few cedars &c Woods on banks 12 ft W and 18 in about. S. Wind little Snow in the valley. Pass on 2 miles to Mound creek 2 ft Wide 6 in deep. Greasewood & sage all around. Camp draws near the settlement. One house up, about 46 families in tents wagons &c 1 P.M. fired off cannon. Bre sing "Some fifty sons of Zion" ["]All is well" ["]Come all ye sons of Zion" while passing the wagons and tents at the encampment of the Sandpitch Settlers. cross city creek & camp South bank 14 ft Wide 18 in deep 130 3/4 miles. Parley very sick to day. Snowed a little. Rocky bottom.

ARMSTRONG: Drove six miles. Just before we got into san Pitch settlement I blew a trumpet for camp to stop, fired off cannon, Played "Corn Cornspese" & Company Sang "The Fifty Sons of Zion,["] All is well All is well etc. etc. Camped on the other side of City Creek from the settlement, found Brothr Parley P Pratt very sick. Visited Brothers Hamilton, potter and Allred and many more, Spent the evening in singing, all went well.

HAIGHT: Got up in the morning found it snowing we went 7 miles to Sampitch Settlement saluted them with the firing of the cannon and a song. Br Pratt quite unwell

BROWN: We reached the settlement and remained one day here five more men joined the company with two wagons. We now have 52 men 15 wagons (ox teams) and 37 horses and mules.

They had reached the infant settlement of Manti in Sanpete County, finding one house already built just two weeks after the settlers had arrived there. On June 14, a delegation of Ute Indians led by Chief Walker had met with Brigham Young asking that Mormons settle in Sanpete Valley to teach the natives to farm and build homes. In August, W. W. Phelps, Joseph Horne, D. B.

---

34. Joseph Smith, *History of the Church*, 1:52–57. See also Book of Mormon, introduction.

Huntington, and Ira Willes, all of whom but Willes would later join Pratt's party, were sent to explore the valley. At this time Phelps drew his rough but fairly accurate sketch of the territory. Their report was favorable, and a company of fifty families under leadership of Isaac Morley left in late fall to establish the first settlement away from the Wasatch Front. In fairly mild weather, they built a road up Salt Creek Canyon and reached the site of Manti on November 22. They first called the settlement Copenhagen since so many settlers were Danish, but Morley soon named it Manti for a prominent city in the Book of Mormon.[35]

The singing of Pratt's group as they passed the settlement was characteristic of the Mormon pioneer experience; indeed, the company would sing at campsites throughout the exploration whenever circumstances permitted. Of the songs mentioned: "Some fifty sons of Zion" apparently was composed for this expedition and has since disappeared. "Come all ye sons of Zion" would be either "Come, All Ye Sons of God," composed by Thomas Davenport (1815–1888), or "Come, All Ye Saints of Zion," composed by W. W. Phelps and included in the first LDS hymnbook, 1835. Since Phelps was on the expedition, it was probably the latter. "All is Well" was the original title of the famous Mormon hymn "Come, Come, Ye Saints." While crossing Iowa in the Mormon exodus from Nauvoo in the winter of 1846, William Clayton composed it to celebrate the birth of a son.

Tuesday, December 4

CAMPBELL: T 28 Bre repairing wagons, Greasing, fireing up. Phelps & Jones at noon try to calculate Lat & Long. Lat 39 10" Long 15' East of G.S.L. City. Parley quite well today. R.C. Writing at Fa[ther] Richards all day. 5 Bre come from Sandpitch with us their names r Madison D. Hambleton, Gardner G. Potter, Edward [Eward?] Everett, William [John] Lowry[Jr] & Sylvester Hewlitt. Captn Walker and his Indians are 70 miles from here up the Sevier river on our way. Bre here busy getting wood, rock building, sawing and fencing. Went with fa Richards to the place designed for Fort on the South of a Rocky bluff—beautiful building sledge, any quantity 6 rods from the building spots for their houses. Rocky naturally designed for building. Showed me on a Rock projecting over and jutting out some characters engraved on stone, plain, visible representation of a man, something on his head not unlike a bird

---

35. Van Cott, *Utah Place Names*, 244.

with wings, one hand behind him with fingers, other hand before
him holding on to something—pushing it strait South, the South
end of which rock is defaced or worn away that the "something" aint
all perfect. Apparently cut on the stone with a punch. Thousands of
cedars within 1 mile of the Fort, & thousands more another mile &
Good rich feed South of creek, cows increase in milk here Cattle fatten fast—Redish earth clayey soil, Ther 22. 2 Wagons & 6 yokes of
cattle & a tent. Now fall in with the Sandpitch Bre.
ARMSTRONG: Stayed all day here. Got some bread baked, Spent the
time well.
HAIGHT: Br Pratt some better weather very cold remained all day
with the Breathren

Campbell's favorable view of Sanpete Valley, including "Good rich
feed . . . cows increase in milk here Cattle fatten fast," was not uni-
versally shared. One settler, Seth Taft, grumbled that "This is only a
long, narrow canyon, and not even a jackrabbit could exist on the
desert soil."[36] Nor did Campbell foresee the terrible winter the settlement was about to endure. Armstrong's journal reports that on
December 7, "It came on a very heavy snow storm." *The History of
Sanpete County*, published in 1898, confirms that report:

> In a few days snow began falling and continued almost incessantly
> until the ground was covered to a depth of three feet or more, and
> the colony changed quarters to the south side of temple hill, where
> some families had dugouts, while others occupied their improvised
> wagons and tents. That winter was most severe and the snow fell to a
> greater depth than ever was known to the Indians, and the equal
> has never since been recorded. Men and boys were engaged daily in
> shoveling snow in winrows to bare the grass and furnish shelter and
> food for the starving cattle. Even the horns of cows and oxen were
> sharpened by filing, to give them better means of defense in fight-
> ing wild animals, and enable them to break through the crust of the
> frozen snow in search of the dry grass. Of the two hundred and
> forty head of cattle brought in by the colonists, only one hundred
> and thirteen were living the following June.

A twelve-man company sent to Salt Lake City for fresh supplies was
snowbound in Salt Creek Canyon, not returning to the settlement
until March, wagons being dragged by hand "over snow ranging in
depth from 8 to 20 feet."

---

36.   Albert C. T. Antrei, ed., *The Other Forty-Niners: A Topical History of Sanpete County* (Salt
      Lake City: Western Epics, 1982), 9.

Spring brought its own miseries.

In the evening following the first warm day of early spring, the peaceful colonists were startled by a continuous hissing and rattling of myriads of rattlesnakes . . . wriggling and writhing about in the boxes, beds, cupboards and everywhere they could get inside the homes of the settlers. A general warfare was inaugurated by the aid of pineknot torches, and many hundreds of the reptiles were killed, nearly five hundred being slaughtered in one night. The strangest thing connected with the raid of these deadly serpents was that not one person was bitten. . . . In the spring of 1850, when time for plowing and planting came there was but one team able to draw a plow through the native desert, until feed was obtained from the growing grass.[37]

On the "Rocky bluff," just south of which the fort was to be built and where the settlers dug in for that first winter, now stands the Manti Temple. The "beautiful building sledge" Campbell mentions is the lovely cream-colored limestone of which many early Sanpitch homes as well as the Manti Temple were built. Of this limestone, geologist Halka Chronic writes: "The limestone is oolitic—made of small spheres that look like fish eggs but that are really formed as sandlike grains roll around in agitated water. . . . The formation contains fossils of fish, alligators, turtles, and other inhabitants of the early Tertiary lakes."[38] Much of it came from a still-active quarry just below the north slope of temple hill. On a nearby outcropping of dark conglomerate rock are the petroglyphs Campbell was shown.

Before leaving the settlement, Parley sent a short letter to the First Presidency. The journal he mentions is a slightly different version of the journal kept to date by Robert Campbell and is included in the appendices under Related Papers. Parley's letter follows:

Sandpitch Settlement
Wed 5 Decr 1849

Prest. Y[oung] K[imball] and Richards
    Enclosed we send herewith sketch of Camp Journal &c up to yesterdays date. We have been successful &prosperous so far in all our undertakings &Journeyings. The Providential hand of the Almighty has been over us for good since we left and to him we give

37. Antrei, *The Other Forty-Niners*, 13–15.
38. Halka Chronic, *Roadside Geology of Utah* (Missoula: Mountain Press Publishing Co., 1990), 150.

the honor &humbly entreat of him to guide us by day &by night, that we may do much good for Israel.

We start this morning &may reach the Sevier to night, perhaps not till to morrow but we crave an interest in your faith &prayers, as our Camp continually pray for you and all the household of faith.

All is well, all is well

Rob Campbell Clerk   Parley P Pratt

Sanpete to the Little Salt Lake

Wednesday, December 5, 1849

CAMPBELL: Left copy of Journal, Letter to the Presy & letter to Dr. R and T. B. with Phinehas Richards. Also 2 copies of Epistle of the Presy for this branch. Phinehas promised to send the letters on as soon as he could to GSL City. Left the nigh ox in the yoke Brigham bought for this expedition in care of Bro. [Jezreel] Shoemaker it being deemed wisdom to leave it & take from Bro Shoemaker one instead till we return, he said to Fullmer he would not consider himself responsible, but would take care of the ox like his own cattle. Ther 21 10 A.M. cattle up & hitched, horses also, cold clear morning, 11 start, & make a new trail. find where Barney Ward & Shumway had went with wagons—go on their trail to low swamp at the end of the valley. 133 1/2 miles. Go thro the pass & strike down to the right 1/2 mile to cross South creek 10 ft wide—20 in deep 136 1/2 miles 200 yds above where it flows into the Sandpitch some pine, cedar & small Birch on its banks, Poor Sage land all round, Red clayey earth. Cold day T 42 in shade—rocks of gravel & Red earth on the right. Mts On the left black with cedar groves, see the peaks of the Mts above the dense white clouds. Dimic Pioneering— to Reed creek 139 1/4 3 ft wide 12 in deep we have traveled from the crossing of South creek on the East of Sandpitch creek, on the creek bottom plenty grass, but we travel thro small sage & Red earth—tolerable good road all day. Camp 1/2 mile past Reed creek 3 P.M. Good feed on the bottoms of Sandpitch a few rods to the right. T 21 R C. on Guard midnight watch—Camp prayers & singing

ARMSTRONG: Started from camp about 10 oclock this morning. Joined by five from this place, Brothers Hamilton Potter and Lowrie. Traveled 9 miles from San Pitch just in the mouth of Sevier valley. A very dreary place and very cold, have two toes frozen.

HAIGHT: Proceed on our journey five of the breathren go with us from Sampitch come 9 miles and camp on Sampitch creek

Parley had planned to complete the roster of the fifth ten by recruiting three men in Manti. Five joined instead. Two of the party would be sent home from Little Salt Lake Valley, leaving the company at the planned strength of fifty men.

Elijah Barney Ward, an early mountain man, was a fascinating character in Mormon history. Born in Virginia about the year 1820, he went to the Rocky Mountains at age 15 and helped Nathaniel Wyeth and his band of trappers build a trading post on the Snake River near the mouth of the Portneuf. They called it Fort Hall and it became an important stop on the Oregon and California Trails. Ward worked at Astoria at the mouth of the Columbia River; trapped and traveled with Jim Bridger, Kit Carson, and other mountain men; and lived several years with the Flathead Indians. He married one of them, by whom he had two daughters, who, after he died, were adopted into the family of Brigham Young.

After the Mormons arrived in Salt Lake Valley, Ward joined that church and became a friend of and Indian interpreter for Brigham. Though not listed among the original settlers of Manti, he clearly was in the area at the time. But he did move around; a few weeks earlier, in the wagon train of '49ers led by Jefferson Hunt, O. K. Smith said Barney Ward had given him a map drawn by mountain man Bill Williams, showing a shortcut to the gold-fields. Smith persuaded most of the party to leave Hunt near present Newcastle, Utah, to strike out on the shortcut; a number of them died in Death Valley and beyond. Ward fought in the 1850 Indian battle at Fort Utah (Provo), lived at Fort Supply near Fort Bridger from 1853 until the approach of Johnston's army, then settled in central Utah towns Payson, Fairview, and, finally, Gunnison. During the Black Hawk War, still acting as Indian interpreter and thinking he was safe from the Utes, he went unarmed up Salina Canyon and there, on April 10, 1865, he and a young man, James Anderson, were killed and scalped.[39]

Charles Shumway was born August 1, 1806, in Oxford, Massachusetts. Joining the LDS Church in 1840, he was a member of the Nauvoo police, defended the city against mob violence, and was among the first to cross the Mississippi in the February 1846 expulsion from that city. He was with the Pioneer Company that arrived in Salt Lake Valley July 22, 1847, returned with Brigham

---

39. Jenson, *Bio. Enc.*, 3:552–54. See also LeRoy R. and Ann W. Hafen, *Journals of the Forty-Niners: Salt Lake to Los Angeles* (Glendale: Arthur H. Clark Co., 1954), 35.

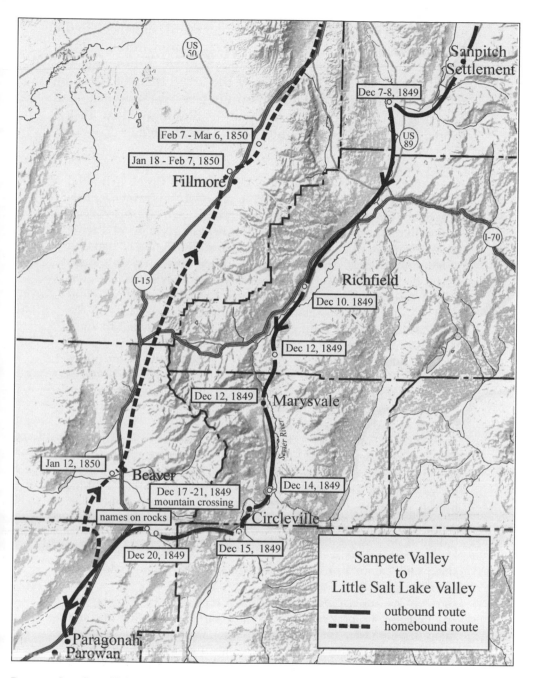

Base map from Peter H. DeLafosse, ed., *Utah Historic Trails* (Utah State Historical Society, 1998), cartography by David H. Vaughn. Used by permission.

Young to Winter Quarters later that summer, and came back to the valley in 1848. He was a counselor to Isaac Morley in the original settlement of Manti and represented Sanpete County in the Territorial Legislature. He was one of the first settlers of Mendon, Cache County, in 1859; assisted in founding several southern Utah towns; and in 1880 erected a gristmill at Shumway, near Taylor, Arizona. He died in Kane County, Utah, May 21, 1898.[40]

Thursday, December 6

CAMPBELL: T 34. N Wind. Start at 1/2 9 A.M. To Fir Creek 20 ft wide, 15 in deep 141 1/4—Fir, cedar, & Pine on its banks. Travel over barren, clayey land. Some places, but very little, Sage or Greasewood, not unlike the land between the South pass, crossing of Pacific creek & and the Dry Sandy. excellent road all day, follow Indian trail & Shumway's track, Capt Brown & few others fixing any little steep places in the road. R. C. Teaming to day. Ther they say at noon was 27 very cold day. Cloudy. strike towards the Sevier Angling. Wind cold, blowing S.W. up the Sevier. See fires a head travel up the Sevier, which is to the right a few hundred yards. Descend to lower land and cross small creek 3 ft Wide 10 in deep 119 1/4—Camp at 2 1/2 P.M. on the Sevier. Many willows, some feed at this point [illegible] yards wide [illegible] ft deep 152 1/4. Five Utes in Camp tell us Walker up the Sevier hunting. Shumway camped a few miles a head of us, has sent for Walker to come and trade. See the Wasatch Mts a head of us to day above the clouds. T 28

ARMSTRONG: Traveled 11 1/2 miles along a good road but no feed. Ought to be called "Severe Valley" A large dreary wilderness, A complete barren waste; Camped about half past one oclock. Camp upset by five Indians, They tell us that Walker the Indian chief is a long way off. The boys got out a fiddle and amused themselves with dancing on account of the cold. The Indians were very pleased to see and hear the singing and dancing.

HAIGHT: Travelled 12 1/2 miles over a barren plain covered with small sage camped on the Severe River. Some Indians waded the river and came to our camp.

BROWN: We moved down San Pete Creek and in two days we reached the Sevier River here Walker came to us with his band many of whom were very sick with measles, we got information from him about the country south Barney Ward and others came to us also and we spent the day in camp. We concluded to continue up the Sevier in a southerly direction. Walker sent one of his men as an

40.   Jenson, *Bio. Enc.*, 4:718.

interpreter and guide but he was taken sick and turned back in a day or two.

On this bitter cold day, the party reached the Sevier and camped near present-day Redmond. It is ironic that Armstrong thought this "large dreary wilderness . . . complete barren waste" should be called "Severe Valley." Others long before had the same impression. Travelers on the Spanish Trail called the river Rio Severo, or Severe River. Sevier is a corruption of that name. One traveler on the trail, Orville Pratt, did not agree either with Armstrong or whoever named the river. "Seeing Sevier valley in its late September gold," he wrote, "it was truly the loveliest spot, all things considered, my eyes have ever looked upon."[41] Earlier it had still different names. Domínguez and Escalante, who crossed it near present-day Yuba in September 1776, named it "Santa Isabel" in honor of the Spanish queen.[42] Jedediah Smith, who followed the Sevier from present Aurora to Joseph (near the route of I-70) and described the Indians there in uncomplimentary terms, called it Ashley River "in compliment," he wrote, "to my friend, the enterprising Genl. W. H. Ashley."[43]

Friday, December 7
   CAMPBELL: T 10 Snowed a little during night, cold day cloudy start at 20 to 9 A.M. as the Wagons started Capt Walker & another Indian rides into Camp said Glad to see us knew he would see us soon, for he dreamed he would, told us he had lots of trade, wished us to go back down the Sevier about a mile where there was good bottom with feed. Parley wishes him to go a head & camp with us. Said no feed. Parley send messenger after the wagons to tell them come back & go down stream to where Walker would shew us. Camp had gone on nearly a mile, turn back & camp on the Sevier 1 1/2 miles below this mornings encampment. cold day, 155 1/2 miles. Parley reads letter from Brigham to Captn. Walker Dimic interprets it tells about the sack of Flour for him, he makes no answer till he sees Arrapin his Brother, all the band is coming & will encamp with us tells Parley no pass over these mts S.E. & no good country over there, little Water, don't run far, Rocky, Shewed him the map he showd points in it &

41.   "The Journal of Orville C. Pratt, 1848," in *Old Spanish Trail: Santa Fe to Los Angeles*, ed. LeRoy R. and Ann W. Hafen (Glendale: Arthur H. Clark Co., 1954), 352.
42.   Warner, *The Domínguez-Escalante Journal*, 269.
43.   George R. Brooks, ed., *The Southwest Expedition of Jedediah S. Smith: His Personal Account of the Journey to California, 1825–27* (Glendale: Arthur H. Clark Co., 1977), 48.

told what country he was acquainted & what he was not, like an experienced geographer, all astonished at him point out on the map, says some country where we could raise corn on the Rio Virgin, says the pi Gads [Piedes, or Southern Paiutes] dying off fast, whole wika up die in one sleep. Coy start off with Parley to make a Ford. Parley and Captn Brown start to hunt a pass over the mts. Ther 28— Indians come in by the dozens, good many nice horses and packs, & Dogs &c blowing from the West & snowing cold, many of them sick with the meazles, hear them making medicine, see them sucking one anothers feet, forehead &c. Stabed a Dog because their village sick Barney Ward gives Parley some information.

ARMSTRONG: Left camp at nine oclock. Got one mile on the road, met Walker the indian chief who turned us back about two 1/2 miles. Told us we couldnt go over the mountain at the head of the Sevier. The company all dissatisfied with the back track. Held a Council in the afternoon. Walker advises us to cross the river and go up a canyon to the Western mountains. Parley P Pratt and Capt. Brown went to explore the canyon. It came on a very heavy snow storm, had to fire the cannon to guide them to the camp. Wind blowing very cold. Brother Pratt and Brown got into camp in half an hour afterwards. Shumway, Allred, Ward and others come in, Ward told Parley that we could cross the mountains the way were going and it rejoiced the boys again.

HAIGHT: Just after we started on we met Walker the Indian Chief the train turned back and camped on the river for the day the Indians seemed sick with the Measles some had died

James Allred, one of the Manti pioneers, had been president of the LDS High Council east of the Rocky Mountains and had spoken in the church's October 1849 general conference. He established Spring City, Sanpete Valley's second settlement, in 1852.

Walker, or Wakara, was the dominant Indian figure in the Great Basin during the mid-nineteenth century. Born probably in 1815 in the vicinity of Spanish Fork, he became chief not by inheritance but through the horses he accumulated in raids to southern California.[44] By the time the Mormons entered Salt Lake Valley in 1847 he had become respected as the major Ute chief. He had traveled and traded with such mountain men as Jim Bridger, Joe Walker, Old Bill Williams, Pegleg Smith, and Jim Beckwourth.

---

44.   Julian H. Steward, *Basin-Plateau Aboriginal Sociopolitical Groups*, Bureau of American Ethnology Bulletin 120 (Washington, D.C.: Government Printing Office, 1938), 229.

With the latter two he collaborated on horse-stealing raids to California ranches, continuing those raids after the Mexican War made California part of the United States and the mountain men gave up the practice. These raids and much other traveling gave Walker the knowledge of Great Basin and Virgin River geography that so impressed the Pratt party.

According to contemporary accounts, Walker was an imposing figure and a proud, jealous, avaricious man. Thomas L. Kane, a friend of the Mormons who would later negotiate a peaceful settlement of the Utah War, described him in 1850 as

> a fine figure of a man, in the prime of life. He excels in various manly exercises, is a crack shot, a rough rider, and a great judge of horse flesh. He is besides very clever, in our sense of the word. He is a peculiarly eloquent master of the graceful alphabet of pantomime, which stranger tribes employ to communicate with one another. He has picked up some English, and is familiar with Spanish and several Indian tongues. He rather effects the fine gentleman. When it is his pleasure to extend his riding excursions into Mexico, to inflict or threaten outrage, or to receive the instalment of his blackmail salary, he will take offense if the people there fail to kill their fattest beeves, and adopt other measures to show him obsequious and distinguished attention.[45]

Walker's early friendship with Brigham Young led to his invitation for Mormons to settle in Sanpete Valley, which the Mormons inferred was a welcome to settle elsewhere in Ute country. He was baptized a Mormon by Isaac Morley in Manti March 13, 1850, and later ordained an elder in the Mormon priesthood by Brigham Young himself—acts likely more a matter of diplomatic expediency than of conversion.[46] Friendship grew thin as Mormon settlements began to crowd the Utes and frictions grew. Tensions worsened after Brigham's order, backed by an act of the legislature on January 31, 1852, outlawed the traffic in slaves that had been a part of the Ute economy and source of much of Walker's personal wealth. Finally, in July 1853, James Ivie, a Mormon settler near Springville, attempted to stop an Indian from beating his wife. In the ensuing fight the Indian was killed—the spark that touched off

45. Journal History, March 26, 1850.
46. Conway B. Sonne, *World of Wakara* (San Antonio: Naylor Co., 1962), 105, 130.

a year of killing that forced the temporary abandonment of many of the infant Mormon settlements. The so-called Walker War killed some twenty whites, including U.S. Army captain John W. Gunnison and seven of his surveying party, killed on October 26, 1853, on the Sevier River near present-day Deseret. Brigham Young and other Mormon leaders negotiated a peace settlement with Walker at Chicken Creek near Nephi on May 12, 1854. Walker's prestige faded quickly, and within nine months he was dead. He was buried in a talus slope on the side of a mountain above Meadow Creek in a pit that also contained his blankets, rifles, robes, and buckskin clothing. Accounts of the burial vary. Some of his best horses—accounts vary from twelve to twenty— were killed for the occasion. So were two of his wives—or perhaps captive women. A young Paiute girl was killed and put in the pit, along with a Paiute boy who was tied by the chief's corpse and left to die.[47]

That Walker wanted to wait for Arrapin (Arapeen or Arrapine) before accepting Brigham's gift of corn is not surprising. Arrapin was the closest of Walker's six known brothers, serving as his lieutenant and counselor, and, following Walker's death in 1855, was elected chief of the band.[48]

The geographical information given by Walker and Barney Ward during the December 7 meeting was accurate but critically incomplete. Certainly, as Walker said, the party couldn't cross the mountains at the head of the Sevier; that would put them into the wild country of the Pink Cliffs in the vicinity of Bryce Canyon. The mountains to the southeast of their campsite were the high, steep Wasatch Plateau; crossing it, even if possible, would put them into Castle Valley and the San Rafael Swell country, accurately described by Walker as "no good country over there, little Water, don't run far, Rocky." Barney Ward's assurance that "we could cross the mountains the way were going" was encouraging. But either he didn't tell them the right place to cross, they didn't understand him, or they failed to recognize the place when they got to it. The best place was the natural passage up Clear Creek over the foothills of the Tushar Mountains towering to the south.

---

47. Whitney, *History of Utah*, 1:539. See also Sonne, *World of Wakara*, 219–21, and Paul
    Bailey, *Walkara, Hawk of the Mountains* (Los Angeles: Westernlore Press, 1954).
48. Steward, *Basin-Plateau Aboriginal Sociopolitical Groups*, 220.

Jedediah Smith had found that route on his 1826 expedition to California, and I-70 generally follows it today. With their guide sick, the Pratt expedition missed that route and pushed another fifty miles up the Sevier River until forced to make the desperate winter crossing the journals will shortly describe.

Saturday, December 8

CAMPBELL: T 21 A horse traded for few Buckskins & very high priced. James Allred, Charles Shumway [both Sanpitch settlers] came in last night, find coal, Salt & iron ore, their iron ore questioned & other curiosities which Shumway was going to inform Brigham of. Parley, Dan Jones & Dimic goes & prays for Indians at Walkers request, rebukes their meazles, by laying hands on them in the name of Jesus. Walker makes long speech, said he'd come with us but his ppl r all sick the best he can do for us send his Bro Ammomah with us—he wished to do right that he might come back on the earth and live with Shinaub [a Ute god] after he died & his Spirit went to Shinaub who gave it, he always listened to the good words of ours, wished all to come American and Mormon & live in peace, he would not fight any more, had done fighting. Start about 10 A.M. Dimic brings Indian guide Ammomah along with 2 horses, reach Coal creek. Difficult turn in crossing, 18 ft Wide, 14 in deep gravelly. Willows on banks Walkers mother laying here sick, 162 miles. cold cloudy. Indians shoot a Pi Ute boy, they had bought for a Gun because they were sick & afflicted in camp, sing over one another, & suck their feet and hed. Parley gives instructions to Camp about travelling together. Coy going with him to explore. Capt Green & some of his ten a head fixing roads to day, good hard claying soil Beautiful prairie road, through sage & greasewood. Ravine, steep 164 1/4—Pass over small creek 10 ft wide 4 in deep & Camp on banks of the Sevier 165. Willows, sage & greasewood, Sevier nearly froze over. Indian guide sick. Camp prayers & singing.

ARMSTRONG: Traveled six miles, very cold, men and animals feel it very much..

HAIGHT: Got an Indian guide and started on our way as we left the Indian camp they shot a young Pah Utau Boy as a Sacrifice that the sickness may stop There is Salt, Coal & Iron Ore in the mountain east of the River came 9 miles

BROWN: We left Walker and took up the east side of the river we crossed a creek where coal has been found specimens of which Ward and company showed us we crossed another creek which had very salt water camped at its mouth.

These journal entries give insight into health problems as well as practices of the Utes and other Indians. Measles, introduced by contact with whites, devastated many tribes who had built no immunity to this disease. Despite the blessings given Walker's people by Pratt, Dan Jones, and Dimick Huntington and despite the Indians' own treatment of singing and sucking feet and heads, the epidemic continued and many died. Some weeks after the Pratt party moved on, Walker sent to Isaac Morley of the Manti settlement for medical help, which was given. In a letter to Brigham Young, Morley reported Walker's statement that without this help all the band would have died.[49]

The killing of children, usually slaves, to ward off sickness or as a form of mourning was not unknown. Though contemporary journals don't mention it, John Lowry, one of the Manti settlers who had joined the expedition, recalled years later that Walker wanted to sell a number of Paiute children, and that when the offer was declined he threatened to kill them, saying it was because of them so many of his people were sick. He did kill one child. Lowry stated that only the persuasion of Parley saved the lives of the others.[50]

The discovery of Walker's aged and ill mother raises the question: had she been abandoned to die as was sometimes done? One account claims that on one occasion Walker had tried to hasten the process. Mrs. A. B. Sidwell, an early Manti settler, wrote:

> Walker . . . deciding that his mother, a withered, wrinkled scrap of a woman, who looked as if the first mountain breeze might annihilate her, had cumbered this earth long enough, attempted to end her life. She was a quick, wiry, plucky little creature and though well advanced in years, after receiving several very severe cuts and bruises at his hands, any one of which would have ended a common mortal's career, made good her escape, and remained hidden among the bullrushes of Sanpete Valley swamps for a week or more with no known means of sustenance. When she concluded his wrath had somewhat subsided, she came crawling back to the wickiups, and was permitted to drag out a sort of attenuated existence a few years longer.[51]

---

49. Journal History, February 20, 1850.
50. Olive Anderson, "Sketch of the Life of John Lowry Jr.,1829–1915," typescript, Manuscript Division, University of Utah Marriott Library, Salt Lake City, 5.
51. Andrew Jensen, comp., "Sanpete Stake Historical Record," manuscript, LDS Church Historian's Library, Salt Lake City, 5.

That the account was written many years later raises a question as to whether it was history or folklore.

Sunday, December 9

CAMPBELL: T 5 below zero. N Wind, start 9 A.M. Sun breaks thro. Good feed up the river. descend to Sevier bottom 168 1/4— Excellent feed few willows. Snowed last night, inch deep all over. Red butte on the Mts to the right & cedars plentiful, nice feed on the top of smooth Mt. 169 To crossing of Sevier 20 yds Wide 14 in deep, few Willows To Dry creek 172—Plenty drift wood, rotton & dry cedar laying along the road some few cotton woods to the right of road—within one mile you cross several dry creeks with dry cedar laying in them & to the left of road is some good dry feed. River, suppose 1 mile distant, T noon 18 in shade strike down to the left. Camp at an isthmus Carrel in front of it good feed. Sevier pretty near froze over. Good road all day, 176 1/4 Willows & burnt bull-berry, for fuel. Camp prayers reading & singing T 6 below zero.

ARMSTRONG: Traveled 11 1/4 miles. Camped in good season, but very cold, All well. Rabbits, grouse and deer but none killed. This night one of the coldest we have had. Both of my feet frozen.

HAIGHT: Weather very cold crossed the River ice running in the River come 11 3/4 miles

BROWN: We reached a place where the mountain came down to the river on the east. We had to cross over to the west we found a good ford and camped on the Sevier the ground was still covered with snow

Camp this night was in the vicinity of Venice, on the Sevier River five miles northeast of present Richfield.

Monday, December 10

CAMPBELL: T 21 below zero, extreme hard frost, river froze over hard. Cattle all on the Peninsula. Good feed, but too cold for to eat. Indian guide getting better. Start at 9h 25m. Pass good feed, & nice bottom David Fullmer says would be a good place for a settlement. Snow 1 in deep all over. Sun strong. Slough froze over 179 1/4. Have never yet turned many rods from the road to camp. Parley thinks this good loamy soil & some Red Clayey soil believes the Water could be brought from the river up above. Timber on the mts West 5 & 6 miles off could not be easily obtained. Two tenpenny Utes come into Camp recognize Dimic speak to him and Ammomah, they over the high ridge of Mts on the East. see the Sevier a head angling up to the right. We cross the Mts to the right where small ridge, bear to the right. nobody being ahead we have to avoid the bluff or descent on the left. Strike the Sevier 186 3/4. Bre turn out their teams Parley comes & hunts ford with Captn Brown 3h 25m. Camped. T all day 28 snow 2 in deep—Greasewood, Sage, Dry Willows abundant, S wind—camp singing and prayers—Parley finishes Hymn "O come come away" T at 9 P.M. 10 below 0—find good ford 1 3/4 miles above no ice—better feed above, & more, dry brush for fuel.

HAIGHT: Thermometer 21 below zero. the valley a little more fertile the Mountains high on both sides of the Valley on the west they contain Quicksilver come 10 miles

BROWN: The Thermometer stood at 21 below zero. It was a pretty sharp morning. Traveled up the west side of the river, met a few Indians camped on the bank we were more on the old Spanish trail but the ground being covered with snow could only see it once in a while.

The "good place for a settlement" with "good loamy soil" passed this day would become Richfield. Calling the place Omni for a character in the Book of Mormon, the first settlers spent the winter of 1864–1865 in dugouts before building Fort Omni of rock the following spring. The name was later changed to Richfield. The timbered mountains Campbell noted to the west are the Pavant Range. The "high ridge of Mts on the East" over which the two Indians came is the Sevier Plateau soaring 5,800 feet above the valley floor.

Since striking the Sevier, the explorers have been more or less on the Old Spanish Trail, called the longest, crookedest, toughest pack trail in North America. It wound 1,120 miles from Santa Fe to Los Angeles, passing through southwestern Colorado into Utah, crossing the Colorado River near Moab, the Green River near the present town of Green River, through the San Rafael Swell into Castle Valley, and over the Sevier Plateau near the present route of I-70 to reach the Sevier River in the vicinity of Salina. Over it, for twenty years in the 1830s and 1840s, New Mexican traders drove mule trains loaded with woollens to trade in California for the horses and mules they would drive, thousands at a time, back to Santa Fe. But since it was a trail for horses, not wagons, and was frequently indistinguishable under the snow, it was of limited use to the Pratt party.

Camp this bitter cold night was near the present site of Central. Parley, a prolific creator of hymns, finished another one this night. The present LDS hymnbook contains eight of his hymns. This one, "O come come away," is not one of them, however.

Tuesday, December 11

CAMPBELL: T 13 below zero. Sun breaks thro at 9 A.M. T 40 start 10 AM. Pass thro large Sage, reach Ford find ice collected & damd it up 1 1/2 feet deep. Pass on, search above for a Ford, 189 1/4—crossing, best place to Camp below 1 1/2 miles on account of feed and fuel. Sevier 18 yds Wide, 1 1/2 in deep. Snow 2 inches deep. Strike to the left, sage & greasewood all along on the banks of the Sevier. at this point we leave the river to cross the mts where the Spanish trail crosses them. Large hollow 193. Ascend snow gets to be 2 & 3 inches deep—sage all over, reach Dry Kanyon creek 1/2 hour before sundown. Camp in hollow. Plenty fuel. Snow for water, feed on bench foot of Mt South side of creek. Band of Indians camped above us on creek 198 T noon 20 Parley comes into Camp, having been a head exploring, sings Extempore

> O Boys we've found out the trail, Leading thro' a beautiful vale
> We've found the trail boys where over we go
> Tis' a rich grassy vale mid the mountains of snow
> And the meadows beyond it look pleasant and fair
> And the evergreen forest is flourishing there
> O come come away to this sweet Southern vale
> Through the mountains of snow boys we've found out the TRAIL

Ammomah says we don't make enough medicine for him, an old medicine squaw at Indian Camp, he is going there, & if gets better in 2 or 3 days he will come on & overtake us—S. Wind

ARMSTRONG: Traveled 11 and 1/4 miles. Had to go two miles up the river to cross. The snow from three to six inches deep. My feet very sore, I have had to walk all day and could hardly get along. Camped in the cedars upon the first rise of the mountain. It is a long way up. No water and little feed. Brother Pratt has been out exploring to find the way that we have to go. We are making a new road all the way. All well and in good health. When Brother Pratt rode into camp he took off his hat and sang the following lines [not recorded] and the boys gave a loud huzzah for it. There were some indians in camp and did not know what to think of it. We have passed through valleys and between mountains of nothing but Desert and brown land.

HAIGHT: Crossed the River travelled 11 1/2 miles and camped at the foot of a Mountain Snow one foot

BROWN: We crossed the river again to the east side, and started for a
gap in the mountain east of the canyon through which the river
passed, we camped on a dry creek among the cedars near an Indian
camp.

Camp this night was in the foothills east of the river near Sevier
Junction. Just upstream from this point, Maryvales Canyon pinches
closely on the Sevier River, making a passage so narrow and difficult that Jedediah Smith, on his 1826 expedition to California,
found it prudent to leave the river and strike west up Clear Creek
to cross the natural pass between the Pavant Range and Tushar
Mountains—a route later followed by I-70. The Spanish Trail also
left the river here, but turned to the east instead, ascending Long
Valley to cross the Antelope Range before returning to the river
near Marysvale. This was the trail of which Pratt sang and that the
expedition would follow fifty miles farther south toward a much
more difficult mountain crossing into Little Salt Lake Valley. The
route up Clear Creek was well traveled by Indians in the region,
and it is difficult not to believe that this was what Barney Ward had
in mind when he told them they could cross the mountains the
way they were going. If so, they misunderstood and, with their
guide sick, missed this important passage.

Disenchanted with the white men's healing power, Chief
Walker's brother Ammomah now gave up his guide duties to seek
healing the Indian way. He promised to return if he got well soon
but never did.

The quiet farming community of Sevier, near where the expedition camped, was once a rowdy mining and railroad town. In the
late 1880s, gold was discovered in Clear Creek Canyon. The
Kimberly mine produced $3 million in gold and silver over the
next two decades. Sevier boomed with a railroad station, a hotel,
and saloon, but the vein pinched out, the buildings burned or
were moved elsewhere, and Sevier now doesn't even qualify as a
ghost town.

Wednesday, December 12

CAMPBELL: T 20 Cattle got away down to the bottom, this is the end
of the Sandpitch Indians land—Pi-eads over the Mts East Pi Vants
over the Mts West (this was told by Dimic yesterday before we
crossed the Sevier) Strong South Wind—been windy all night, these
r Lake Utes camped above us. The Indians call the Pi-eads Pi

Utch—or Pi Utes. Sunny morning. Start 20 to 11. cedars plenty in creek & on the sides of the Mts. Small white oaks on the creek—Snow 3 to 4 in deep—T 40 in shade. sun strong. Ascend narrow steep kanyon 199 3/4—the last 1/4 mile very steep, large rock in the way—narrow pass Summit 200 1/2—doubled teams. Snow 7 in deep, drifted in places to 1 foot deep. Cut some cedars out of our way, otherwise, a firstrate Mountain pass, nothing in comparison to what we anticipated, crossing it being so easy. foot of the Mountain 204 enter Merry vale, a beautiful valley, covered luzuriantly with dry Grass all over, not a sage brush scarcely to be seen while flowing thro' the valley is the Sevier, which is froze over & Pine growing in the bottom. Mts black they say its iron ore. Put up 200 mile board at 204 1/2 miles. Pass half mile further on & encamp near Willow patch by wayside—no Indian trail nor Spanish trail can I discover. said to be a great deer country by Mountaineers, discover many D tracks Camp on the bend of Sevier, near Willow patch 205 miles. Sun 1/2 hour high, hemmed in here by Mts sun sets soon—Willow feed, after dancing a little—Parley said a name for this valley came into his mind—"Merry vale"—Cannon fired for the party who with Captn Brown went in pursuit of the horses & lost ox. 1/2 hour after, Captn & Coy come in with all the horses which they found on the Sevier opposite where we camped Tuesday night, the lost ox belong to M D Hambleton could not be found T 38 Camp prayers & singing—Parley said he had not seen much of this valley yet, but he never felt so like home since we left the Yohab valley as here, has no doubt but this will be settled, intends to look into it, explore it & report it, felt thankful to find ourselves so comfortably situated to night with thousands of feed for our animals & sheltered by these high, Rocky rugged Mts The grass here richly mixed with fine rushes. Cattle like them—The valley white with grass, which is so deep, where there is snow, you can't see it, but the soil hard froze.

ARMSTRONG: Very cold morning, wind blowing very strong, blew hard all night. Left camp at 10 o'clock this morning, 24 horses and mules missing and two oxen. Commenced to ascend the mountain almost knee deep in snow. After a long and troublesome drive got to the top with doubling teams. Five of us men went ahead and cut down trees and rolled them to one side to let the wagons pass. Plenty of timber, pine and cedar. Passed down a hollow and two more ridges when a splendid view burst on our sight. A small valley with abundance of grass and stream of water with timber in the mountains. There is a great quantity of Iron ore in these mountains and they are both high and steep. There was a company of men sent out with Capt. Brown to find the horses. About one hour after dark

the cannon was fired and in half an hour they came into camp with
all the horses but the ox they could not find. The indians had got
one horse and they caught them with it.

HAIGHT: Lost an ox last night. high winds, crossed over a Spur of
the Mountain and camped on the Severe again in a beautiful little
fertile valley which we called Merry Vale come 8 1/2 miles.

BROWN: Our animals were scattered all over the hills and some of
our horses and one ox gone it was very cold and the snow quite
deep, the camp moved and I took some men and went in search of
the animals which we found on the river except the ox who could
not be found we pursued the camp and after travelling sometime
after dark and the report of the little brass piece announced them
nearby. They were camped on the river above the canon in a beautiful little vale.

John W. Van Cott's book, *Utah Place Names*, suggests several sources
of the name Marysvale: that it was named by Catholic miners for
the Virgin Mary, that Brigham Young named it for his wife Mary,
that Brigham named it Merry Valley because his party sang and
danced there on a trip south, or that Parley Pratt named it
Merryville.[52] Campbell's journal entry that "Parley said a name for
this valley came into his mind—'Merry vale'" would seem to settle
the question. The town was settled in 1863 but abandoned tem-
porarily during the Black Hawk War of 1865–1868.

Marysvale is tucked between two great mountain ranges, the
Tushar Mountains soaring over twelve thousand feet elevation to
the west and the Sevier Plateau rising to ten thousand feet on the
east. Both are formed largely as a result of Tertiary volcanic activ-
ity.[53] Armstrong's observation that there was "a great deal of iron
ore in these mountains" is questionable; none has been developed.
But Marysvale became the center for other kinds of mining and
became the southern terminus of a railroad to service the mines.
Rich lead-zinc, copper, gold, and silver bodies have been developed in the Tushar Mountains, though the remote and rugged terrain and complex geology have limited the industry. During World
Wars I and II, decomposed volcanic rock five miles south of
Marysvale was mined for alunite, used to make alum and fertilizer.
And in the 1950s and 1960s the Antelope Range over which the

---

52.   Van Cott, *Utah Place Names*, 245.
53.   Chronic, *Roadside Geology*, 144–46.

Pratt explorers climbed became a major source of uranium ore—tragically, because many Marysvale miners have died of lung cancer contracted in the deep tunnels in which they worked.

Thursday, December 13

CAMPBELL: T before sun up 31 mild pleasant morning. Parley with Coy going exploring. start 10 A.M. cross the Sevier on the ice 15 yds Wide 205 3/4 Captn Green & Bro J. Packer, keeps specimens of these black Mts. Bro Arnold says there is iron ore in the blackish Rocky Mts. Go on something less than mile cross a deep stream, 3 yards wide ice breaks thro, bad descent for the want of a very little fixing. ground froze hard, ox got run over owned by Bro Williams nigh ox being slow, its foot was caught by the wheel—the bow key broke, & both nigh Wheels run over it laying on the Willows which was put on the top of the ice in the creek. Pass thro thick sage, cross over, small creek 207 miles, & come into beautiful valley, rich in feed. Soil light & loose no soot, saleratus however dispursed all over, come to Sage & Greasewood—then into beautiful feed again. travelling to day on the bottom near the river, Willows on its bank, this bottom from 1/2 mile to 1 1/2 & 2 miles broad. T 46, the bluffs which rise above the bottom bare, with little Sage & Greasewood. see at the mouth of one kanyon, apparently some large Fir & Pine 2 miles distant, near the same spot on the Mts & bluffs, good deal of cedar, as there was in the kanyon we came down into this merry vale. Camp on Sevier 211 1/4 Three & 20 P.M. excellent feed, some snow on the ground but its at the roots of the grass, river not quite froze over here T 37 South Wind, blowing down thro' this valley, all day. Quite breezy at times Parley & Exploring Coy went about 10 miles a head—did not find forks of river Camp prayers & singing. Killed California cow this morning.

ARMSTRONG: Traveled six miles today, had hard work breaking the ice to cross the river. One ox fell down in the river and the wagon went over it and broke one horn and cut it but it sustained no other damage. I went out with Bro pratt to explore the mountains, Rode hard all day and when we got back to camp I was so tired I cant stand nor sit down. I could not lift my leg up to step in the wagon, I walked as well as I could and blew the trumpet for prayer—slipped off to bed, rubbed my limbs trembling all the time with cold, my teeth chattering in my head. Truly I thought of home and a good comfortable bed.

HAIGHT: Weather more moderate come over a rich Aluvial Soil covered with a heavy groth of vegetation skirted with timber come 6 miles

BROWN: We had to cross the river again to the west on the ice soon
after we crossed a little creek running in from the west in doing this
a wagon ran over an ox, broke off his horn and otherwise injuring
him but he continued in the team. Bro Pratt road out to the west
mountain and saw some Pahutah Indians who were very wild and it
was difficult to get them to come near him.

Parley's ten-mile advance exploration stopped six miles short of
the confluence of the East Fork with the main Sevier River. In view
of Campbell's and Haight's observation that it was a pleasant day
of moderate temperatures, Armstrong's complaint about his
exhausted and chilled state is puzzling.

Friday, December 14
CAMPBELL: Mild S Wind. T 31 horses loosed, being tied & hobbled
round camp last night. 9 A.M. starting 213 Rabbitt kanyon creek.
[illegible] Wide 8 in deep. cotton woods on banks. reach river bottom again—216 m. Pond of water left of road leave bottom again
few hundred yards—small creek Kanyon, 220 miles cotton woods on
it. Bunch grass feed, 1 yard wide 4 in deep, Willows plenty. Camp on
South West bank of Sevier, S.W. fork, 3/4 mile from the forks, good
feed, willows abundant. Dry cotton woods by going to the Forks—4
P.M. camped—on the other fork discover cotton woods all along
banks. Passed over some tolerable good bench land 223 1/4 m.
Ther 36 at 6 P.M. Camp prayers singing & dancing, Snowing
HAIGHT: Come 12 miles camped at the forkes of the River
Mountains high covered with Evergreen forests valley narrow
BROWN: We came to the forks of the Sevier where we camped here
we had another fall of snow which continued until noon

Camp this night was in the vicinity of Junction, settled in 1880 and
so named because here the East Fork of the Sevier joins the main
river.[54] It is, however, also the junction where a summer version of
the Spanish Trail, coming from Castle Valley past Fish Lake and
down Otter Creek, joins the main Spanish Trail.[55]

Saturday, December 15
CAMPBELL: T 27 Snowing 2 & 3 inches snow all round, Contemplated
sending mission up the left hand fork, but too cloudy and snowing.

---

54.   Van Cott, *Utah Place Names*, 209.
55.   Crampton and Madsen, *In Search of the Spanish Trail*, 62.

225 Slough or Warm Spring—bad crossing to Kanyon creek 12 feet wide 1 foot deep, Plenty of Willows & bulberries at crossing 226—recross Sevier—228 1/2 travelled thro' some good bottom land Go up Sevier to 232 1/4—turn back & camp on Sevier at 233 1/4 Snow 4 inches deep—T 30 South Wind—W W Phelps & others report the road ahead impassable—Parley goes up to the left but finds no pass.

HAIGHT: Proceeded up the west fork crossed it twice and camped where it comes out of the mountain come 7 1/2 miles snow 8 inches

BROWN: We travel up the western fork and after going some eight or nine miles we came to an impassable canyon through which the river ran, we camped for night brother Pratt road out some ten miles to the left to find a pass but did not succeed the mountains were very high on either side.

Camp this night was about two miles south of Circleville, very near the boyhood home of George LeRoy Parker, later to be the infamous outlaw Butch Cassidy. Circleville, settled by Mormons in 1864, was a tough place. Four settlers were killed in November 1865 in the early days of the Black Hawk War. The following spring, the settlers rounded up a small band of Piede Indians who probably had nothing to do with the earlier killing and were on friendly terms with the whites. Disarmed and bound, they were put in the meetinghouse under guard, while eleven women and children were guarded in an empty cellar. During an escape attempt, the men were all killed. The women and older children were then brought up, one at a time, and their throats slit. Only three or four small children were spared, and adopted into white families.[56] Brigham Young condemned this atrocity, declaring the valley would be cursed because of it. Shortly thereafter, escalation of the fighting forced abandonment of the settlement, which was not reoccupied until 1873.

Here on the Sevier just below Circleville Canyon, Pratt's party was obviously confused, since they "contemplated sending mission up the left hand fork [East Fork]." That would have taken them in the opposite direction from their goal of the Little Salt Lake Valley. So would Parley's exploration ten miles to the left, probably up Lost Creek, which would have dead-ended him

---

56. Albert Winkler, "The Circleville Massacre: A Brutal Incident in Utah's Black Hawk War," *Utah Historical Quarterly* 55 (winter 1987): 18–19.

against eleven-thousand-foot Mt. Dutton; no wonder he found no
pass. But their frustration was understandable. Circleville Canyon
to them seemed impassable. With eight inches of snow on the
ground, they apparently did not see that the Spanish Trail continued up the river through the canyon, and so determined they had
to find a way over the mountains to the west. Whether the decision was a good one is debatable; the Spanish Trail route over the
mountains twenty miles farther south was no picnic. Orville Pratt
described it in 1848: "a very hilly & rocky country—Sometimes up
the steepest of hills, then down places which it would seem almost
impossible to descend, again in deep and precipitous canions."[57]
That was in the pleasant days of early October; in the winter it was
worse. In 1830–1831, William Wolfskill and George C. Yount
headed a party of New Mexico traders, the first known to have traversed the entire Spanish Trail. Crossing the Markagunt Plateau,

> they encountered the most terrible snowstorm they had ever expe-
> rienced—During several days, no one ventured out of camp—
> There they lay embedded in snow, very deep, animals and men
> huddled thick as possible together, to husband and enjoy all possi-
> ble animal warmth, having spread their thick and heavy blankets, &
> piled bark and brush wood around & over them. . . . After the
> storm subsided, Yount & Wolfskill ascended a lofty Peak of the
> mountains for observation—In the whole range of human view, in
> every direction, nothing could be discerned, in the least degree
> encouraging, but only mountains, piled on mountains, all capped
> with cheerless snow, in long and continuous succession, till they
> seemed to mingle with the blue vault of heaven and fade away in
> the distance—It was a cheerless prospect. . . . Several of their ani-
> mals had perished in the piercing cold.[58]

Comparing that with the ordeal about to be faced by the Pratt
explorers begs the question which route was the worst?

Sunday, December 16
    CAMPBELL: Fitting out exploring Coy & Captn Brown, to go & find a
    road—Coy start at 10 A.M. Camp rests, Cattle driven to feed—good
    mountain bunch grass. Sevier has a swift current here. Cedars

---

57. "The Journal of Orville C. Pratt," 353.
58. Orange Clark, from a biography of George Yount as quoted in "The Trail Makers,"
     Old Spanish Trail, 150.

plenty round. beautiful day. 20m 6h Exploring Coy return R.C. composes the following when coming home & sings it to camp:

> We've found out the trail boys where over we go
> It lyes thro the mountain, deeply covered with snow
> It's a rough rocky road, the rout we have been
> But there is plenty of Deer, for them we have seen
> We looke'd away far beyond, but nothing could see
> Save the blue expanse of Ether so clear & so free
> But to a high Mountain some of us did go
> And we spied out a trail where the Mormons can go.

[A note at the side running crosswise says, "This route is 'Brown's Pass' named by Bro Stewart."]

Parley had it sung again, then Captn Brown makes report of the rout, as being impracticable but barely passible, rocky road all along for 6 miles, winding over a succession of kanyons, steep ascents and descent, cobble stones all the way, nearly perpendicular in places. Snow drifts where the horses could not pass, we had to get off & stamp the snow away & make a track. The snow being collected in drifts on the lee side of the ascents—Southerly Wind—Camp in high Spirits to go & try it. Parley prays, singing in Camp. R.C. being absent WW Phelps keeps Thermometrical observation &c, being Topographical Engineer, many camp songs making. T at 6 A.M. 2 below cipher

HAIGHT: Remained in camp weather cold. a party went to find a pass over the Mountain returned after dark report a pass but rough and difficult

BROWN: I took two or three men and went to examine a pass to the right we road all day and found a pass over which I thought we could go, it was a long way through the mountain and very difficult snow 1 1/2 to 2 feet deep. We returned at night the brethren were anxious to hear our report as we did not know but we were to the end of our row when we reached this place. after hearing a description of the pass, the cry was we can go it. It was a great undertaking and a very hazardous one to cross so large a mountain at this season of the year. There was danger of being snowed under.

The terrible ordeal of crossing this southern end of the Tushar Mountains, described so dramatically in journals of the Pratt expedition, was confirmed four years later by another exploring expedition—that of John C. Frémont. In the winter of 1848–1849, his fourth expedition had lost ten men and 130 pack animals in a horror of starvation, freezing, and cannibalism in the San Juan Mountains of western Colorado. Obsessed by his goal of finding a railroad route through the central Rockies along the thirty-eighth parallel, Frémont tried again. By February 1854, following the summer branch of the Spanish Trail, he had struggled past Fish Lake, down Otter Creek to reach the forks of the Sevier, and on to the mouth of Circleville Canyon. He now faced the mountain crossing. Solomon Nunes Carvalho, an artist with the expedition, wrote:

> Four days before we entered the Little Salt Lake Valley, we were surrounded by very deep snows; but as it was necessary to proceed, the whole party started, to penetrate through what appeared to be a pass, on the Warsatch Mountains. The opening to this depression [Chokecherry Creek[59]] was favorable, and we continued our journey until the mountains seemed to close around us, the snow in the canon got deeper, and further progress on our present course was impossible.
>
> It was during this night, while encamped in this desolate spot, that Col. Frémont called a council of Capt. Wolff and Solomon of the Delawares [Indian guides-hunters with the expedition]—they had been sent by Col. Frémont to survey the canon, and surrounding mountains, to see if a passage could be forced. . . . Capt. Wolff reported it impossible to proceed, as the animals sank over their heads in snow, and he could see no passage out. The mountains which intercepted our path were covered with snow four feet deep. The ascent bore an angle of forty-five degrees, and was at least one thousand feet from base to summit. Over this, Captain Wolff said it was also impossible to go. "That is not the point," replied Frémont. "We must cross, the question is, which is most practicable—and how can we do it."
>
> We commenced the ascent of this tremendous mountain, covered as it were, with an icy pall of death, Col. Frémont leading and breaking a path; the ascent was so steep and difficult, that it was impossible to keep on our animals; consequently, we had to lead them, and travel on foot—each man placed his foot in the tracks of the one that preceded him; the snow was up to the bellies of the

---

59. See "Diagram of the 6th Standard Parallel and Exteriors in the Territory of Utah, Surveyed by Joseph Gorlinski, U.S. Dep Sur: Under His Contract No 13 Dated January 11th, 1871," Bureau of Land Management, Salt Lake City.

animals. In this manner, alternately toiling and resting, we reached the summit. . . . When I surveyed the distance, I saw nothing but continued ranges of mountains of everlasting snow, and for the first time, my heart failed me.[60]

The crossing cost the life of one man, Oliver Fuller, left frozen in the snow while the survivors staggered on to the tiny Mormon settlement of Parowan. Carvalho wrote, "We had now triumphantly overcome the immense mountain, which I do not believe human foot, whether civilized or Indian, had ever before attempted." Apparently his rescuers at Parowan had not told him—or in his youthful pride he forgot or ignored—that four years earlier Parley's fifty men had attempted and accomplished exactly that, not on horseback like the Frémont expedition, but with wagons, a far more difficult task.

Monday, December 17
CAMPBELL: T 31 South Wind—mild, Parley exhorting to early start, 9 A.M. start, large Coy with Parley breaking roads, levelling steep pitches, removing rocks &c strike out from Sevier West up kanyon, Rocky road, about 2 1/2 miles up, perpendicular descent, road fixed & Mormon team hold back with ropes, both wheels locked. Pass some good feed but 8 & 9 in snow. Plenty cedars. Camp with one half of the wagons at foot of steep long hill 4 3/4 in Deer Kanyon, double teams with the other half & ascend, then descend &c &c to kanyon creek where we leave the wagons & bring back the teams. in the ravine or kanyons coming from the Mts to the right of us perhaps 1 mile or 1 1/2 to Summits, there is Clear Water & plenty timber, especially up above where we cross then some large Fir & Pine trees. Boys cold & tired, snow so deep to wade thro holding wagons back, pulling oxen up steep pitches then the oxen pulling the wagons, tedious work. Wind, & small frozen flakes of Snow on the tops of the ridges like to blow thro a fellow. Cloudy day—Hambleton and Brown kill 2 Deer in this kanyon, both near each other—return teams get into Camp nearly 5 P.M. Parley & Captn Brown come back—T 31 The wagons who r camped on N side of the Mts have come 4 3/16 miles. 237 1/2.
HAIGHT: Commence to cross the Mountain had a long heavy hill snow one foot. come 4 1/2 miles and left half of the waggons and

---

60. Donald Dean Jackson and Mary Lee Spence, eds., *Travels from 1848 to 1854*, vol. 3 of *The Expeditions of John Charles Frémont* (Urbana and Chicago: University of Illinois Press, 1970), 458–60.

put all our team on the other half and went on. had to let the waggons down into some deep ravines with roaps and help our cattle up
out the same way had to shovel through the snow in some places
went about 3 miles forth and camped in a deep hollow

BROWN: Early morning we started with all the courage and united
exertion possible for us to command knowing we had a severe job
on hand, bro. Pratt led the way being followed by all the men who
were not driving teams or loose cattle armed with axes, picks, shov-
els, spades &c. We worked our way four miles without much difficulty here we left half the wagons and put all the teams on the
others, continued on some three miles further to a little creek
where night came on. This part of the road was very difficult we had
to use ropes to let the wagons down some places and other, to pull
them up. It was intensely cold. We took the teams back to the wagons and turned them out for the night, there was good grass but it
was under the snow, after dark the snow began falling very fast and
continued till noon next day

The route taken by the party as it left the Sevier River to cross the
mountains to the west has not been certainly known. The only previous attempt to identify the route was in a master's thesis by Rick
J. Fish.[61] His text and map have the route ascend part way up present Highway 20, then double sharply back north to Fremont Pass
and on down Fremont Canyon. That route would require John
Brown and his companions exploring for a pass on December 16
to ride thirteen miles up the Sevier, then another seven or eight
miles into the snow-choked mountain to find the pass. The round
trip would be more than forty miles—clearly impossible in the ten
hours the explorers were absent from camp. By that route the wagons would have traveled thirty-five miles to complete the crossing;
their odometer registered nineteen miles. Further, the terrain on
that route in no way resembles that described in the company's
journals.

    From a close comparison of the journals with contour maps
of the area, and from personally exploring the entire route, the
editors are convinced that from their campsite on the river a couple of miles south of Circleville, Parley and his men struck directly
west, up Birch Creek. Two and a half miles up, they climbed out of

61. Rick J. Fish, "The Southern Utah Expedition of Parley P. Pratt, 1849–1850," master's
     thesis, Brigham Young University, Provo, Utah, December 1992, 82 and accompanying
     map.

that canyon to the left and began a grueling struggle cross-grain along the flanks of eleven-thousand-foot Circleville Mountain. To appreciate the incredible labor of that crossing, the country must be seen close up. An extremely rough jeep road contours south from the Birch Creek campground at about the eight-thousand-foot level, close to the explorers' route. Six times the road plunges in and out of ravines and deeper canyons, often at grades only manageable in the lowest gear of four-wheel drive. Wagons don't do well on sidehills, so Pratt's wagons had to be hauled up the ascents and lowered down the descents, not at an angle as the road goes but directly up and down, on much steeper grades. In a typical understatement, Campbell's journal mentions "plenty cedars." There are, indeed; much of the way, especially on steep canyon slopes, is covered by dense pinyon-juniper forest. Add cutting of trees to the back-breaking labor of shoveling snow, clearing rocks, and hauling oxen up, and the heroism of their accomplishment becomes more clear.

The journals don't mention all the smaller ravines they traversed, but the deep, snow-choked canyons into which they lowered wagons on ropes and from which they doubled teams to climb out were the steep-walled canyons of Pole, Little Pine, Pine, and Chokecherry Creeks—the latter three called in Campbell's Dec. 18 journal entry 1st, 2nd, and 3rd Kanyon creeks.

"Deer Kanyon," where half the wagons were left so other wagons could be double-teamed up the "steep long hill," is an unnamed tributary of Birch Creek. "Kanyon creek," where men with the advance wagons camped, is Pole Creek. Aspen and fir forest start at about eight thousand feet in this area, so their campsite was somewhat below this elevation.

Tuesday, December 18

CAMPBELL: Snowing nearly all night, T 33 10 A.M. Brethren come in from the other Camp, say it snowed 1 foot more last night at their encampment. ceases snowing 11 A.M. Horn blows 1 P.M. starting. ascend steep Rocky long hill. Wind blowing the Snow in our faces on the ridge. Cloudy, Snowing a little. Descend steep hill, 12 men hold back with ropes & both wheels locked, then ascend, wind to the right & ascend long hill, snow on the lee side of the hills drifted from 1 to 2 1/2 feet high. sideling & Rocky, but the snow so deep Rocks covered—then descend sideling steep Rocky hollow, men with ropes hold back, ascend, & strike to the right, steep, Rocky, &

snow drifted very deep. then descend, Steep Rocky pitch to 1st Kanyon [Little Pine Creek]. Birch, Pine, fir on creek, which is frozen & covered with snow, so the Water running can be heard easier than seen, ascend nearly perpendicular, snow drifted very deep on the ascent side of the hill. Wind from the South & blowing on the ridges. between these divides we cross like to tear our wagon covers away & cold on the sides of our face, descend to 2nd Kanyon creek [Pine Creek], timber plenty, some feed to be seen above the snow but not much, the snow shovelled away up this ascent & on each side of the oxen, snow as high as the oxen, nearly perpendicular ascent, hitch rope round the oxen yokes & men stand on the summit & pull the oxen up, then they pull the wagons up, that is the oxen. descend into 3rd Kanyon creek [Chokecherry Creek], where the wagons camped. Plenty timber, Fulmer & Phelps, make a temporary bridge over the creek—2 1/2 miles from where we started this morning—start up, & keep to the right round the Mts. Snow very deep, being drifted all along where we pass thro' men a head breaking road, shovelling the snow, others holding their wagons, move down sideling into Hollow & Camp turn the cattle out no water. Snow 2 feet deep at encampment, Plenty of dry timber, T 30 1 1/2 from the last Kanyon where the other encampment. 241 1/4— Parley calls R.C. into carriage where Dan Jones & Wadsworth were—Sings hymn. Parley said he felt like praying. he prayed, asked the Lord to forgive the camp for their vanity, folly, & wickedness— interceded with the Lord not to hedge up our way, but to enable us to get out of these Mts & to find a pass, to have mercy & compassion on this Camp, & to treat us kindly & for the sakes of those in Camp who keep thy name sacred, & seek to fulfill our mission &c &c— Schyler Jennings swore & dam'd Captn Jones in Gods name to take his horse away from near his waggon & threat him with club in hand—Witness Captn Jones, Wadsworth & others. had pleasant talk till nearly 10 P.M.

HAIGHT: Got up in the morning found it snowing and the wind blew a gale on the hills went back and brought up the other waggons the snow two feet deep and drifted in heaps we took the waggons two miles beyond the others and camp stormed continually.

BROWN: Some were almost ready to dispair, the snow was now one foot deeper than before half of the wagons were in the midst of the pass and the others just entered, however, discouraging as it was we hitched to the wagons and moved on, it was still cloudy and looked as though it might continue to snow for days. We took these wagons some two miles beyond where we had left the others the previous night and camped in the canyon at the foot of the last hill. During the night the wind blew at a tremendous rate covering us with snow in our tents and wagons. This was quite discouraging to a faint heart. We were now all in the midst of the mountain.

This day's journals reflect the expedition's hardest day. They speak of incessant snow, winds piling up huge drifts, threatening to blow off wagon covers and engulfing wagons and tents at night. They speak of exhausting labor, shoveling through drifts higher than the oxen, hauling oxen up steep pitches with ropes so the oxen could then haul up the wagons. No wonder stalwart John Brown wrote of discouragement and Parley felt the need to beseech the Lord not to hedge up their way out of these mountains. And no wonder that Schuyler Jennings, probably exhausted and with nerves frayed by incessant labor, would curse and threaten with a club over what would seem a minor annoyance. Remarkably, this and a similar outburst the next day are the only indications in any of the journals of a breakdown of morale or civility.

Wednesday, December 19

CAMPBELL: T—clear Beautiful morning. Sun rises, shines strong, cattle go out from camp, (whither they had come in last night for shelter) & find little feed on Mt sides. Capt Haight & others arrive from the other Camp, 11 A.M. Cattle gathered up yoking & some have commenced starting back for other wagons—Parley, WWPhelps Nathan Tanner & RC. go a head to explore & beat track. R.C. goes 1/2 mile down Hollow running S.E. where WWPhelps stopped to inform the camp, that, some feed above the snow here, & cedars on the right, up the Mtn. large Buck Deer, with large horns, turns up hollow running North Parley asked R.C. to shoot him, followed him, shot him, knocked him over, but got up & bounded off. snow so deep my mule sometimes drowned in snow drifts, see other Deer, track them on to our road again. Wagons get doubled up last hills by 3 1/2 PM Pass over beautiful level road. Get next into a small Basin, no outlet but Southerly to the Waters. Snow 1 foot deep on level, then pass down narrow hollow at the foot of which, you turn down hollow to the left 1/2 mile then Camped at the last point where cedar is on the Mt on the right. Camped at 5 P.M. 244 1/4 boys packing wood from the Mts shovelling snow away from where they intend to have fires & camping spot. Parley comes back before 6 P.M. Found the only place where they can pass down, went to where the waters run the other way. These hollows where we camped run down into the Sevier

winding to the left—afterwards made a long exhortation & preach
to the Bre told them, the Lords spirit grieved on account of the
folly, nonsense, & vanity in camp, said some had threatened to
knock one another down & cursed in the name of God. it was
wrong to use the name of God have no fellowship for those who
take our God's name in vain & especially to curse their Bre, said
need for us all to pray & ask God's forgiveness, said he felt to do so,
pleased at the kindness & love evinced at first, but too much folly,
lightmindness & nonsense. Yet the Lord has lead us, our Guardian
Angels vexed but have not left us, brought us to the only pass in
these Mts very thankful to the Lord. Prayed. T 21 While Parley
speaking Jennings said in hearing of George Matson & John Lowry,
that he'd a good mind to black his mouth, &c using the word
damd.
HAIGHT: Sun rose clear with much labour and toil we got our waggons all together upon the summit of the Mountain. came 3 miles
and camped as usual without water our cattle almost exhausted for
want of feed and water the cold was intense every man froze his feet
more or less we killed some deer.
BROWN: Clear and handsome but very cold we sent the teams back
and brought the other wagons up and just before sun set we were
on top of the last divide where every team could take its own wagon;
we camped in a wide hollow that runs west

With the last wagons finally double-teamed out of the canyon of
Chokecherry Creek, the party now finds easier going. The "small
Basin" with an outlet to the south is the lovely Little Dog Valley.
From there, through a narrow gap in Cougar Ridge, they enter
and camp in the two-mile expanse of Dog Valley, level, thickly covered with grass, but at 7,500 feet choked with snow so deep it
required double-teaming. Here they were on the route Frémont's
party would follow four years later after ascending Chokecherry
Creek. Campbell says this night's camp was on the Sevier River
drainage, Brown that they camped "in a wide hollow that runs
west." The confusion is understandable; the valley is so level and
broad that both are correct. Fremont Pass, which should be called
Brown's Pass since he discovered it, is at the western edge of Dog
Valley after a slope so gradual it is difficult to discern, especially
under snow. Even with the relief the party must have felt at seeing
safety ahead, Parley's prayer of thanksgiving apparently didn't
soften Schuyler Jennings's heart.

Thursday, December 20

CAMPBELL: T 25 some feed above the snow down this hollow, no water here but the snow. Coy of hunters sent out of each Ten as directed by Parley last night. Cloudy day. Wind blowing down the hollow some cattle missing, hitch up whats here & start about noon T 45 Sun shines away South, & often does while it is cloudy all round we must be on bottoms whose altitude is higher than the Mts we have passed. the land now hilly & knolly a head S & W many miles, not even cedar timber. left a high valley, The Sevier running down thro' it. Plenty Wheat Grass on these vallies, & other Grass which is covered with Snow about 1 foot deep on these plains, 8 or 10 miles a head the bench land (beyond which we can see no high rugged Mts) covered with tender cedar I presume beyond this surely it's the basin, to the right of us these high Rocky rugged peaky Mts (at the foot of which we have been passing these 4 days) level down to hills where there may be a pass down some-where, foot of Hill 245 1/2 200 yards doubled on acc of the deep snow Pass a fine Doe the hunters have killed & brought to the road for the wagons to pick up. further down this hollow good deal of Wheat grass, & bunch grass on each side of us—the hollow frequently 100 yds broad, Pass open space from where the water may flow to the left down to the Sevier & some of the hollows would only admit of their waters flowing down the hollow (West) we r travelling. Snow only 6 in deep, gets less as we go down the hollow, Camp at elbow in the kanyon to the right. Cedars plenty, considerable grass above the snow, no water, in the Creek bed. 249 1/4—T 30 Breth come in who were hunting lost cattle, say they found them on the Sevier, down near where we camped Sabbath last—unable to drive them here in the night so they left them— Parley arrives—eats supper. Calls Camp together by the Horn as usual for prayers, said he wished to report & he'd begin at the date, "Wasatch range of Mts, Mormon pass, 4 miles (or 1 hours ride) above Summer gate. Lat 38 (only guessed at) Dec 20th 1849—Bre we ave been down into the valley where the waters flow to ~~the Colorado~~ Little Salt Lake ~~or somewhere else than the Basin~~. 4 miles below here r huge rocks nearly closing up this kanyon but when you get to them, you'll find room enough for a wagon to pass—below these rocks (which we av called Summer Gate) the weather is mild, the sun shines, but few inches of snow. above 2 miles further there is a large Rock, the most beautiful cornishing on it you have seen in large cities got a few miles further down, went on the side hill discovered a valley 60 miles long, or more, no snow on the bottom land save where there is a Gopher hill, or on the benches, there is some water, about a mile (1 1/2) from this encampment, but steep banks to it, & it sinks in little ways could discover no water in the valley, a head, therefore want an early start to morrow, so that we may get to water in the valley, tho' it is 60 miles long that we can see does not appear to be broader than 1 & some places may be 2 miles. Camp prayers & singing. Practicing Music

HAIGHT: Our cattle badly scattered 13 missing but the camp moved on down the Mountain I with three others went to hunt them found them just at night but had to leave them and found the camp in a narrow valley that leads to Little Salt Lake Valley came 5 miles Br Pratt & Capt Brown returned after dark from exploring the road through to the valley. We were all very glad that we were so near through the Mountains.

BROWN: 13 of our cattle had wandered off into the mountains and could not be found we hitched on and moved out in a westerly direction, leaving four horsemen to hunt the missing cattle. Bro Pratt and myself pioneered ahead of the camp, we followed down a little narrow canyon which led us into the upper end of Little Salt Lake Valley. The pass was so narrow between perpendicular rocks that in many places it was just wide enough for a wagon to pass. We returned to camp at night. They had followed our trail and traveled six or seven miles that day. The men who went in search of the lost cattle had returned without them one man found them but could not drive them alone.

Campbell's entries this day are puzzling. Fremont Pass, at 7,522 feet elevation, is far lower than 11,000-foot Circleville Mountain they have been passing the past four days; perhaps he was thinking of some low mountain they had passed earlier. If the "high valley" to the left refers to Dog Valley, east of Fremont Pass, it indeed contains water draining toward the Sevier, but not, of course, the Sevier itself. Parley's report of his exploration—or Campbell's recording of it—also contains a surprising misstatement, that the waters of Parowan Valley flow to the Colorado River. John C. Frémont's second expedition of 1843–1844 had circumvented the Great Basin, including travel through Parowan Valley. His map of the expedition contained this notation about the vast area between the Wasatch and Sierra Nevada Mountains: "Diameter 11 of latitude, 10 of longitude: elevation above the sea between 4 and 5,000 feet: surrounded by lofty mountains: contents almost unknown, but believed to be filled with rivers and lakes which have no connection with the sea."[62] He had concluded that the region was a land of interior drainage, a "great basin," and so named it. Brigham Young knew it, too; he had carefully studied Frémont's reports before the exodus from Nauvoo. Moreover, Jefferson Hunt, lately released from the Mormon Battalion, had made a round trip to Los Angeles in 1847–1848, understood the drainage, and had reported to Brigham. Whether Parley misstated or Campbell misunderstood is impossible to tell. In any event, the entry about drainage to the Colorado was later crossed out, as was that about drainage "somewhere else than the Basin."

Camp this night was about three miles down Fremont Canyon after crossing Fremont Pass.

At the end of Campbell's journal, in his handwriting, is a poem, apparently written by Campbell since no other author is indicated. Though apparently unfinished, it is a vivid description of one man's feelings about this mountain crossing:

> Tis Winter i' our Mountain
> Tis mantled in snow
>
> The Winds o'er its Glaziers
> Unceasingly blow
>
> Tis the home of the storm-cloud–
> Its rival–the skies
>
> And its proud towering summit
> our passage defies
>
> Shall the sons of the Prophets
> now shrink from the task
>
> And a 50 of Israel
> be conquered at last?
>
> No–Never tho legions
> should dare to oppose

---

62. "Map of an Exploring Expedition to the Rocky Mountains in the Year 1842 and Oregon & North California in the Years 1843–44 by Brevet Capt. J. C. Frémont of the Corps of Topographical Engineers," Bancroft Library, University of California, Berkeley. A copy of the map is reprinted in Donald Dean Jackson and Mary Lee Spence, eds., *The Expeditions of John Charles Frémont* (Urbana: University of Illinois Press, 1970), map no. 3.

Tis the motto of Jacob
    to conquer the foes.

Then arise with the signal–
    The sound of the horn

And we'll scale yon proud Mountain
    our breasts to the storm

A shout from the Fifty
    Exultingly rung

And the following morning
    the toil was begun

At first mid the cedars
    Full slowly they rose

And the rocks rough & ready
    Their wagons opposed

The clouds on its bosom
    Betoken dispair

And the hurricane tempest
    Is revelling there

The storm-God enthroned
    In his palace of white

Beheld their approach
    and exclaimed with affright

Our castle invaded!
    Then foaming with rage

He gathered the tempest
    his foes to engage

It was night and the watchfires
    Gleamed bright on the hill

The notes of the bugle
    were merry & shrill

Glad songs broke the silence
where solitude reign'd

For the Fifty of Israel
A summit had gained

The Winds roared like thunder!
The hurricane burst

The fires were all quenched
And the cattle dispersed

The storm demons raging
Attacked the foe

And reared as by magic
new breastworks of snow

Friday, December 21

CAMPBELL: T 28 All rise at the blowing of the horn as Parley wished last night, men go right off & herd the cattle start nearly 9 A.M. 251 miles. Water, running in bed of creek, little brackish, Cattle can get easily to it, many of the crossing of this creek or bed of creek, steep, rugged & Rocky. Pass lots of good feed, side hills to the left bare from snow, good bunch grass on them. Sun shines clear sky T in shade 44—at Summer Gate, about noon, 252 3/4—Cornishing rock 254 1/2. Hollows gets wider feed more plentiful. Carriage tongue breaks. Hambletons wagon comes uncoupled. Rocky going, but the snow helps us along among the rocks, & had it not been for the deep snow coming over these Rocky divides or hollows or kanyons. our Cattle's feet must have been severly injured if not many of them rendered entirely disabled to travel. Cattle getting very poor & reduced many of them—Camp at 257 miles in Little Salt Lake Hollow or Kanyon—Breth come in from a head, suppose they can see nearly to the Colorado, thot the little Salt Lake is over these Mts to our right, see other Lakes in the valley ahead of us &c—Bro. Isaac Hatch says he knows there is Gold & Silver in these Mts his mineral rod is attracted the strongest kind, is sanguine that he could find Gold. Isaac Brown kills a Catamount, wild cat, is dressed very fat. Bre come in bring 13 head of Cattle, from about 1 mile beyond where we turned back on the Sevier Saturday night last, had not got to drink on the Sevier (supposed) Good feed here, on this bottom & some bench land to the right covered with cedars. Bre pick up curiosities & keep them from time to time, T 42. Camp prayers & singing, moonlight.

ARMSTRONG [after eight days of silence]: The camp aroused at or before six oclock by sound of horn; Traveled seven and 1/4 miles, as we have had new arrangements. Left camp at 15 to nine oclock, descended the canyon, I must mention here that we have fought with the storms and tempests and it must have been by and thru the divine interposition of providence of God who led Nephi of old, that we were brought over these mountains. To look at them it would be said that no white man could do it or be rash enough to undertake it or have enterprising spirit enough to attempt it. The Mormons are the boys for such expeditions. They fear neither canyon, mountain snow storms, gulleys or rivers, Because they know they are led by the mighty God of Jacob. About three and 3/4 miles from camp we passed through the Summer gate, It is a place where rocks of the mountains rise perpendicular above our heads as if bidding defiance to man. After passing through the canyon it began to widen all the way down, at about a half mile farther the rocks at some sides very much like the ramparts of some Baronial castle such as was used in feudal times. Brother Isaac Brown killed a wild cat upon these rocks, One was named Cornish rock on account of its resemblance to a Cornicework done by stone mason and cut to put over doors. I cut my name on the face of these rocks, and may more had I the time. We got along in good season to a camp. Out in front us about three miles is a large rock to look at it, it looks impossible to climb up to the summit. We have named this "Brown's Pass." A little snow about two and one half inches under foot over mud.

HAIGHT: Came down the canon which is quite narrow with perpendicular rocks some hundred feet high of the most curious formation called the pass Summer Gate as the snow decreased and the weather moderated after we got through Camped where it widens out into the valley had good feed for our cattle for the first in a week but no water came 7 1/2 miles in the evening the last cattle were brought in.

BROWN: Another detachment of 4 men were sent back for the lost cattle. The camp moved down into the valley here the snow was only 3 or 4 inches deep At night the men returned with the cattle We were now safe over the mountain without any loss save the reduction of our animals that had to eat snow or do without water they had very little feed and worked hard every day. We saw plenty of deer on the mountain but had little chance to hunt succeeded in getting three or four of them.

The resumption of Armstrong's journal is welcome because of the richness and exuberance of its entries. Whether the eight-day gap was due to exhaustion and exposure from his day-long ride on December 13, to the difficulties in crossing the mountain, or because this portion of it was lost, is hard to say. There are several other gaps in his account of the expedition. They are now on the route Frémont will follow four years later. A dirt road running east from I-15 exit 100 now follows that route up Fremont Canyon. "Summer Gate," the narrow gap through strange formations of rock, is five to six miles from the freeway up this road. Though the canyon is narrow, with columnar formations of conglomerate rock towering overhead, no place where wagons could barely squeeze through is now apparent. The "Cornish rock" into which Armstrong and others carved their names is three and a half miles up the road from the freeway. The name "John C. Armstrong 1849" is cut large and deep and is clearly visible. Surrounding it are several other Armstrong names cut later, presumably by descendants. Barely visible is the name Henry Heath. Below it someone much later carved "Henry Heth," neatly enclosing it within the outline of a simple cabin. Among many names added later are other names and initials, dim in the soft and erodible rock, that may have been carved by the Pratt explorers. "Homer" may be Homer Duncan. "Wadwo" (rest illegible) may be William Wadsworth. "C E Williams" may be Christopher Williams. The initials "J H" may be John Holladay; "W (or H) G," Hial Gay; "S T," Seth Tanner; "J R (or A)" Josiah Arnold; "J M" and "W M," carved close together, Joseph and William Matthews.

Isaac Haight's mineral rod, mentioned by Campbell, may have indicated the presence of gold and silver in this area, but, unlike the highly mineralized northern Tushars near Marysvale, none has been found here.

"Little Salt Lake Hollow" where camp was made this night is now called Fremont Wash.

Saturday, December 22

CAMPBELL: T 20 Start about 9—clear sunny morning—Snow melting fast. R.C. & Edward Everett takes right off to the right over these Mts, see where the California road comes into this Little Salt Lake valley—find lots of crockery ware. Red Rocks with curious holes & cavities in them. Plenty deer tracks. Isaac Brown strike into

The name "H, Heth" on rocks in Fremont Canyon, where Henry Heath and the Pratt party passed after their ordeal crossing over the mountains into Little Salt Lake Valley. This name and the house enclosing it were probably carved later, perhaps by a descendant of Heath. A barely discernible "Heath," not shown here, is carved above it and is more likely Henry Heath's original signature.

John C. Armstrong's name inscribed on the rocks in Fremont Canyon.

California road, comes down it nearly 3 miles noon T 56 Breth kill 21 Rabbits, 1 Wolf, 2 Fox, another Catamount. see the Little Salt Lake, wind round to the left of this valley, near the bench land, beautiful day, scarcely a cloud to be seen. Camp among the Greasewood & Sage which we have pased thro' all day at 267 miles. feed on the bottom, a head & to the right, no water, little snow—T warm day. travelled (when exploring) over green grass on the Mts & large groves of cedars, some think about 32 horses in the crowd— many cattle foot sore so lame they have to be drove.

ARMSTRONG: Traveled ten miles up this valley, It is the Little Salt Lake A great number of rabbits at the entrance, 20 killed one wolf and one fox. Camped among the sage, no water, had to melt snow for cooking, plenty of sage for cooking but no wood otherwise, Well and in good spirits. They [the animals] are getting very weak

HAIGHT: Proceeded down into the valley came 10 miles over a smooth sage plain snow mostly gone off feed poor cattle almost worn out.

BROWN: We passed through a barren sage plain in which were a great many rabbits we killed and used many of them for food which were very palatable, we camped in the centre of the valley near the migrant road. had sage fuel and snow for water

They are now in Parowan Valley, named by the Indians for the Little Salt Lake the explorers could now see to the west. The name evolved from the Paiute "paragoons" meaning "marsh people" and "bad, salty, or harmful water."[63] Little Salt Lake, once marshy and rich in waterfowl, supported substantial native populations, of both the prehistoric Fremont culture and historical-era Paiutes. It was a well-known landmark on the Spanish Trail. Orville Pratt, traveling the trail in 1848, wrote of crossing the mountains from the Sevier, when "suddenly broke upon us one of the finest and most extensive valleys I have seen in the whole western country! In the center of it was a fine lake full of fish, with gravelly banks, and into which run 4 fine mountain streams from the south."[64] The lake being salty, the fish may have existed only in Pratt's imagination, but otherwise his description stands in contrast to the desolate, usually dry playa that is Little Salt Lake today.

In early 1848 Porter Rockwell with twenty-five discharged Mormon Battalion men managed to cut the first wagon tracks over

63. Van Cott, *Utah Place Names,* 288.
64. "The Journal of Orville C. Pratt," 353.

the old Spanish pack trail, dragging to Great Salt Lake Valley a single wagon loaded with seeds, fruit tree cuttings, and other foods from the California ranch country. The more well-established wagon road the Pratt party found so welcome had been made only a few weeks earlier by the California-bound gold-seekers being guided, for a fee of $10 a wagon, by Mormon Battalion veteran Jefferson Hunt. They were preceded by 23 wagons of what is known as the Gruell-Derr party, people who could not or would not pay Hunt's fee and so left Utah Valley in late September, a week or two before the Hunt train. The two groups were only a few days apart as they traveled through Parowan Valley and arrived in California almost together.[65] Their wagon tracks saved the lives of Frémont's explorers when, four years after the Pratt expedition, they emerged from the mountains starved and half-frozen, found the tracks under the snow, and followed them to safety at Parowan.

Sunday, December 23

CAMPBELL: T 20—Beautiful morning—scarcely a breath of wind 10 A.M. start, strike to the right, angling across the bottom of the valley. Plenty feed, cattle very dry, middle of the valley, no sage nor greasewood Plenty dry grass, high perpendicular rock to the right, then low ridge of Mts or knolls studded with cedar. Mts been black with cedars these 2 days. Ground hard froze on the bottom, good travelling, little snow in places, melting fast. Slimy [?], strong, clayey soil, muddy walking. Come to join Cal road 269 1/2 T in shade 58 sloppy 273 3/4 Two Springs 40 yds left of road. Boys in their shirt sleeves— Warm in the sun. Cattle lick the snow. Water them 1/4 mile on, near Sulphur Springs Left of road on a small round knoll 20 yds from road, where the ice has thawed. Sage & Greasewood all round, 274 3/4. Spring by wayside to the right—good water, feed ahead & to the left 1/4 mile & also other Springs. Pass thro some good feed & soil, strike to the left up to Red Creek or Rogcaw & camp North side, little feed at crossing. Sundown 278 miles beautiful star light night Freezing—Camp prayers & singing. T 38 when we know its Freezing, the fires must have influence, &c. Stream spreads into many branches. Wolves howl during night.

HAIGHT: Came 11 miles and camped east of the Lake on a creek called Red Creek three oxen gave out.

BROWN: We came into the wagon road which we were prepared to appreciate having traveled without any road ever since we left San

65. Hafen and Hafen, *Journals of Forty-Niners*, 51ff.

Pete. We went as far as Red Earth Creek here we found some good land, grass and water, the first running water we had found since leaving the Sevier.

Just before reaching their campsite, the party crossed Little Creek, down which the Spanish Trail descended into Little Salt Lake Valley. That trail left the Sevier River at today's Bear Valley Junction and followed Bear Creek along the route of State Highway 20, then swung southwest up Upper Bear Valley to cross the saddle between Cottonwood Mountain and Little Creek Peak, then descended Little Creek to the valley.

The Pratt camp this night was on Red Creek below where it emerges from the Hurricane Cliffs. A few families from Parowan settled here in 1852, establishing the town of Paragonah. A year later they fled back to Parowan at the outbreak of the Walker War, but returned in 1856 and built a fort. The site had been a Fremont village centuries earlier. The site was studied by an archaeological team from the Smithsonian Institution in 1919,[66] and later excavations there in the 1950s and 1960s yielded much of the material now on display at Southern Utah University in Cedar City.

Monday, December 24

CAMPBELL: T 28 Parley calls meeting of all, see Minutes. South wind, beautiful day, cattle find good [feed] up towards the Mts, many exploring, after minerals & precious stones, find Emery in the creek, ox killed, jerking meat for those who pack from this point, T at noon in the shade 60 in the sun 75—Breth fixing up their Pack saddles, &c &c for journey—Horses brought up at night & tied to wagons. Parley judges this to be a good settlement for 30 families T 32

HAIGHT: Br Pratt come to the conclusion to leave the waggons and take the Mules and horses that were fit and pack on to explore over the rim of the Basin. Dried a beef to pack

BROWN: Our teams were so reduced that we had to stop and let them recruit. It was finally concluded in council to take the wagons no farther, but to go on with pack animals leaving a portion of the men with the wagons

The decision was a wise one, and not only because the "teams were so reduced." Without the extensive road-building that would be

---

66. Neil A. Judd, *Archaeological Investigations at Paragonah, Utah* (Washington, D.C: Smithsonian Institution, 1919).

done over the next few years, the route ahead, down the gorge of Ash Creek where I-15 now runs, was far too rough for wagons. The 108 wagons Jefferson Hunt was guiding to California had not gone that way but, following the Spanish Trail, had swung west through Mountain Meadows. So had other wagons on what became the California Trail.

Tuesday, December 25

CAMPBELL: T 28 Bre preparing to start T at noon 58 meeting of Camp, see minutes &c Jos Matthews & Schyler Jennings have an honorable furlough to go home, & that they carry our mail—voted that David Fulmer be Prest Isaac C. Haight Capt & see to clerking— Parley gives Camp instructions about guarding Camp incessantly, never more than half of Camp leave at once, can send out exploring parties for 10 days if needful, exhorted them, told them equal share in the glory whether go or stay—R.C. writes letter to Presy— Cotillion parties, dancing—T 31 Many letters Writing.

HAIGHT: Some went out to explore for minerals but found none in the evening a meeting was called David Fullmer was chosen president of the company that remained with the waggons and I was chosen Captain & clerk

BROWN: At this encampment we spent Christmas day. We also fitted out a mail to go back to Salt Lake City to be carried by Joseph Mathews & Schuyler Jennings. We were at this place, by the rout we came 272 miles from G.S.L. City by our Rodometer.

In view of Jennings's quick temper and Parley's December 19 remonstrance that he would "have no fellowship for those who take our God's name in vain & especially to curse their Bre," it seems clear why Jennings was invited to return home. Obviously, he could not be sent home alone; Matthews was chosen to accompany him, probably because he was captain of the Second Ten, to which Jennings belonged, and because of his experience and reliability.

The letters sent home include two to the First Presidency, from Campbell and Pratt:

272 miles from G.S.L. City, Red Creek
Dec. 25, 1849 Little Salt Lake Valley
Prests Young, Kimball, and Richards
Dear Brethren,

There is talk in camp of Brethren returning from this point, if so, you expect some news. I tried at first to keep (aside from my journal) a copy of camp proceedings and to be ready at any moment to send back, but lately have failed in doing so. If cooking, guarding, keeping camp journal, nursing Roadmeter [are] excuses enough for the failure, then can I be justly excused. While fixing up to start with pack animals from this point, being around about today, I have heard many family letters eloquent, grand, sublime and sympathetic: truthful, elaborate and poetic to which I would refer for many particulars. We have about used up our oxen in getting our wagons thus far, and it is considered absolutely necessary to leave them here to recruit. The last 45 miles from the Sevier to this point, over the mountains of snow, in places from 2–4 feet deep, which has taken us a week, with water only in two camping places. Nearly perpendicular pitches where men had to draw up the oxen, then the oxen draw up the wagons and as steep places for to take our wagons down, all this road strewed with cobbled stones and large rocks, feed mostly all covered by the snow has tended in a great measure toward disabling the camp farther with teams. The thermometer has been at 21 below zero on the Sevier bottom, been nearly in snow 3/4 of our time, seen but few Indians, different Utes had a good time with Capt. Walker, whose band family were much afflicted with sickness (measles), gave him the flour, but seen his brother Ammomah who in two or three days got so sick, he was compelled to stay with some lake Utes who had a medicine squaw that could make medicine for him to cure him, he to come on, if got better soon. We have passed thro' since we left Sandpitch, a barren, rugged, mountainous country, at present fit only to be a habitation for those who live by idle Indian arts and that of the scantest kind. We took up the s west branch of the Sevier, where there is a few hundred acres in places with rich feed. [This would be the Circleville area.] Land black and loamy, but considerable saleratus, which tests more salty than the saleratus on the soil in the valley. The mountains and some bench lands where we have passed thro is thickly studded with cedars. The mountains exhibit the action of fire and may have specimens of rock along that contain iron ore, some 1/4 inch, some has been found today along with emery from the bed of this creek, washed from the mountains. Father Arnold sends some home. This place [future site of Paragonah] deemed good and suitable for a settlement, say from fifty to eighty families, only thing lacking is building timber, not much explored yet only one man been to the lake. The camp has generally enjoyed good health, been mindful, killed on 22nd 21 rabbits, one wild cat, one wolf and a fox, some deer killed two days before, so that some of us have had plenty of wild meat lately, killed 4 beefs, since we started, the meat of one we killed yesterday being jerked for the packers who each carry 40 lbs flour, coffee and half of our beefs are yet preserved. 9 ocl pm a meeting held a few minutes ago voted that David Fullmer be president of the camp who stay, Isaac C. Haight be capt. and see to clerking. Capt. Brown reports 20 men fitted out with 30 horses and mules to go 5 animals remain with the party who stay here, voted that we give Joseph Matthews and Schyler Jennings an honorable furlough to go home and carry our letters taking each of them one of their animals, and their arms, provisions enough to last them home. We sent from Sandpitch our doings up to that time, expect you have received them ere' thus.

Parley is now calling who is ready (26th noon) to start. I am ready and must close—before I have the chance of expressing a good wish for all the saints, which is in my heart continually.

Yours in meakness
Rob Campbell

To the Presidency, Dear Brethren

I have just heard the foregoing letter, and do not consider it necessary to add a great deal to the information therein contained. Myself and the camp are in good spirits and have been thro' all weather, and all circumstances unexpected snow storms extraordinary cold together with weak teams many of which had been worked down before we started have retarded our progress far beyond our expectations and may prevent us from accomplishing as much as is desired, but we will do the best we can.

The place where we now are is well adapted to the sustenance and convenise of a small settlement, say 50 to 100 families, and we suppose most of the country from here to the Utah on the main line of travel, which is west of the Wasatch range will admit a continuous line of settlements, but of this we can speak more fully when we return. This location is immediately east of the little Salt Lake from which may be 6 miles distant in the same valley and at the western foot of the Wasatch range. The land is rich, is beautiful and undulating westward, and the best calculated for watering of any place we have seen of late. Two small streams rather less than city creek come out high run nearly on a level with the top of the ground on the highest levels and throw out their surplus floods in times of high water dispersing fertility in every direction. The grass, willows, weed and other grasses grow exceedingly dense over thousands of acres. Pasture land extend for miles north and south of the farming land and the foot hills at from one to two miles distant and ablacked with inexhaustible supplies of fuel easy of access and consisting of shrub pine and cedar about 12 feet high. Good building timber will be harder to obtain but shows itself in abundance among the mountains. There is also free stone in abundance near a good town site and water power running thro' with any desirable amount of fall and being on the immediate line of travel is certainly a desirable location. The weather here is like spring thermometer 60 in the shade and the evening sky for days in succession remind us of the trade winds at sea or the West Indies. The nights, mornings and midday reminds us of April. The valley still opens to the south, as far as the eye can reach and we hope to find other streams and more land in the vicinity.

We must close by wishing you all through out the church a happy new year, to say nothing of Christ mass or other masses, remember us in your prayers, and God bless you all our friends forever.

I remain your brother in the N and E covenant
Parley P. Pratt[67]

Parley's reference to "a continuous line of settlements" is responsive to Brigham Young's plan to establish Mormon settlements along the Southern Route to California and also to a proposed "seaport" on the Colorado River above the Gulf of California.[68] The "two small streams rather less than city creek" are today called Little Creek and Red Creek. City Creek, to which these two creeks are compared, is the stream flowing from the canyon north of Salt Lake City and is the creek the Mormon pioneers dammed on July 23, 1847, to flood land at today's State and Third South Streets to begin the irrigation that made possible their settlement of the Great Basin.

The "N and E covenant" is defined in the *Encyclopedia of Mormonism*: "The sum of all gospel covenants that God makes with mankind is called 'the new and everlasting covenant.'. . . Baptism, marriage, and all other covenants from God necessary for salvation are new and everlasting. . . . Thus, celestial marriage [marriage in LDS temples] is a new and an everlasting covenant or the new and everlasting covenant of marriage."[69]

Even with their sketchy description of Parowan Valley, these letters were sufficient to confirm to Brigham Young his intention

---

67. Campbell, Southern Exploring Expedition Papers.
68. See Brigham Young to Orson Pratt, Journal History, March 9, 1849.
69. D. Cecil Clark, "New and Everlasting Covenant," in *Encyclopedia of Mormonism*, ed. Daniel H. Ludlow (New York: Macmillan Publishing Co., 1992), 3:1008.

to colonize the area. On January 31, 1850, five days before receiving Pratt's official report, the General Assembly created the territory's first six counties. Five of them—Great Salt Lake, Weber, Utah, Tuilla (Tooele), and Sanpete Counties—were to some extent settled or adjacent to settlements. The sixth, Little Salt Lake county, was more than two hundred miles away and would not know its first settler for nearly a year. In October 1850, after Pratt's full report to the assembly disclosed the richness and extent of the iron ore and the feasibility of establishing an iron industry there, the name was changed to Iron County. Its area, as defined in 1852, stretched six hundred miles from California to the crest of the Rocky Mountains.[70]

70. James B. Allen, "The Evolution of County Boundaries in Utah," *Utah Historical Quarterly* 23 (July 1955): 261–65.

Over the Rim to Dixie

Wednesday, December 26, 1849

CAMPBELL: T 26 Beautiful morning. Parley hears my letters read
sanctions & dictates another to the Presty. refer to letter Minutes &c
for particulars done here. Matthews & Jennings start T 80 on Phelps
bosom. Packers start at 12 1/2 P.M. all the Camp was turned out to
catch Smiths mule "Camanche." R.C. volunteered to ride it, seeing
Parley wanted to pack R.C's riding pony, R.C. got on; with his legs
tied he followed the others but about 3 miles a head he stumbled in
a Gopher hole, & jumped clean out of his Saddle backwards, there
being no crouper. pass over Big Creek 14 ft Wide 6 in deep, swift
current. feed plenty here, Willows plenty. Go on 2 miles farther,
find a Brindle 8 year old ox, white spotted on each side of his back
& down the hind parts, whitest spade on his forehead, short horns.
R.C. sent back on the "Camanche" to camp with it. Eats supper at
camp a little after sundown then starts and make the forward camp
by 8 P.M. at ~~Centre~~ South Creek 8 ft Wide 6 in deep. plenty willows
& some cotton wood Good feed up stream. T 32 at sundown. this
creek runs down on a ridge, or the highest ground soil excellent 10
miles. comes out of the range of Mts East (Wasatch) flows down into
the valley. Camp prayers & singing

BROWN: All things being ready the mail started for home and 20 of
us, including bro. Pratt with pack animals started south to continue
our explorations beyond the rim of the basin, leaving the camp in
charge of David Fulmer counsellor and Capt Haight. Within five
miles of camp We came to a pretty creek running parallel with the
first, on which the soil appeared to be good and about five miles farther we came to another but not quite so large. Hear we encamped
for the night; a company of Emigrants had left this place about 10
or 12 days previous they had lost some cattle and burnt up a wagon
here.

Those chosen to go by horseback on to the Virgin included Parley
P. Pratt, Nathan Tanner, Dan Jones, John D. Holladay, John H.
Bankhead, Ephraim Green, William W. Phelps, William Brown,
Robert Campbell, Madison Hambleton, John Brown, Homer

Duncan, William Matthews, George B. Matson, Robert M. Smith, Alexander Wright, Charles Hopkins, Benjamin F. Stewart, Dimick B. Huntington, and Gardner G. Potter.

"Camanche" must have been quite a mule—wild enough it took the entire camp to catch him, high strung enough to jump out of his saddle when spooked, yet sound enough to be sent, with the embarrassingly thrown Campbell aboard, to take the found ox back to camp.

They are camped tonight on Summit Creek just north of the low ridge separating Parowan and Cedar Valleys.

> HAIGHT [in camp with the wagons]: Br. Pratt left us to go over the rim of the Basin with 20 men and 30 horses.

Thursday, December 27
> CAMPBELL: T 29 Beautiful morning. 9 A.M. Pass on 3 miles, good feed good soil. Packs come loose, some flour lost—beautiful place for a Settlement, rich feed, Plenty cedar easy of access, we now strike thro heavy sage all round—go on a mile or two to the South outlet of this valley which ushers us into a large extensive valley—Springs of water to the left of road, good meadow down to the right, beautiful thick grass. Mt range still continues to our left & if anything more thickly studded with cedar, can see in places up the kanyons either Fir or Pine T 50 we leave the road Wet and muddy walking in this big valley, strike road again then leave it & Camp on Muddy creek. Plenty cotton wood timber for 1 mile down, Large trees, Goodly number of them, & can see them scattering on Creek banks which run down Northerly for many miles. The Land here is a Red wash from these Mts on our left, this Muddy creek is [illegible] & comes out of passes on these Mts. some Cloudy. Boys this morning found 3 Wagon tires, the irons of a wagon, notice written on a board—"Captn Fly's Coy passed here 16th Decr 12 in deep of snow. M Beardsell of St. Louis left wagon here" signed by "Sand". Find here to night, a chain. Thousands of cedars on the Mts left, some good feed here, 12 miles to day T 30

The wagon tires and irons found this morning, the brindle ox and burned wagon found the day before, and the chain found near tonight's campsite probably belonged to the Jefferson Hunt wagon train or another large California-bound party with whom Pratt and his group will camp and trade near Mountain Meadows ten days later while returning from their exploration of the Virgin River country.

The springs to the left of the road are the springs at Enoch, a
favorite campsite on the Spanish Trail. Though the springs are
largely dried up today, Orville Pratt, traveling the trail in 1848,
called them "one of the finest fountains and streams of water on the
entire route."[71] Here the Spanish Trail swung west through Cedar
Valley, past the Three Peaks, which motorists on I-15 can see across
the valley to the west, past Iron Springs, then into the Escalante
Desert and on to Mountain Meadows.[72] From where Parley's group
first encountered it near Paragonah to the springs at Enoch, the
wagon train of gold seekers Jefferson Hunt was guiding to California
followed the Spanish Trail. But in the broad valley west of Enoch,
Coal Creek loses itself in swampy ground easily traversed by the
Spanish Trail's horses and mules but difficult for wagons. So the
'49er wagon trains continued south to cross Coal Creek six miles
north of present Cedar City, then turned west to rejoin the Spanish
Trail near Iron Springs.[73] Parley's mounted explorers followed the
wagon road to Muddy (Coal) Creek, then continued on south to
cross the Great Basin rim, exploring a shorter route to the Virgin
where a more direct wagon road would later be made. Of the two
groups, Parley's fared better. Riven by dissension and beguiled by a
map that supposedly showed a five-hundred-mile shortcut to the
goldfields, all but 6 of the 108 wagons in Hunt's party rebelled and
separated. After days of suffering while finding the "shortcut" too
difficult and too dry, some of the travelers returned to follow Hunt
on the Spanish Trail. The rest pushed on west, with several perishing
in the waterless wastes of southern Nevada and Death Valley.

The "Mt. Range" that Campbell said "continues to our left" is
the Hurricane Cliffs, which begin here and extend two hundred
miles deep into the Arizona Strip. The colorful cliffs, composed of
Jurassic and Triassic rocks, mark the line of the major Hurricane
Fault that separates the Colorado Plateau from the basin-and-
range country to the west.[74] Pratt and his explorers would follow
along the base of these cliffs all the way to the Virgin River.

Camp this night on "Muddy creek"—now Coal Creek—is
near the site of Cedar City, in the heart of Cedar Valley, which

---

71. "The Journal of Orville C. Pratt," 353.
72. C. Gregory Crampton, "Utah's Spanish Trail," *Utah Historical Quarterly* 47 (fall 1979):
     361–83.
73. Hafen and Hafen, *Journals of Forty-Niners*, 78.
74. Chronic, *Roadside Geology*, 243.

Parley's report to the legislature extolled as the "'firstrate good' place we were sent to find as a location for our next Southern colony." His report was heeded. By December 1850, 118 men, thirty with families, called by Brigham Young were on the way south to establish the Iron Mission. They first established Parowan, where the wagon company had waited for return of Parley's mounted party exploring the Virgin River country. In 1851 a group left that infant settlement to build a fort at Cedar City, closer to the iron ore they had been sent to mine. The following year one hundred families, including skilled English, Scotch, and Welsh miners arrived to strengthen the enterprise. They built a crude blast furnace and in the summer of 1852 produced the first pig iron made west of the Missouri River. In 1853 an Indian uprising and a flood closed down the operation. It was resumed briefly in 1854. In 1868 another attempt to establish an iron industry succeeded in producing pig iron used to cast stoves, grates, pots and frying pans, flat irons, and other items. But completion of the transcontinental railroad brought cheaper and better products into the territory, and after fifteen unprofitable years the operation closed. The first financially successful use of southern Utah iron ore began in 1922 with Columbia Steel Company's construction of a blast furnace at Ironton, south of Provo. This was followed in 1941 by construction of the Geneva Steel plant on the shore of Utah Lake. That plant continued to use southern Utah ore until the mid-1990s, when market conditions reduced production. Geneva Steel retains its holdings there and is currently researching ways to remove the phosphorous with which southern Utah ore tends to coat the interior of blast furnaces.[75] Cedar City meanwhile thrives as a college town and tourist gateway to southern Utah's national parks.

> BROWN: We went about six miles and came into a larger valley from the south varying a little west of north, we camped on another creek the largest we have seen in this region. It ran in several channels to the north west and appeared to sink forming a vast meadow of several thousand acres of land. There had been a very deep snow but was now all melted which made the ground very soft and mirey Leaving the road at this place we continued directly south through

---

75. Geneva company brochure, undated. Also conversation with K. C. Shaw, Geneva director of engineering and technology, February 10, 1999.

a high wide pass, mostly covered with sage. About noon we crossed a small creek that formed a small lake. In the valley west of us and in the afternoon we crossed another, all coming out of the mountain on the east. This last creek is on the divide and runs into the basin but could be very easily turned. We camped in a dry cedar hollow on the south side of the rim here it snowed two inches deep.

Brown has compressed two days' travel in this entry. His "small creek" is what Campbell in his journal the next day calls "Lake creek."

Friday, December 28

CAMPBELL: T 32 Horses 3 1/2 miles on the Mts right [?] Left R. C. & others went for them, excellent feed, start about 9—Good morning. Pass over this Muddy creek where it flows in 2 considerable streams each about 12 feet wide, 5 or 6 in deep, down a little ways it flows apparently in about 40 or 50 streams overflowing all round, bringing down floodwood. Red wash, or alluvial & depositing it all over cedars abundant, & easy of access, leave the road & strike to the left, aiming to travel at the foot of the benches for this Red alluvial, clayey deposit, coming from the Redish Mts is miry & muddy, horses sink 3 & 4 inches every step. Pas over sage The valleys with this Red deposit is all made soil Parley finds some whitish flints, silver blossom, mountain (or mourning) crystal, good black streaks in it. reach Lake creek 2 1/2 feet Wide, Water flowing in it. this creek runs on a ridge, beautiful piece of farming land above & where we cross rash fed [rich feed?]. Red clay sandy soil, some soap masqual [agave or yucca], cedar abundant & plentiful all along the hills & Mts on the left. the Lake is about 3 miles down judge it to be nearly 1 1/2 miles long 1/4 broad. Plenty Willows on creek banks, the Soil or Clayey land apparently has never been froze. keep up pretty near the Mts had some very muddy walking hard on our animals. Clouds begin to be heavy & while passing over us [leave?] Some of their contents. cold—Ther 29 at noon, come up to where Parley calls it Summit Creek. Rock gate, not so high as Devils Gate the washes & floods from this creek apparently flow both ways in this long valley. looking South we can see no end to immensity. whether this is the rim out of the Basin or not cant tell, we have passed over so many rims, but this creek flows Northerly into the Lake just before described. Thunder. Good feed. Plenty fuel, Indian Wika ups see tracks of a man, valley continues Southward. Pass on a mile & camp in Dry cedar hollow where it comes out of a kanyon with pretty high Rocks at the Gate. Snow falling, Parley says we come 24 miles, nearly all the Camp say 17 miles. But Parley told 13 yesterday & it was only put down 12, so this to day be 15 & therefore makes Parleys distances. animals tired going thro this clayey land. T 31. keeps snowing, get crotches, build Mormon wika ups [wickiups] with cedar carpeting, comfortable bed under. Parley & Dan takes shelter with us. Horses go up towards the cedars. Plenty fuel. Snow plenty

Campbell's "Lake creek" is Shirts Creek, named for Peter Shirts, an early Mormon settler. It drains into Quichapa Lake, a Paiute name meaning "laxative waters," either because of the antelope and bighorn sheep bedding ground through which Quichapa Creek flowed before entering the lake from the west, or because of the stagnant, brackish water of the lake itself.[76] "Summit Creek" is today Kanarra Creek; at that time it may have flowed north into the lake, being about on the imperceptible rim of the basin, but now flows south to join Ash Creek and eventually the Virgin River. On this day the party passed the site of a present-day marker noting the passage of the Domínguez-Escalante exploring party of 1776, heading back to Santa Fe after abandoning its assigned task to reach California. From here to the Virgin River, Parley's company will follow Escalante's route, though, of course, no trace of that passage would remain.

Saturday, December 29
    CAMPBELL: T 28 cloudy morning South Wind, Jones dreams about the Indians coming to meet us. Thunder heard many times yesterday. Passed high Mts yesterday afternoon perpendicular. to day move on at 10 1/4 A.M. Snow considerable last night Strong Northerly Wind blowing down this valley which may here be 3 miles broad, a few hundred yards creek coming from Mts on the left, flowing over perpendicular rock. Travel near the base of these Red Clayey Mts rocky, studded thick with cedar—2 miles brings to large creek steep banks, flows down thro this valley Southward. 3 in of old snow. clayey walking—noon Cupola creek, 3 ft broad 3 in deep Pass in between the Mts or where the creek flows out of the Mts & see high Red cupolas their tops buried in clouds, but can see them when the clouds pass away, see about 80 miles a head, 1/4 to 1 P.M. Sun breaks thro. Waters still flowing over Rocks making hollows & a few dry ravines to cross. some packs required fixing again 1 P.M. cross Southern creek 12 ft wide 17 in deep. Cotton woods on banks, ascend hill 1 1/2

---

76. Van Cott, *Utah Place Names*, 307.

miles, snow having dissolved the animals would sink 6 & 7 in every step, save when they put their feet on rocks, which r thickly studded all along, miserable travelling. steep hill. mule gets thrown at the cedars with its pack, Parley finds it impracticable to travel farther so, & strikes to the left over creek again. Green grass, see Indians fire & tracks. rough steep Rocky hill to go down. My mule's feet gets so deep in the clayey earth, throws itself twice to get out. cross southern creek again, which gathers many streams (from these high snowy Mts 2 or 3 miles to our left). in a short distance, travel down on the left hand of the creek nearly 2 miles, good going but rocky. Would be difficult (if possible) to bring a wagon down from 1st crossing of Southern creek. Camp on banks of creek. Plenty feed, some green at the roots. High bluffs or overhanging Mts 20 rods from the foot of which is our Camp, very high, Camped about sundown. Parley reckons 11 miles cold N Wind—T 34

BROWN: After going about five miles we came to a creek about 1 1/2 ft deep and one rod wide running south it is a branch of the Rio Virgin and came from the North west; we crossed it at the head of a canon and ascended a low mountain that lay in our course. The north side was covered with snow but the summit and south side was bare and very mirey our horses went in to their knees every step right among the stones. The men had to dismount and some of the pack animals had to be relieved of their burdens. However we succeeded in getting over and camped on the creek below the canyon. We were now entirely out of the snow.

Campbell's "large creek steep banks, flows down thro this valley Southward" is Ash Creek, whose course the party will follow, more or less, to the Virgin River. About where they reached Ash Creek, John D. Lee, Richard Woolsey, William R. Davis, and others in 1852 would establish Harmony, the first Mormon settlement "over the rim" and the county seat of Washington County until 1859. Missionaries arrived in 1854 to join Lee in teaching the Indians Mormon farming methods, and built Fort Harmony nearby. Here Lee was living at the time of his involvement in the 1857 Mountain Meadows massacre, and here the twenty-eight-day rainstorm of 1862 melted the adobe walls of the fort and his home, killing two of his children. Fleeing in midwinter with what food they could save, the settlers lived in tents and "Mormon wickiups" until the next spring when they started building the present town of New Harmony. Remains of the fort, including stone gate pillars on the south side and stone pillars marking each corner of the three-hundred-foot-square walls, can be seen

in a sagebrush flat a few hundred yards south of the road leading
from I-15 to New Harmony.

"Cupola creek" is Taylor Creek, flowing out of the Kolob section of Zion National Park. The "high Red cupolas" are the Kolob
Fingers, beautifully sculpted and colorful ridges of Navajo sandstone jutting west from the Kolob Terrace.[77] After the Mountain
Meadows massacre, John D. Lee is said to have hidden out among
these cliffs, looking down on his ranch at Harmony and watching
for a signal of clothes hanging on the line telling him it was safe to
come down for a visit.

Motorists going south on I-15 see to the left the gorge of Ash
Creek cutting through the Black Ridge. Others, both before and
after the Pratt party, noted the difficulty of travel in this section.
Escalante in 1776 wrote of entering "a ridge—cut entirely of black
lava rock which lies between two high sierras by way of a gap." This
was the entrance to Ash Creek Canyon. Here their Indian guides
disappeared, and Escalante wrote, "Bereft of a guide, we continued
south for a league with great hardship on account of so much
rock."[78] And among the Mormon pioneers sent by Brigham to settle
St. George in 1861, one disgruntled settler wrote home of the
wagon road over the Black Ridge and down Ash Creek that there
was only one bump on the road, but it was forty miles long. Parley's
camp this night was about at the present site of Pintura, a tiny fruit-
growing town established in 1863.

Though they completely circumvented it in their travels from
December 27 to January 6, the party's journals strangely do not
mention the Pine Valley Mountains, the most dominant geographic
feature in southwest Utah, or Dixie, by which the area became
known. From these mountains came the lava flows that made
Parley's travel so treacherous down the Ash Creek gorge. From
them flow Ash Creek, which Parley followed into Dixie, and the
Santa Clara up which he later traveled most of the way in returning
to the Great Basin. The Pine Valley Mountains are said to be the
largest known example of a laccolith—mountains formed by vast
masses of magma forced upward from deep within the earth, pushing up and fracturing the overlaying rock but never quite breaking
through and becoming a volcano. That happened perhaps thirty

77.   Chronic, *Roadside Geology,* 243–44.
78.   Warner, *The Domínguez-Escalante Journal,* 77–78; Chronic, *Roadside Geology,* 244.

million years ago. Subsequent eons of erosion have washed away the overlying rock, leaving basalt peaks up to ten thousand feet high. The flows that formed the Black Ridge are much younger, less than two million years ago. This basalt is the same age and composition as that atop the Hurricane Cliffs, indicating they were part of the same lava flow. The difference in their elevation dramatizes the enormous displacement of the Hurricane Fault.[79]

Sunday, December 30

CAMPBELL: T 24 cold N Wind, Parley dreams about talking with the Indians down a little ways who grow corn. Sandy soil here. lots of Emery on this creek, 9 1/2 camp starts. Recross crick, Pass green grass 6 in high, Pass Prickly pears, Soap Maskal, & cactus also Tamimump, a weed the Indians use for Tobacco, Green leaves, branches feel like they were varnished. Pass thro' scattering cedars Pass over a rugged stoney, sandy, almost indescribable country, thrown together in dreadful confusion, bad passes a wagon could scarcely ever be made to go thro there. The country reminds me of that near the South pass of the Sandys only a hundred times more so, follow a dry rivine, Winding to the left for 2 1/2 miles then strike on to hill, see three Indians, running apparently to head us. Parley stops on the hill till we all come up, conclude to go down & camp on the river 12 miles, go down Kanyon & camp on river banks. Plenty ash & cotton woods. 3 Indians come into camp, Dimic talks to them, say there's no Water between here & Colorado to go South. Walker comes this way to go to California. say village one sleep from here. Plenty horses they 2 Pi Utes, called by the American Pi eads, have corn cut down. Navahoes have Wheat, they grow it don't know anything about the White Indians. Smoke the pipe of peace. Dimic asks them to stay till morning, they say yes. They r fat, tolerably clad for this warm climate, one of them has a Cassimere coat. Black hair, no beard nor whiskers nor hair under their arm pits, all under the medium size, have bows made of Mt sheep horns, wound round with sinew of which their bowstring is. Their arrows have 3 large feather in the buts & piece cane break [?], then ash wood points, round the tip of the arrow, sinew is wound to prevent their arrows from splitting, some have arrow points of Iron. been warm day T 64 at night T 39 the Indians asked if Walker along with us. Dimic tells them we were Mormons not Americans. Horses feet sore with walking over the rocks, one of the Indians says he sold

79. Chronic, *Roadside Geology*, 244.

his wife to Walker when he gets any its from a horse. They cry for their companions to come, but they either don't wish to come or r afraid. 3 guarding the horses at a time & one guards the camp. Plenty bunch grass, tho we have passed thro some barren land.

Brown: We continued down the creek which runs through another canyon and we had to wind around through the hills and strike the creek below again we camped on this creek the second time. Soon after we camped three Indians came to us they were Pahutah and were a little shy at first but soon got acquainted our interpreter could talk with them in the Utah language We told them who we were and what we wanted. They were almost naked, and they were glad we had come into their country and wanted us to settle here and teach them to farm and make clothing. They had heard of us from the Utah Indians.

Here we find the first of several descriptions of southern Utah flora unfamiliar to the exploring party. James E. Bowns, professor of biology and range ecology at Southern Utah University, believes Campbell's "Soap Maskal" is *Yucca elata*, commonly known as soap-tree yucca or Spanish dagger. Or it could be *Yucca angustissima* or narrowleaf yucca. Yucca, he notes, is an important food source for Indians in the Southwest. The plant looks like mescal, and its buds, flowers, and emerging flower stalks and fruits are roasted like mescal, which may be where Campbell got the name "maskal" or, as he writes later, "masqual." Yucca roots, known as amole, are used as a sort of soap, as a laxative, in treatment of diabetes, sore joints, and arthritis, and as an aid in childbirth. The fibers are used for baskets, mats, cloth, rope, sandals, and dental floss. Of "Tamimump," Bowns writes that this is probably canaigre, or Indian tobacco, both common names for *Rumex hymenosepalus*. "This plant has bright green, smooth leaves, a slick, reddish stem, and red flowers and fruits. The seeds have been used as a substitute for tobacco, and are apparently a reasonably good substitute. The ripe seeds are also ground-up and used as meal for bread and mush. The tender leaves are eaten raw in salad, but they do contain toxic alkaloids. The powdered roots are sometimes referred to as ginseng."[80]

Campbell's report of "bad passes [where] a wagon could scarcely ever be made to go thro there" proved prophetic; none

---

80. James E. Bowns to editors, April 17, 1998.

ever did. Seeing the difficulty, the first Mormon settlers swung to the right, away from Ash Creek. That route, through Anderson Ranch, Leeds, and Harrisburg, became the pioneer wagon road. The Arrowhead Highway built from Los Angeles to Salt Lake City in the century's second decade followed that route, as did Highway 91 later and finally I-15. Until I-15 bypassed it, Anderson Ranch, where Highway 17 exits I-15, became a favorite stopping place for lodging and the delicious fruit raised there. Parley's explorers, however, continued to struggle down or around Ash Creek, as had Escalante in 1776. But that route was so difficult, even for horses, that Jedediah Smith in 1826 abandoned it, finding another route over Black Ridge, possibly turning southwest from Ash Creek in the vicinity of present Anderson Junction, crossing Cedar Ridge and descending Quail Creek to the Virgin River.[81] Parley's camp this night may have been in the vicinity of Toquerville, as Brown seems to indicate, or four miles downstream on the broad flood-plain at the confluence of Ash and La Verkin Creeks with the Virgin, as Campbell's journal implies.

These Indians, the first encountered in the Virgin River basin, were from the small band of Paiutes led by Chief Toquer, from whom Toquerville got its name. Both names refer to the black lava rock so abundant in the area.[82] Campbell's is the first and most complete Mormon description of the appearance and weapons of these Indians. The account of one Indian willingly selling his wife to Chief Walker raises a question. The Paiutes occasionally obtained a horse (which they usually ate) by selling children—or a wife—to Ute or Mexican traders, but whether the Indian's statement that "when he gets any its from a horse" refers to a method of sexual release or to further trading is unclear.

Chief Toquer persisted in the invitation to settle there, and Toquerville became the third settlement in the Virgin River basin, after Santa Clara and Washington, when families from Harmony moved there in 1858. Finding that grapes flourished in the warm, dry climate, Brigham Young encouraged wine making and sent John C. Naegle, a convert who had been a vintner in his native Germany, to get it started. Naegle also became a prosperous cattle-man and built an imposing two-story stone home housing his large

81.   Brooks, *The Southwest Expedition of Jedediah S. Smith*, 56, n50.
82.   Van Cott, *Utah Place Names*, 373.

polygamous family, with a winery in the basement. The wine was to be used for the Mormon sacrament and as a cash crop to sell to outsiders, but when Brigham learned how the locals were also enjoying it, he put a stop to Dixie wine making as an industry. The Naegle home is now on the National Historic Register. For a time, between 1869 and 1880, Toquerville was the Kane County seat, but conditions were spartan as evidenced by the Jail Rock, a large lava stone with a chain bolted to it, where, lacking a jail, prisoners were handcuffed to the rock while awaiting trial.[83]

Monday, December 31

CAMPBELL: Indians cry for their companions one old man comes into camp, says he was afraid of us, little while other 4 come say they were afraid. T 23 cold, sun rises, beautiful morning, 10 start, cross the Rio Virgin. Pass a small garden spot with some stacks of corn & many semalins & some grape vines. C. Hopkins sees 3 flocks of Quails, cross a large branch of the Rio Virgin 18 yards wide 1 foot deep. Rocky bottom. Indians guide us but Dimic don't understand them well, some of them talk too much Pi Ute. Pass over a large track of barren, some Greasewood & sage, cactus, & Soap Mesquit strike on to the Virgin again & cross it. Camp on bottom on the (other) river. Good bottom feed, Watch horses closely 3 on guard at a time all leave but one Indian whom we detain in camp. T 50 Some cotton wood on banks & Willows, broken, barren land some places on the bottoms might be farmed come 12 miles, beautiful night T 38

BROWN: Six more Indians came into camp and we gave them something to eat, two of them went to show us the trail that led down to the Rio Virgin we saw many little Indian plantations where they raise corn they varied in size from a few rods and up to an acre, having their irrigation ditches &c. We camped on the river two of the Indians yet with us, soon after we eat supper one of them said he wanted a blanket to sleep on one of the brethren gave him his saddle blanket he wrapped it around his shoulders and after a while stepped out to one side and was seen no more taking the blanket with him leaving his bow and arrow in camp. The other one stayed all night.

Of the "semalins" Campbell found growing in garden plots, James Bowns writes: "There is no doubt in my mind that he is referring to *Curcurbita foetisdissima*. This plant has common names of

---

83. Lavoid Leavitt, longtime resident of St. George and guide to historic trails, on-site interview by editors.

Buffalo-gourd, calabazilla, stinking gourd, stinking cucumber, and coyote gourd. This plant is native and grows wild in Washington and San Juan Counties." Anthropologist Mark Stuart agrees and reports that the ancient Anasazi as well as the Paiutes ate both the seeds and the pulp, and used the shells as containers, some of which have been found in Anasazi dwellings and middens.[84]

Guided by the Indians, the explorers learned that shortly below the confluence of Ash and La Verkin Creeks with the Virgin the river enters a narrow, precipitous gorge, so they crossed the river near the confluence, climbed the bluff to the south, and found themselves on the present site of Hurricane. Escalante had crossed here three-quarters of a century earlier, naming the river Rio Sulfureo because of the hot, sulfurous water pouring into the river from the hot springs just upstream, now the site of the Pah Tempe resort. Escalante climbed the bluff to the site of Hurricane as Pratt did but continued south over Sand Mountain, into Warner Valley, and on into the Arizona Strip.

Hurricane was not settled until 1906, after water had been brought to the bench by the Hurricane Canal. The building of this canal was one of Mormondom's heroic epics. For eleven years settlers labored with primitive tools to carve an eight-mile canal along the cliffs of Timpoweap Canyon where the Virgin has cut a gorge through the Hurricane Fault. The task required building trestles and extensive rock work along the cliff faces to support flumes. Nine tunnels were cut through solid rock. The canal, now listed on the National Historic Register, brought the first water to the bench in 1904. After nearly a century as a quiet Mormon town surrounded by orchards and fields, Hurricane has exploded into one of the nation's fastest-growing communities. The "large track of barren, some Greasewood & sage, cactus, & Soap Mesquit" Campbell described as they headed west now contains million-dollar homes surrounding Sky Mountain golf course.

After traveling south of the Virgin most of the day, the party crossed it and camped at or near the present site of Washington, the second Mormon settlement in Dixie. Only seven years after the Pratt expedition, Brigham sent colonists, most of them from the south, here to raise cotton. Survival in the early years was a terrible ordeal, best described in Andrew Karl Larson's *Red Hills of*

---

84. Bowns to editors; Mark Stuart, on-site interview by editors.

November. Malaria sapped the colony's strength. So did hunger, since much land was planted to cotton instead of food crops. Worst was the struggle to control the unruly Virgin River. Floods washed out dam after dam, silted up the canals, washed away whole fields. Tired of the annual washouts, the community labored three years to build a dam that would last. They called it the "pile dam" for the pilings driven deep into the river bed. It washed out the first year. Not until 1890, at a site two miles upstream where a rocky reef provided a solid foundation, did they manage to build a dam that would hold.

In 1865, construction began under Brigham's direction on a massive three-story stone building housing a factory to process Dixie cotton into textiles, clothing, and blankets. It did so for thirty years, but never very profitably. By 1910, the industry was finished, the machinery sold off, and the building little used, until its rebirth in the mid-1990s as a reception center. Mill Creek, which furnished the factory's water power, is now chiefly known as one of the natural hazards on another of the area's golf courses, Green Springs.

Tuesday, January 1, 1850
CAMPBELL: T 38 cloudy morning Rainy, 9 1/2 start Raining Pass over broken rugged country red sand, cross the Virgin which is a swift, rocky stream, recross Virgin strike on to a large bottom. Parley said before we crossed it would make a good Settlement. Sandy soil, Plenty greasewoods, & cane break. Cotton wood & some ash timber on the creek strike a knoll where lots of hard earthenware, streaked. strike stream come down from the right. Lots of willows on banks and cotton woods. Indians tell Parley & Dimic about the land ahead, road &c. Go right a head & cross stream, very bad crossing, & strike up to the right 2 miles & camp, 10 miles to day. Raining the most of the time. Indians accompany us from where they met Phelps alone, when the rest of us had gone down on the bottom, then Phelps being alone they jumped up from the sage, come with him & talk to Dimic, said afraid, did not know whether came in peace or war, mean, dirty almost naked creatures—many come into camp. Rain so hard I had to hurry and now stop writing. Parley calls on R.C. to sing, gather round & sing, all the Indians join & try to sing with us—say they have no families died in sickness about 17 of them, move some of the animals, 2 rods from camp Hopkins finds corn stalks 11 feet long, some Pumpkin & squash vines Indians say (& Ward said) if we go down the Virgin we must go round many

kanyons, Red Knolls, high Red bluffs perpendicular like Mts no timber, for a long way South East nothing but barren land. Indians say they willing we should come & live with them, this stream we r camped on to night well timbered. Indians, all talk at once, rude, dirty mean & filthy. they see we r prepared for them guard them closely wanted us to feed them which we have done always when we eat ourselves. But now they wish us to make beds for them, seeing it Rains so say Walker is a good Indian, they have not killed any American cattle this year, they adhere to Walker, love what he says, the land is all ours if we come & settle among them, glad to av us.

BROWN: Our Indian traveled with us a short distance this morning and disappeared but we were not long alone as four others came to us pretty soon they traveled with us and served as guides. It was very muddy owing to the late rains. We camped on the Santa Clara a little above its mouth in a little grass bottom. Some of our animals mired down in getting to camp it had rained through the day and at intervals all night. Here we had 27 Indians in camp until ten P.M. They then disappeared in different directions but where they went we never knew for we saw no lodges or wickiups except some old ones.

The explorers this day passed through the heart of what is now the greater St. George metropolitan area, reaching the confluence of the Virgin and Santa Clara Rivers in the area now covered by St. George's new convention center and an extensive public park. Two miles up the Santa Clara, where Campbell says they camped, would be about halfway between Southgate golf course and the Green Valley subdivision. Where Brown says, "Some of our animals mired down in getting to camp," or where Campbell, the next day, reports mules had to be lifted out of the mire, may have been in the wetlands area now containing the Tonaquint nature preserve.

Parley's report to the legislature speaks of two fertile valleys divided by a range of hills, the two containing "3 or 4000 acres of very desirable land." This refers to the valleys now occupied by Washington and St. George, divided by the Black Ridge whose skyline is now marred by luxury homes. In 1857 Brigham Young visited the area and noted the miserable conditions of the struggling settlement of Washington. Typically, instead of abandoning the effort, he expanded it. In the October 1861 LDS general conference he called three hundred men and their families to settle in the St. George Valley in an expanded Cotton Mission. Response to the call was typically Mormon. Elizah Averett, for example, recalled his father's response. Learning of his call after a hard day in his prospering fields, he "dropped in his chair and said: 'I'll be damned if I'll go!' After sitting a few minutes with head in hands, he stood up, stretched, and said, 'Well, if we are going to Dixie, we had better start to get ready.'"[85] Arrival in Dixie stirred little optimism. Robert Gardner's journal records that when he saw the malaria-stricken residents of Washington, "This tried me more than anything I had seen in my Mormon experience, thinking that my wives and children . . . would have to look as sickly as those around me."[86]

But they stayed, naming the infant settlement of St. George for LDS apostle George A. Smith, a leader in settlement of southern Utah. They completed, in 1877, Utah's first Mormon temple, using a lead-filled cannon barrel to pound hundreds of tons of lava rock into the swampy ground to provide a firm foundation and hauling huge ponderosa pine timbers eighty miles from Mount Trumbull near the rim of the Grand Canyon. During the same period, while still struggling to survive, they built a tabernacle and a county courthouse, both of beautifully cut native sandstone. It was an epic feat that led to fulfilment of Brigham's prophecy, when he visited the unpromising site in 1861, that "there will yet be built, between these volcanic ridges, a city, with spires, towers and steeples, with homes containing many inhabitants."[87]

Wednesday, January 2

CAMPBELL: Raining T 39 Cloudy, strike up to the right start at 9 A.M. Miry bad going. Some mules mire down Breth lifting them out with their packs on, cross this stream, 2 mules with packs get mired crossing. Flour not hurt any. Indians pilot Dimic. Pass wika ups, corn patches see one corn stalk 11 feet long, the top of which was broke up Grape vines. Pass cinder Rock 50 yards square on the left & nearly as large on the right. Stream well timbered Cotton woods & ash, Pass a bottom 1 1/2 miles long 1/4 Wide would be a good farm, Red sandy soil, grass green belly weed, kinds of Sage & Greasewood, Rabbitt wood &c. Plenty timber all along banks of

85.   Quoted in Richard Poll, et al., *Utah's History* (Provo, Utah: Brigham Young University Press, 1978), 136.
86.   Andrew Karl Larson, "The Diary of Robert Gardner," in *The Red Hills of November* (Salt Lake City: Deseret News Press, 1957), 61.
87.   James Godson Bleak, "Annals of the Southern Utah Mission" (Manuscript in Church Historian's Office; copied by Utah Writers Project, WPA, 1991), book A, 75. Quoted in Andrew Karl Larson, *I Was Called to Dixie* (Salt Lake City: Deseret News Press, 1961), 102.

creek. Indian Wika ups, sun breaks thro, rain stops. Sandy soil good going. Kanyons on this creek, Rocky & Steep, strike round & avoid them, see creek again, Plenty cotton wood timber, Pass up stream, or creek, which is in places rapid current 15 ft Wide, 1 foot deep, clear water, narrow going over Rocks, & steep ascents & descents Indian trail (they suppose we can go with our horses, where they go on foot) Red bluffs, rise like a fortifications 5 or 600 ft high. 2 miles long, we r going to day W & N West over barren land, sandy, Pass Pebble rocks, good building Rock, & thousands of huge piles of Mts hills, rugged declivities, Rocks, petrified wood steep bluffs, caverns, see ahead of us West, very high Mountains, covered with snow. T at noon 74 very warm Indians about 20 all men, run along side of us, Camp on stream, on a Pi Ute garden patch, plenty semlin vines & semlines on them, 3 P.M. 13 miles see their water furrows or rows between their corn Pass Grass green, nice common Prairie Grass, blades 2 inches & 3 high near bunches of Weeds, &c. T 40 rained about 9 P.M.

BROWN: They [Indians] were back next morning by day light had no women no children they said they had sold them to the Spaniards. We were now about 85 miles from Little Salt Lake. This whole country is a dreary waste of table mountains and barren hills destitute of timber, soil or grass nothing to be seen but rocks, clay and sand there is some cottonwood timber and willows on the river and some grass in the bottoms but they are very small, some of which the Indians cultivate, they grow corn, pumpkins and squash I bought about a gallon of corn from an Indian and gave him some flour for it—we also gave them some presents

Indians the previous day had advised not to go down the Virgin because of the "many kanyons . . . high red bluffs perpendicular . . . no timber," etc. They referred to the Virgin River Gorge, impassable even to horses, as Jedediah Smith had learned seventy-five years earlier on his first expedition to California. Not until recent years, when I-15 was blasted through at the greatest per-mile cost of any in the interstate system, was travel possible through the gorge. With that advice about the useless country ahead and with their horses giving out, Parley's explorers decided to go home. They traveled up the Santa Clara River and over Utah Hill, as Jedediah Smith had done on his second expedition and as did other pre–I-15 travelers on what became the Old Mormon Road, the Arrowhead Highway, and ultimately, in 1930, Highway 91. Parley's route passed through what is now Sunbrook Golf Course and on to Santa Clara.

The Santa Clara settlement, the first in Dixie, was established in 1854 with the arrival of Jacob Hamblin and other missionaries who had been called to teach the Paiutes to farm the Mormon way. Among them was Rufus Allen, who would have passed that way four years earlier with Parley had he not been assigned to stay with the wagons at Little Salt Lake. The original Santa Clara settlement was destroyed in the devastating flood of 1862, and the town was built on higher ground. Here Jacob Hamblin, who narrowly escaped drowning in the flood, built the two-story stone house that today houses a small museum. Visitors standing between the front stoop and a huge cottonwood that shades the house may reflect they are standing squarely on the route of the Old Mormon Road and the Arrowhead Highway—and perhaps in the footsteps of Parley himself.[88]

After a day of negotiating the rocky canyons of the Santa Clara or scrambling over the lava flows that form the canyons, Pratt's group camped "on a Pi Ute garden patch" at what is now Shivwits on the Paiute Indian Reservation. These cornfields were well known to travelers on the Spanish Trail; Orville Pratt called them "the Piute cornfields," and noted, "The Piutes at this place are said to be the worst on the rute. Bought some corn of them & made them some presents." Cornfields along the Santa Clara were so numerous that Jedediah Smith named the stream Corn Creek.[90] The "plenty semlin vines & semlines on them" are the same as the gourds grown there by Paiutes today. The "very high Mountains, covered with snow" are the Beaver Dam Mountains.

Brown's comment about the pathetic condition of a Paiute band that had sold off its women and children reflects the devastating effect of the slave trade along the Spanish Trail. Daniel W. Jones (not the Dan Jones of the Pratt expedition) describes how the trade worked. New Mexican traders setting out for California, pack trails loaded with woollens, would also carry a few trade goods with which they would buy horses from the Utes or Navajos. "These used up horses were brought through and traded to the poorer Indians [the Paiutes] for children," Jones wrote. "The horses were often used for food. This trading was continued into

---

88.   Leavitt, interview.
89.   "The Journal of Orville C. Pratt," 354.
90.   Brooks, *The Southwest Expedition of Jedediah S. Smith*, 60.

Lower California, where the children bought on the down trip would be traded to the Mexican-Californians for other horses, goods or cash. . . . All children bought on the return trip would be taken back to New Mexico and then sold, boys fetching on an average $100, girls from $150 to $200."[91] Brigham Young's opposition to this practice, including a law passed by the 1852 Legislature forbidding it, infuriated the Utes and helped bring on the Walker War.

Thursday, January 3

CAMPBELL: T 40 beautiful morning, sun breaks thro Warm. Indians left last night, don't make their appearances this morny 9 1/2 A.M. Start. Pass semlins, mule gets mired. Cotton woods & bushes plenty on banks of creek. Pass many engravings on Rocks, come up the bottom of this creek. Indian trail, cross it, going Westward, & strike road. Mts Westward high & covered with snow. Cotton wood timber continues plenty, come to Rocks overhanging, large cave about 6 or 7 feet high 50 feet long, cross the creek (Santa Clara) frequently, swift stream, Rocky bottom. 14 feet Wide 1 foot [deep], some of the crossings very steep, strike to the left up Mt to avoid, kanyon, very steep, Go along. Indians hollows out & comes & meets us, tolerable good looking fellow. The creek here forks, take the left hand fork, on the bottom before the creek forks, East side of the river, a Pi Ute farm a long irrigation furrow, creek dam'd up not the best land however. Corn seems to be small, Hopkins sees this, who walks afoot every day since we left the wagons 12 miles large Prickly pears, he also sees 5 flocks of Quails, have seen crows almost every day for 2 weeks indeed very frequently since we left the city. Some Willows and stumps in the way, see encampments & writing of Date Decr 20th T 29 Camp near forks 15 miles 3 P.M.

BROWN: We now bent our course up the Santa Clara in a north westerly direction there is a great many Hieroglyphics out in the rocks on this river also pieces of broken crockery scattered around going up this stream about 16 miles we came to the California road here we concluded to go home.

Where Campbell reports they "strike road" they again reached what was first the Spanish Trail for horses and mules and later became the wagon road to California. Here the Santa Clara bends

---

91. Daniel W. Jones, *Forty Years among the Indians* (Salt Lake City: Juvenile Instructor, 1890; reprint, Salt Lake City: Bookcraft, 1960).

sharply north, and the party followed it all that day, past what is now Gunlock Reservoir and the town of Gunlock, established in 1857 by Will Hamblin, Jacob's brother, who was nicknamed "Gunlock" because he kept his guns in such good condition.[92] Pressing on, they reached the confluence of the Santa Clara and Magotsu Creek, where they camped.

Friday, January 4

> CAMPBELL: T 28 Horses guarded on the Mt. Some bunch grass, traveled good hard rate yesterday about 5 1/2 hours. Tho we had many crossings, but mostly good road (Parley called it 12 miles) start to day at 1/4 9 A.M. 2 Indians come into Camp. Some Hawks, Madison shot one on New Years day with a rifle at the Indians request Cotton wood timber, & poles on the Santa Clara which now is but a small stream. Willows in the road & good many stumps, but tolerable good Sandy road about 8 miles then ascend & leave the [Santa] Clara, Steep going up, thro cedars, reach small run of water where the road turns to the right, round a hill where some wagons have gone over. excellent green grass on the hill, 6 miles to this small run of water from the Santa Clara, cold day. Snow drifted, chilling breeze, very cold, animals weak, ascend steep & go 5 miles on the rim, strike up to the left in Valley up to the cedars & camp, come about 19 miles—build good bowers, or houses in cedars, snowy cold, cloudy day, Mts manufacturing snow from the clouds on their bosoms, Camp at 3 1/4 P.M. No water. Plenty old snow. Mt. feed. snowing.
>
> BROWN: We passed over the rim of the basin and camped in the pass. Here it snowed on us three or four inches.

The "Mts manufacturing snow from the clouds on their bosoms" refers to the ten-thousand-foot laccolithic Pine Valley Mountains east of the trail. John C. Frémont on his 1844 expedition wrote of these mountains: They "showed out handsomely—high and rugged with precipices, and covered with snow for about two thousand feet from their summits down."[93]

If they followed the Spanish Trail, travel this day was not, as Campbell indicates, up the Santa Clara to the northeast but north up Magotsu Creek until it is pinched up by impassable cliffs. They

---

92. Van Cott, *Utah Place Names,* 170.
93. Frémont, *The Exploring Expedition to the Rocky Mountains,* 270.

there turned right and climbed up through cedars, which are still much in evidence, to the vicinity of Central, on Highway 18. The "small run of water" six miles from where they left the Magotsu is probably Kane Springs, named for Thomas L. Kane, a longtime and valuable friend of the Mormons. He traveled through southern Utah with his wife, whose journal of the trip is a delightful description of the life and times of early Utah Mormons. Parley's expedition camped this night on the southern edge of Mountain Meadows, a favorite campsite for travelers on the Spanish Trail and California Road to rest and fatten horses before tackling or after emerging from the desert wastes to the southwest. Here, in 1857, would occur the darkest, most shameful tragedy of Mormon history—the massacre of 120 California-bound travelers by Indians and Mormons. Tensions leading to the tragedy, the event itself, and its aftermath are best detailed by Juanita Brooks in her book *The Mountain Meadows Massacre.* After decades of bitterness, a closure of sorts was achieved when descendants of the victims cooperated with the LDS Church in 1990 to erect a monument on the hill overlooking the site.

Saturday, January 5

CAMPBELL: T 29 Snowing, start at 19 min before 10 A.M. Strike to the road. Snow a foot deep, for 4 or 5 miles Animals walk on the top of the snow, sometimes sink in. come to crossing of creek. Snow bridge over it good water Springs apparently to the right over crossing, passed a wagon left in the snow—2 miles back from this water, find Purbelow & 4 or 5 wagons encamped near here in the snow this water flows North, snowing large flakes cedars on the hills. Passed a good valley with lots of dry feed Pass over ridges upon ridges, plenty cedars, get into a large valley, some good feed to the left, can't see the extent of this valley. Clouds so dense & snowing come to Kanyon creek, good little stream, Plenty cedars at the right, beautiful feed up the kanyon. Capts Fly, Owen & large Coy with families encamped here. Pass on 1/4 mile past creek up to cedars & Camp at 3 1/2, clears up ceases snowing, find Iron ore 3/4 rich, heavy—15 miles. Fly's Coy 84 men, 25 wagons, many families T 34

BROWN: We arose and shook off the snow and shoved on we soon came to a small company of gold diggers and 10 miles farther we came to a large company of about 50 wagons we camped near them they had a rodometer by which we learned we were 319 miles from G.S.L. City this company had been here recruiting their animals and shoeing their cattle, they had specimens of iron ore which they

had obtained near their camp and 34 miles farther we found more
of the same kind of ore which was said to be first rate.

Travel the first part of this day was through the snow-covered
Mountain Meadows, on the divide between the Colorado drainage
and the Great Basin. Magotsu Creek, up which they have traveled,
flows south to the Santa Clara, Virgin, and Colorado Rivers. Spring
Creek, which they now cross and follow through historic Holt
Canyon, flows north and loses itself in the Escalante Desert.
Purbelow with his four or five wagons is apparently the same horse-
stealing mountain man in pursuit of whom, on November 28, ten
of the Pratt explorers had joined Colonel John Scott's posse. That
Campbell here makes no mention of the chase or of stolen horses
is probably due to the fact that, almost three hundred snow-covered miles from the nearest law officer or courthouse, nothing
could be done about it short of administering frontier justice at
the end of a rope.

Kanyon Creek, the "good little stream," is today named Pinto
Creek and emerges from the mountains at the site of Newcastle, at
the south end of the Escalante Desert. Its name probably comes
from a Paiute band, the Pintiatas, who lived along the creek.[94] The
large company they found camped there was undoubtedly that of
the Pomeroy brothers, freighters from Missouri, with a number of
California-bound gold-seekers who joined them. According to
LeRoy and Ann Hafen's definitive book, *Journals of the Forty-Niners*,
that fall only two wagon trains followed the road cut a few weeks
earlier by Jefferson Hunt and the 108 wagons he was guiding to
California.[95] One was a small group with three wagons, led by the
Mormon scout Howard Egan. The other was the Pomeroy company, comprised of about fifty wagons, which left Salt Lake City
November 3, 1849. None of the accounts written by members of
the company mention either a Captain Fly or Owen, but there can
be little question this was the group.

The samples of iron ore found both by the emigrants and the
explorers led within the year to Brigham Young's call to colonize
Parowan and Cedar City and establish the Iron Mission. Only eight
miles up Little Pinto Creek from the January 5 campsite are the

---

94. Van Cott, *Utah Place Names*, 296.
95. Hafen and Hafen, *Journals of Forty-Niners*, 43.

ruins of Old Irontown. On nearby Iron Mountain is the Columbia
Mine that has provided ore to the Geneva Steel mill on the shore
of Utah Lake.

Off a dirt road six miles southwest of Newcastle a small monument marks the place where on November 3 all but a few of the five
hundred people following Jefferson Hunt rejected his guidance
and, despite Hunt's warning that "I believe you will get into the jaws
of hell," struck out on their ill-fated "shortcut" to California. Leader
of the defecters was a Captain O. K. Smith. David Seeley Sketch of
the Pomeroy company recalled: "at Iron Springs in Cole [Iron]
County Utah we picked up nine men that had at one time formed
part of the Company that suffered and perished in Death Valley,
Nevada. They was trying to get back to Salt Lake they had experienced such suffering for want of food and shoes we brought them
safe to California."[96] If that account is accurate, Smith and his companions were with the company Pratt found camped on Pinto
Creek. Edwin Pettit of the Pomeroy company later wrote of the
O.K. Smith rescue: "They reached the Muddy Desert just at the
time that we did—ragged, starved, and almost perished."[97]

The name "Muddy Desert" for the Escalante Desert is apt, as
Escalante himself had discovered three-quarters of a century earlier.
Bogged down in the desert by a snowstorm, Escalante wrote: "On
the 7th [of October] we could not depart . . . although we were in
great distress, without firewood and extremely cold, for with so
much snow and water the ground, which was soft here, was unfit for
travel." And on the next day: "We travel only three leagues [nine
miles] with great difficulty, because it was so soft and miry everywhere that many pack animals and mounts, and even those that
were loose, either fell down or became stuck altogether."[98] That day,
the goal of establishing a trail from Santa Fe to Monterey, California,
was abandoned. Three days later, at a site twenty miles northeast of
the Pratt campsite, the decision was confirmed after seeking God's
will by casting of lots. From here Escalante's party headed south
through Cedar Valley. In the vicinity of the Three Peaks their trail
crossed at right angles what would become the Spanish Trail, the
only spot in Utah where the two trails would touch.

---

96.   Ibid., 296.
97.   Ibid., 294.
98.   Warner, *Escalante Journal,* 70.

Sunday, January 6

    CAMPBELL: Beautiful morning T 31 exhibit beautiful iron ore, got
in the Mt South of creek, Plenty thousands of it so says Flys
[Pomeroy] Coy. Bre sell a little Flour at 20 cents per lb, several
Mormons in the Coy. They write off a table of distances from the
Southern rim of the Basin to Utah, measured by Church's roadometer, been laying bye 2 weeks shoeing cattle, intended to start middle
of week. 10 A.M. start, look NW to the eye can see no farther, very
extensive valley good deal larger than Salt Lake & Utah vallies
stream apparently heads in the Mts West or N.W. travel round a
curve, large Mound out in the valley which from the North would
hide from the eye the extent of the valley, sage & greasewood.
Rabbitts any quantity of them, Indians say the Deer go away N..W. to
Winter, Walkers [band] comes & runs them in these valleys in
Spring, make. Pass Willow Springs without striking to the right to
them, & Go on to creek, cross it, & Camp at foot of hills under a
cedar, few yards past crossing, nearly Dark come 25 miles, thousands
of cedars, easy of access to the right & left, Good day. T noon about
40 no snow. Judge Phelps & Bro Green gets in 2 hours after dark,
Judges Mule slow, & Greens horse about given out T 29 Matson gets
drunk, boys bring him in on Hollidays horse

Campbell's reference to the "Church's roadometer" in possession
of the Pomeroy company is intriguing. The first Mormon odometer was made on the journey of the Pioneer Company of 1847 and
first installed on a wagon between Council Bluffs and Fort
Laramie. William Clayton, assigned by Brigham Young to keep
track of mileage, grew weary of counting the revolutions of a
wagon wheel; he proposed a mechanical instrument to do the job.
Orson Pratt, a scientist and mathematician, got the job to design
such an instrument. His journal records:

> For several days past, Mr. Clayton and several others have been
> thinking upon the best method of attaching some machinery to a
> wagon, to indicate the number of miles daily traveled. I was
> requested this forenoon, by Mr. B. Young, to give this subject some
> attention; accordingly, this afternoon, I proposed the following
> method:—Let a wagon wheel be of such a circumference, that 360
> revolutions make one mile (It happens that one of the requisite
> dimensions [Heber C. Kimball's wagon] is now in camp.) Let this
> wheel act upon a screw, in such a manner, that six revolutions of the
> wagon wheel shall give the screw one revolution. Let the threads of

this screw act upon a wheel of sixty cogs, which will evidently perform one revolution per mile. Let this wheel of sixty cogs be the
head of another screw, acting upon another wheel of thirty cogs. It
is evident that in the movement of this second wheel, each cog will
represent one mile. Now, if the cogs were numbered from 0 to 30,
the number of miles traveled will be indicated during every part of
the day. Let every sixth cog, of the first wheel, be numbered from 0
to 10, and this division will indicate the fractional parts of a mile, or
tenths; while if anyone should be desirous to ascertain still smaller
divisional fractions, each cog between this division, will give five and
one-third rods.[99]

The task of actually creating a somewhat simplified version of the
instrument fell to Appleton Milo Harmon, a skilled woodworker.
In just five days, while the company continued its journey, he completed the job. His granddaughter wrote: "Appleton Milo Harmon
constructed the iron and wheel work and attached it to the wagon
wheel. Since the pioneers had few tools and little material,
Appleton Milo Harmon took a wooden feed box and some scraps
of iron and by using his pocket-knife, a hammer, and other simple
tools fashioned the crude instrument which was the first
speedometer to pass over the great Plains and the Rockies."[100]

Other odometers were soon made. Assigned to resurvey the
route to Winter Quarters, William Clayton had a second instrument made by William A. King in August 1847. Clayton's *Latter-day
Saints Emigrants Guide* resulted from his resurvey. Peter Derr of the
Gruwell-Derr wagon train to Los Angeles in 1849 wrote that the
company had three odometers,[101] probably purchased from the
Mormons in Salt Lake City. Parley's list of expenditures for his
expedition contains the item: "Willard Snow for rodometer—
$00.25," clearly an important instrument in making their mileage
measurements so accurate. So what was the Pomeroy company's
"Church roadometer?" The fate of the original "roadometer" has
never been known; the one exhibited in the church museum was
made eighteen years later by Thomas G. Lowe while on a Mormon

99. Orson Pratt, "Interesting Items ... from the Private Journal of Orson Pratt," *Millennial
     Star*, February 15, 1850, 49–50. Quoted in Guy Stringham, "The Pioneer
     Roadometer," *Utah Historical Quarterly* 42 (summer 1974): 262–63.
100. Ardelle Harmon Ashworth, "Stories Found in Appleton Milo Harmon's Journal,"
     manuscript in her possession, Provo, Utah. Quoted in Stringham, "The Pioneer
     Roadometer," 264.
101. Hafen and Hafen, *Journals of Forty-Niners*, 52.

mission to the Oraibi Indians in Arizona.[102] Is it possible the instrument created on the plains by Harmon could have fallen into the hands of the Pomeroy brothers?

The "very extensive valley good deal larger than Salt Lake & Utah vallies" is the Escalante Desert, which extends nearly one hundred miles to the north. Following the Spanish Trail, the explorers circled to the north of the Antelope Range and camped just beyond Iron Springs, on the western edge of Cedar Valley. George B. Matson's inebriated condition indicates the nature of some of the trading done with the Pomeroy company. The well-known Mormon prohibition of drinking liquor originated with an 1833 revelation to Joseph Smith, given originally "not by commandment or constraint, but by revelation and the word of wisdom."[103] Adherence to the Word of Wisdom, as the revelation came to be known, was spotty in the early days of the church. Brigham Young strongly preached obedience to its principles, declaring: "I know that some say the revelations upon these points are not given by way of commandment. Very well, but we are commanded to observe every word that proceeds from the mouth of God."[104] But this emphasis came later in his ministry. Not until 1930, in the presidency of Heber J. Grant, had obedience to the Word of Wisdom become a commandment in the sense that it was a test of worthiness to enter a Mormon temple.[105]

Monday, January 7

CAMPBELL: T 28 Boys find Iron ore with Silver I can see little of it 10 1/2 Camp starts. Pass up the crek, which gets to be a Dry creek, strike to the left leave road, & pass thro' an extensive beautiful bottom, rich in feed, hundreds of acres on the bottom, sandy knolls dug up by Gophers, wire grass dense & thick, excellent bottom. Dry hollows apparently have been water furrows. Indians 20 or 30 come & look at us, no families sickness taken them away, said Mormons over North East, they our friends never knew them till now gave us lots of presents, Dimic tells them we r also Mormons they say Mormons coming to live among them & help them to raise corn

---

102. Norman Edward Wright, "The Mormon Pioneer Odometers," *BYU Studies* 37 (1997–1998): 83.

103. Doctrine and Covenants, section 89, verses 2ff.

104. Brigham Young, *Discourses of Brigham Young*, selected and arranged by John A. Widtsoe (Salt Lake City: Deseret Book Company, 1925), 13:3.

105. Joseph Lynn Lyon, "Word of Wisdom," in Ludlow, *Encyclopedia of Mormonism*, 4:1584.

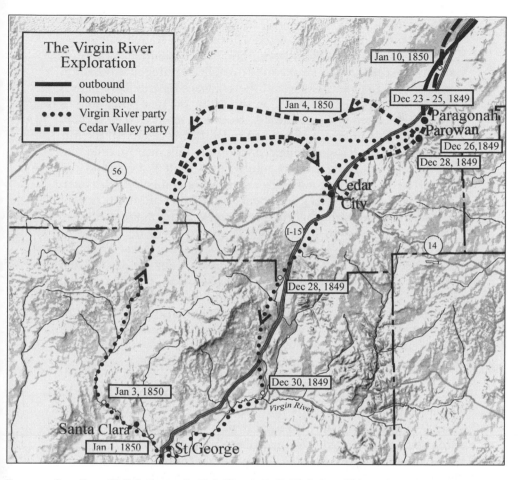

The Virgin River
Exploration
— outbound
▬ ▬ homebound
• • • • Virgin River party
▪ ▪ ▪ ▪ Cedar Valley party

Jan 10, 1850

Dec 23 - 25, 1849

Jan 4, 1850

Paragonah
Parowan

Dec 26,1849

Dec 28, 1849

56

Cedar City

I-15

14

Dec 28, 1849

Dec 30, 1849

Jan 3, 1850

Virgin River

Santa Clara

Jan 1, 1850   St George

Base map from Peter H. DeLafosse, ed., *Utah Historic Trails* (Utah State Historical Society, 1998), cartography by David H. Vaughn. Used by permission.

want we should come give us all the land round here for a knife, accompany us to Camp (4 of them) see lots of Rabbitts & a sage hen, very extensive bottom Dense good feed. Camp at springs on the hill, excellent feed on the hills near, beautiful feed on the bottoms below, Sage & Greasewood, there r many Springs here, 2 or 3 good Springs or runs of water. on the Mt or hill west of us there is thousands of cedar, easy of access, from this knoll to these cedars across the bottom may be nearly 10 miles. Plenty cedars on the Mts 3 miles East & a few scattering cedars on the hills near us. mild day, go thru a swampy place where muddy loses itself as a consolidated stream we av cut off a good many miles by not going up to the road. Great many large cotton woods near the crossing of Muddy extend a mile & half down the margin of the creek. Parley & Jones after we camp, ask permission from Captn Brown to go to the wagons to night they start with Jones' two horses. stop about 3 P.M. Phelps & Green comes in 1 1/2 hours after, mild sunny day. we have passed thru no snow to day. Indians have all black hair, no guns among them, tell Dimic they could understand him, could not the other Mormons only they knew they were coming to raise corn, They pack us 4 large loads of wood, we feed them liberally, good set of Indians apparently. T 26 Camp prayers & singing the boys express their desires to stay a while & explore in this region 19 miles

The area of "extensive beautiful bottom, rich in feed" the Indians offer to sell for a knife is the heart of Cedar Valley, generally northwest of Cedar City. The "muddy," which here "loses itself as a consolidated stream" in the "swampy place" is Coal Creek, which comes out of the Markagunt Plateau down Cedar Canyon, through Cedar City, and here disappears in Cedar Valley. Pratt's mounted party could follow the Spanish Trail through this area, allowing Campbell to report "we av cut off a good many miles by not going up to the road" that Jefferson Hunt's wagon train cut higher up across Coal Creek to avoid the "swampy place." After traveling fourteen miles this day through this pleasant, level valley, they camp at the springs just below I-15 at Enoch, well known to travelers on the Spanish Trail. The name given the springs by those travelers is reflected on Frémont's map of 1845, which labels them "Ojo de San Jose."[106]

The "thousands of cedar, easy of access" Campbell sees looking from the Enoch springs ten miles west across Cedar Valley are the Utah juniper (*Juniperus osteosperma*). If there is a signature tree

---

106. "Map of an Exploring Expedition."

of the Great Basin, surely it is this one. As naturalist Donald Culross Peattie writes, in the vast land between the Rockies on the east and the Sierra Nevada and Cascade ranges on the west "this tree is likely to be the most abundant, as it is the most widely distributed. . . . It dots the mesas, descends the canyons, climbs the mountains. In its namesake state of Utah it is as characteristic a settler as the Mormons, and in its venerable age sometimes reminds you of an old patriarch of the sect—rugged and weathered and twisted by hardship, but hard too to discourage or kill. . . . No other tree it seems is so well fitted as this one to endure the arid, wind-blown, sand-swept land of Deseret."[107]

This is the tree that until recent years federal land managers were intent to uproot by huge tractor-dragged chain to improve grazing for cattle. The Pratt explorers also viewed the vast juniper forests through practical economic eyes. In the official report to the legislature (printed in full in the final chapter of this volume), writing of Cedar Valley, Parley reported: "But the best of all remains to be told, near the large body of good land on the Southwestern borders are thousands of acres of cedar contributing an almost inexhaustible supply of fuel which makes excellent coal. In the centre of these forests rises a hill of the richest Iron ore." Indeed, the juniper was the fuel of choice for the crude early pioneer blast furnaces.

For the native peoples of the Great Basin, the juniper has, from ancient times, played a more central role. Peattie writes that ancient Fremont peoples used juniper bark for cordage, that they strengthened their unfired clay pottery with juniper bark, carried their infants in juniper bark cradles bound with yucca fibers, used the bark as a thatch under their earthen roofs, covered their walls with juniper bark mats, used it in sandals, and wove it into bags. Among the Havasupai and other remote peoples today, Peattie writes, the juniper figures from babyhood to the grave.

> When the child is born he is covered with juniper bark which his mother has rubbed very soft for his tender skin, then swaddled in a blanket and placed in a juniper cradle. From the bark are fashioned the dolls with which he first plays, and he sleeps on an oval mat of the bark. When he is weaned, he begins to eat the berries. . . . When

---

107. Donald Culross Peattie, *A Natural History of Western Trees* (Boston: Houghton Mifflin Co., 1953), 264.

he marries, the young Havasupai brings his wife to a bed of juniper bark. . . . If wounded, he uses juniper gum as a protective membrane over the sore. . . . When a Navajo dies the two men who attended him to the last back carefully away from the grave, sweeping their tracks with juniper bough so that deathliness shall not follow them from the grave.[108]

---

108.   Peattie, 265–66.

Little Salt Lake & Cedar Valleys & Beyond

During the arduous two-week exploration of the Virgin River basin by Parley's mounted party, the men left behind with the wagons were not idle. They explored Little Salt Lake and Cedar Valleys, the mountains to the east and west, and part of the Escalante Desert. Because of their discoveries of the iron ore and other resources in the region, Brigham Young within the year sent a colonizing company to establish an iron industry there. The journal of the wagon company's activities during that two-week period was doubtless kept, as intended, by Isaac Haight, though the manuscript doesn't bear the name of an author.

Little Salt Lake Valley. East of the lake on Red Creek

Decr 25th 1849 a meeting was called in the evening Prayer by Prest Pratt Voted that David Fullmer be Prest of the part of the camp that remained with the waggons & I. C. Haight Capt and to keep the journal. voted that Joseph Mathews and Schyler Jennings have an honourable furlough to go home and that they carry the mail back

25th Wind S. East Weather clear thermometer 26 degres at 6 ocl A.M. 12 ocl M T. 53 J. Mathews & S. Jennings Start for G. S. L. City P. P. Pratt and company consisting of 20 men & 30 horses & mules start on the track after some trouble to catch a wild mule all in good Spirits 6 ocl P.M. T. 45 W. E. 6 1/2 PM. Br Robert Campbell came back to our camp with an ox which P.P.Pratts company found about six miles South of here supposed to belong to Misses Infilt [?] Br C. left for P Prtts camp again about 8 ocl PM Camp came together sung Prayer by Mr. Wadsworth

27th Wind S. Cloudy Thermometer 20 12 M. T 57 Sol [?] 6 ocl P.M. T. 40 came together at 8 ocl Prest Fullmer made some remarks. Sung a hymn Prayer by Father Dustin a good spirit prevailed in the camp. Concluded to move our camp to the next creek

28th Wind South Cloudy 6 ocl AM T. 34 Left red Creek and came 4 1/4 miles and camped at 12 ocl M T. 46 at the Mouth of a large canion on a beautiful creek which we called Birch creek 8 ocl Camp met singing Prayer by Father Gould 6 ocl PM T 33 stormy

HAIGHT [his separate journal this date records]: Moved the camp 4
1/4 miles there being plenty of wood and feed for our cattle.

This was a move from Red Creek, the site of Paragonah, to Birch
Creek, now the site of Parowan, the first Mormon settlement south
of Manti. After Parley's report of a potential iron industry in southern Utah, Brigham Young sent a party of 119 men, 310 women,
and 18 children under leadership of George A. Smith, who left
Fort Utah in December 1850 and arrived at the site of Parowan
January 13, 1851. Their 129 wagons contained "armament, saddles, 'lights of Glass,' carpenter and blacksmith tools, seeds, 'pitt
saws,' plows, 'syths and cradles,' mill irons, cats, dogs, and chick-
ens. Milk cows, beef cattle, oxen, mules, and horses all served as
draft animals."[109]

Jules Remy, passing through in 1855, found the settlement
"nothing more than a poor straggling village, built of wood and
adobes of red earth."[110] Poor it may have been, but its citizens were
strong enough to save the lives of John C. Frémont and the men of
his fifth expedition. After leaving the Sevier River to force a way
over the same snow-choked mountains that had tested Parley and
his men so severely, Frémont's expedition staggered into Parowan
on February 9, 1854, leaving one of their number, Oliver Fuller,
starved and frozen to death in the foothills a few miles to the
north. The citizens of Parowan, themselves struggling to survive,
nursed the party back to health. Of this rescue Frémont wrote: "We
owe our lives to these good Mormons, who not only cared for us
for two weeks, but gave us food and new horses to continue our
journey."[111]

29th Wind S. W. cloudy 6. T. 27 12 ocl M 30 A misty rain froze
as fast as it came 1 ocl P M. clear 6 P.M. 24 W. East. as the clouds
hung heavy on the mountains there was no one went out to explore
in the mountains the most of the boys found amusement in rolling
the ball at 10 pins for a dinner which is to be furnished by the losing
party to eat on New Years day. 8 oclock camp met sung a hymn
Prayer D. Fullmer

---

109. Ward J. Roylance, *Utah: A Guide to the State* (Salt Lake City: Utah Arts Council, 1982),
307.
110. Jules Remy, *A Journey to Great Salt Lake City* (New York: AMS Press, 1861), 2:360.
111. Letter to Jessie Benton Frémont, quoted in Luella Adams Dalton, ed., *History of Iron
County Mission and Parowan* (Provo, Utah: Brigham Young University Press, 1973).

30ᵗʰ W. S clear 6 A.M. 14—6 P.M 32 Wind East. I C Haight Br Horn S. Gould E. Everett went to explore the canion of Birch creek as we passed up the creek we found it forked about 4 miles up to the left which had the appearance of considerable timber about 1/4 miles it forked again to the left Br Gould & Evrett went up it and report large quantity of the best pine timber fit for hewing, Sawing House logs and fence polls. Br Horn & myself went up the main creek and found it to contain a large quantity of pine timbr fit for any purpose tht should be wanted the creek bottoms are wide and practible for a good road it ascends gradually to the hed of the canion

Br Wm Wadsworth & Hulett went up into the Mountains and found Iron Ore in abundance and very rich and also water Lime & plaster of Paris the mountains appear rich with minerals Camp met in the evening had singing and prayer by I C. Haight

HAIGHT [on this date his separate journal records]: I took three men & went up into the Canon to search for timber found a plenty of the best of red pine, easy of access.

This would be up Parowan Canyon. The fork to the left, up which Gould and Everett explored, was Center Creek, which heads on the north slope of Brian Head on the heavily forested Markagunt Plateau. The "main creek" that Haight and Horne explored is Parowan Creek, which heads on the west face of Brian Head. Present Highway 143 follows up this creek and on to Cedar Breaks National Monument.

Wadsworth's and Hulett's exploration was not into the high mountains to the east as the phrase "up into the Mountains" would suggest, but west across Cedar Valley to the low mountains of the Antelope Range. It was there that iron ore was found and where the Iron Mission would soon begin operations. And it was to there that the next day "Some of the Breathren went out to the Mountains and returned without making any farther discoverys."

31ˢᵗ Wind East Clear T. 23 12 ocl M 48 6 P.M. 34 W. East Some of the Breathren went out to the Mountains and returned without making any farther discoverys excepting an abundance of timber camp met in the evening Sung a hymn Prst Fullmer made some remarks concerning our living in such a manner that we should not be ashamed to have angels come into our midst and see our acts &c followed by some others a good feeling prevailed in the camp Prayer by J. Horn Br Arnold reports a plenty of lime Stone.

HAIGHT [his separate journal entry is more revealing of his feelings on this New Year's Eve so far from home]: I remained in camp feel depressed in spirit much lightness prevails in camp. In the evening Br Fullmer made some very good remarks on the necessity of laying aside our folly and living in such a manner that we should not be ashamed to have angels come into our midst and behold our acts I followed him on the same subject. Meet every evening have prayers and singing and enjoy ourselves as well as we can being deprived of our wives and children.

Tuesday January 1st 1850 Wind South Cloudy 6. T. 30. 12 ocl M. 45 6 P.M. T 31 Camp waked by the firing of the Cannon Killed a beef, a company of ten men were organized to go west and explore the mountains and valleys to be absent some ten or twelve days, viz Chancy West Capt Andrew J Blodget, Clerk Rufus C. Allen Sterling Driggs, Edward Evertt ~~Henry Heath~~ James Farrer, Stephen Taylor, Isaac Brown ~~John Armstrong~~ Hial K. Gay, & John Lowry, to start on the 2nd at 2 ocl all Sat down to a dinner prepared according to previous arangement. The dinner conscisted of Roast Beef Biscuit, Apple & Mince pies, pumpkin Sauce, Pickles & coffe got up in a style not easily surpassed, after the company were seated a blessing was asked by prest Fullmer all did ample justice to the repast After it was finished, a sentiment was offred by Br Wm L Wadsworth in the form of a toast relative to the situation of the camp and the prosperity of the church, which was responded to by three cheers and the firing of the cannon camp met in the evening sung a hymn prayer by C. W. West

Wed 2nd Wind West cloudy 6 P.M. T. 31 12ocl M 60 in the sun 6 P.M. 35 Capt C. W. West and company started to explore west of this valley the camp moved across the creek and down it 3/4 miles for the convenience of keeping our cattle and made correll of ceders by hauling the trees and laying them whole in the fence Correlled our cattle camp met had singing Prayer by Father Williams

Thurs 3rd Wind North Cloudy 6 A.M. T 32 12 M T 55 6 ocl P M. T. 32 A company of five men viz Capt J Arnold S. Willis G. Nabiker S. Tanner and J. Packer went to explore the creek & canion some 7 or 8 miles south of this camp met at 7 ocl P.M. Singing Prayer by Br Henry.

The creek "7 or 8 miles south" is Summit Creek. Its "canion" is the extremely rugged gorge through which it emerges from the Hurricane Cliffs.

Frid 4th Wind East cloudy 6 A.M. T. 24 12 ocl M. T. 40 W. South. 6 P.M. 31 Snowing a little Wind South 3 ocl P.M. Capt Arnold and company returned and report a large quantity of timber of the first quality in the mountains and canion of the South creek the canion rather difficult of access 7 ocl P.M. camp met sung a hymn Prayer by Br J Armstrong

Sat 5th Wind East stormy 6 ocl A.M. T. 30 12 ocl M. T. 36 6 P.M. 32 cloudy It being stormy most of the day, all remained in camp. in the evening although stormy camp met and had singing, Prayer by Br J. Arnold aftr which Brs Vance & Hatch being somewhat indisposed requested the laying on of hands which was done by Brs Arnold, Horn & Wadsworth

Sun 6th Wind West cloudy 6 A.M. T. 32 12 ocl M. T 43 Clear 6 P.M. 28 Brs Williams & Arnold went across the valley to explore the gap [Parowan Gap] where the lake passes through the Mountain Ground white with snow. 1 ocl P.M. camp came together and had a meeting for Prayer and exhortation had a good season and enjoyed ourselves very well 3 ocl P.M. Capt West & company came back all well. in the evening had singing Prayer by Br J. Farrer Capt C.W.West reports as follows after leaving the camp they went west to the pass in the Mountains [Little] Salt Lake enters the pass about 50 rods there could be a good waggon rode made through the Rocks one perpendicular either side some 4 miles through the pass as they passed out into the Valley on the west it is very narrow and the Rocks two or three hundred feet high on either side they camped over night the Rocks are covered with Hyeroglyphics on either side especially on the North as high as there was a face stone some of which they drew off. they entred the vally next day and found it to be nothing but a deasert on the North with but little vegetation and no water, but towards the South part of the valley there is a small Lake probably 2 miles North & south and one East & West of fresh water formed by a large creek coming from the South East called Cottn Wood as there is a large quantity of cotton wood timber on the creek. after they left the Lake and between it and the creek there is a large body very rich aluvial Soil which can be watered from the creek The creek sinks before it reachs the Lake except in high water at which time it has an outlet in to the deasert West after they left the Lake they went west some 8 miles and camped for the night on the fourth they travelled about 10 miles West and came to the edge of a great Valley apparently a deasert but as their animals were not fit to go any farther (as they had but 3 for ten men and very poor) they thought it not wisdom to go any farther in that direction as there was no prospect of water or feed but being informed by an Indian (a Pah Ute) that there was water south they went in that direction along the border of the deasert about 12 miles and came to a spring which sinks in about one mile camped over night

PAROWAN GAP PETROGLYPHS

THIS ARCHEOLOGICAL SITE WAS PLACED ON THE NATIONAL REGISTER OF HISTORIC PLACES IN 1969. THE PETROGLYPHS DISPLAYED HERE REPRESENT THE WORK OF PREHISTORIC FREMONT AND SOUTHERN PAIUTE CULTURES. THE FIGURES AND DRAWINGS ARE LIKELY THE WORK OF MANY DIFFERENT INDIVIDUALS OVER A LONG PERIOD OF TIME. WHILE THE MEANING OF THE FIGURES MAY NEVER BE KNOWN, THEY PROBABLY PORTRAY SUCH TRIBAL PURSUITS AS RELIGION, HUNTING AND GATHERING TRIPS, FAMILY HISTORY, SOURCES OF WATER AND TRAVEL ROUTES.

VOLUNTEER PROJECT   BUREAU OF LAND
ALVA MATHESON   MANAGEMENT
PAROWAN EAGLE SCOUTS   CEDAR CITY DISTRICT

Plaque at the Parowan Gap petroglyphs.

The "pass in the Mountains" West's group explored west of Little Salt Lake is Parowan Gap, running through the Red Hills that separate Parowan Valley from the north end of Cedar Valley. Over millions of years it was formed by a stream cutting through a gradually rising fault block. Eventually the stream disappeared, and the fierce winds blowing off the desert continued to shape what is now known as a wind gap. The Parowan Gap Petroglyphs, listed on the National Historic Register, were carved over millenia, first during the Archaic culture, later by the Fremont people, who disappeared some eight hundred years ago. Enigmatic geometric figures cover the rocks, as do images of mountain sheep, bear claws, lizards, snakes, and human figures. According to the expedition's report to the Legislative Assembly, Chief Walker called this place "God's own house."[112]

---

112.   Parley P. Pratt, Report of the Southern Exploring Expedition Submitted to the Legislative Council of Deseret, February 5, 1850, LDS Church Archives, 10.

From their somewhat inexact description it is difficult to be confident about the exploring party's route the next four days. One possibility is that from Parowan Gap they traveled five miles southwest to Rush Lake, which at that time may have had a larger creek than present Johnson Creek coming from the southeast. The next two days they explored eighteen miles to the west, which would put them at the edge of "a great Valley apparently a deasert"—the Escalante Desert. Here, with their pitifully few horses giving out and no prospect of water or feed, they wisely headed south twelve miles to the water the Indians told them they would find, in the vicinity of Newcastle.

> *5th* took a South East course one mile and found the wagon road which they followed East 15 miles and struck the Cotton Wood creek which forms the Lake below. today crossed a range of hills filled with Iron Ore of the richest quality it will yeald probably 75 per cent, a specimen of which they took with them. four Indians came to us today we told them we were Mormons they said Capt Walker had told them about us that we were his friends they said they were our friends and would not kill our cattle or horses Walker told them that the Mormons raised Saunt of Tickup and they wanted us to come and raise it among them Said they loved the Mormons. they are very poor have no horses or skins they live upon Rabbits which ar plenty in this valley and cloath themselves with their skins. we explored the creek 8 or 10 miles there is large quantity of timber fit ^for^ building it is cotton wood the land bordring on the creek very good and fit for cultivation easy to be watered from the creek camped on the creek
> *6th* We took our course back to the camp where we arrive about 3, ocl. All well after travelling about 100 miles[113]

The road they followed on the return trip was the road cut by Jefferson Hunt and other wagon trains earlier that fall. En route they crossed the Antelope Range, finding evidence and obtaining samples of the rich iron ore that would shortly be mined by men of the Iron Mission. The creek they explored was probably Shirts Creek, named for early Mormon settler Peter Shirts. It rises in the Cedar Mountains and flows through the Hurricane Cliffs to feed Quichapa Lake.

---

113. Campbell, Southern Exploring Expedition Papers.

ARMSTRONG [in the camp on Birch Creek; undated but probably January 6]: Looked through the glass along the valley, Saw some more men, they were so far off I could not count them, thought it was Brother Pratt and his camp returning, fired the cannon twice to let them know where we were, This broke up the meeting, all get our guns and pistols and fired them when they got nigher to us we found it was the camp of ten that had gone to explore the valley and mountains West of here, They gave us a good report of water, wood and iron ore, The day they left us they passed thru a gap in the mountains about three miles long with perpendicular rocks, good roads though and all cut with Hyrogliphics from one end to the other, They sketched a few for samples, If Bro Pratt does not return in a day or two we are going to get them all drawn off, The camp is all well, My foot is a great deal better.

Mond 7th [returning to Haight's account of camp activities] Wind South 6 ocl A.M. T 24 clear 12 M T. 46 6 P.M. T. 30 At half past 5 P.M. Prst Pratt & Capt Jones returned from their journey South and were received with the firing of the cannons and Small arms and three cheers from the camp we were all glad to see them well. have some singing and prayer by Br Wadsworth Br Pratt requested in behalf of his company which are camped 12 miles back that we have a publick dinner tomorrow which was unanimously agreed to. Voted that Bros Wadsworth & Griggs to superintend the same also that we have a liberty Pole raised.

ARMSTRONG: A fine warm day, Boys got me to make them some boxing gloves 2 pair of boxing gloves, and spent the day boxing, bowling etc. I made some good apple pudding and it was a treat out here About six oclock in the evening the boys were dancing cotillions, when we heard a gun fired off at a distance, the dancing ceased in a moment and it was laughable to see every man run and get his gun loaded and then the cannon loaded and fired off in less time than it takes me to describe it, The guns and pistols followed so fast it sounded as if there were two or three hundred of us. Then we gave a few loud huzzahs, for we knew it was Parley Pratt, After the tumult ceased Bro Pratt Halloed to us, then the air rent with another shout of joy and the firing of guns, Presently he was among us with Capt. Dan Jones, He told us he had left the camp about eleven miles off and would be in tomorrow. We then gave loud huzzahs. Then the little Captain told us he had a canteen full of whiskey, Then he handed it all around, Then we gave three more loud huzzahs Brother Pratt and brother Jones joining in with all their might. They then took supper, we were all overjoyed to see them. Some went to boxing some to singing, some dancing to amuse them, They told us we must prepare a large dinner for the whole camp tomorrow, Put up a liberty pole and have Jubilee.

HAIGHT [his separate journal]: Nothing worthy of notice occurred till the 7th when Br Pratt returned he was received with the firing of cannon and cheers all was glad to see him.

Boxing, bowling, dancing cotillions, eating apple pudding—life doesn't seem to have been all that hard for the camp during the two weeks they have waited for Pratt's return. The canteen of whiskey he brought with him was no doubt purchased from the Fly-Owen (Pomeroy) company. The detail in Armstrong's account is welcome in view of Haight's brevity.

REUNION AND CELEBRATION

Tuesday, January 8, 1850

ARMSTRONG: It is now three oclock in the morning Tuesday and I am helping them prepare the dinner (I had two or three minutes to spare and noted it down) Here we have large kettles boiling meat to make mince pies, The sky is clear and the stars are twinkling bright and we are in hopes of a fine day At half past five the horn was sounded, the camp got out of bed with one consent and commenced cooking with all their might, I have made 16 Cartridges for the cannon, Mended two pair of pants for the boys, and we all cleaned ourselves for dinner, then hoisted up the Liberty pole with a flag. At one oclock the boys that were returning got within two miles of us, the cannon was fired and then they fired their guns in answer to us, We waited until they got up to camp, We fired the cannon three times again, The boys had got their handkerchiefs fixed on small sticks and attached them to their horses heads and rode up in front of our camp, gave us a volley with their guns and pistols We answering in return gave some loud huzzahs then they heard some wonderful stories.

The Mormon tradition of the liberty pole began with a Book of Mormon account in which Moroni, a military leader,

rent his coat; and he took a piece thereof, and wrote upon it—In memory of our God, our religion, and freedom, and our peace, our wives, and our children—and he fastened it upon the end of a pole. . . .

And . . . he went forth among the people, waving the rent part of his garment in the air, that all might see the writing which he had written upon the rent part, and crying with a loud voice, saying:

Behold, whosoever will maintain this title upon the land, let
them come forth in the strength of the Lord. . . .

And [after his armies had defeated the enemy] he caused the
title of liberty to be hoisted upon every tower which was in all the
land. . . .[114]

Patty Sessions, a Mormon pioneer midwife, recorded the burial of
Jacob Weatherby, shot by Indians near the Elk Horn River,
Nebraska: "he died this morning [June 20, 1847] was ^calculated^
to be caried back to Winter Quarters to burry him but he morti-
fied and smelt so bad they buried him in a buffaloe robe near the
liberty pole. this liberty pole was raised the 14 day of June 1847 and
a white flag put on it another raised here with white flag the 18 day
they have had a meeting under it to day."[115] Patty also recorded the
raising of a liberty pole in Salt Lake Valley on August 10, 1848:
"went to the bowry [a shelter built of upright poles covered with
boughs and brush, the first public building in Salt Lake City] 9 A M
saw the liberty pole raised heard the cannon fired then between 12
and 2 feasted after 2 danced heard the music and the prayers and
preaching."[116] Parley P. Pratt was one of the preachers that day. His
autobiography describes what was the first Thanksgiving Day in
Salt Lake Valley:

> On the 10th of August we held a public feast under a bowery in the
> center of our fort [at what is now Pioneer Square]. This was called a
> harvest feast; we partook freely of a rich variety of bread, beef, but-
> ter, cheese, cakes, pastry, green corn, melons, and almost every vari-
> ety of vegetable. Large sheaves of wheat, rye, barley, oats and other
> productions were hoisted on poles for public exhibition, and there
> was prayer and thanksgiving, congratulations, songs, speeches,
> music, dancing, smiling faces and merry hearts. In short, it was a
> great day with the people of these valleys, and long to be remem-
> bered by those who had suffered and waited anxiously for the
> results of a first effort to redeem the interior deserts of America,
> and to make her hitherto unknown solitudes "blossom as the
> rose."[117]

---

114. Book of Mormon, Alma 46:12, 19–20, 36.
115. Donna Toland Smart, ed. *Mormon Midwife: The 1846–1888 Diaries of Patty Bartlett
      Sessions* (Logan: Utah State University Press, 1997), 87–88.
116. Ibid., 117.
117. Pratt, *Autobiography*, 35.

The Pratt expedition's liberty pole was to be part of a smaller but somewhat similar celebration of thanksgiving. It was erected on a small knoll immediately south of Heaps Spring where Haight and those who remained with the wagons had stayed for two weeks while waiting for Pratt's explorers to return from the Virgin. Here, too, where a fine stream of water emerges from the rocks, the first settlers stayed after arriving January 13, 1851, and while building the Parowan Fort. The Parowan Heritage Park now memorializes the campsite. The liberty pole, at least part of which the locals claim is original, still stands on the knoll above.

CAMPBELL: T 28 cold on this knoll, cloudy. Mts round covered with cedars, start at 10 1/4 A. M. Strike up to South end of Little Salt Lake valley, go up considerable sage on every side. Mts to the right plenty of cedars and easy of access, Pass on to Summit creek. 5 miles See a wagon which has come from our Camp after the wagon irons which were left by the emigrants At this point, Good place for a set-tlement, on the South of creek, Travel on to near Big creek, the Settlers here have called it iron ore creek, find they have erected a liberty pole about 40 feet high, hoisted a white flag, a long red strip of cloth, on the flag "Great Basin, meeting of Rough & Ready club this eveny" & also a banner inscribed on it Free soil, Free speech, free labor & freedom of the Saints. canonading commenced when we hove in sight, & shooting of small arms. Fine pleasant day. See a ten pin alley made at the back of the wagons, with balls & pins, also see boxing Gloves. reach Camp which is on the South margin of creek, above a mile up from the road, near the mouth of the Kanyon excellent feed all round. 15 min past 2 all sat down to an excellent Dinner prepared by Wadsworth & Driggs. Plenty coffee, roast Beef, Pumpkin & Squash, with Pies, minced, apple &c little Sugar, and butter handed round while eating Some sitting on stools, Boxes, others on robes on the ground, Parley prophecied, "while the sun & moon should endure, & so long as a Settlement was here, they should perpetuate this 8th of Jany as the day we celebrate, by this dinner is the first anniversary of the Settlement of this place,["] to which a hearty response was given by three cheers. after dinner was over, the cannon was fired, then Parley said he wished to make a speech, Captn Brown called the attention of the Coy when, he said he rejoiced in the words which headed the flag on the Liberty pole—"Great Basin" to be sure there r climes soil & country whose productions are valuable, he has read of the sunny climes of fair Italy, he had trod Europes shores heard of the fertile & productive

countries in France, but all these things were, where neither the
soil, the elements nor the air, the light of heaven was free, but here
is "free soil free speech free labor free Saints" & free Pumpkin pies,
to be sure west is the country of Gold, but her harbours r so open,
that she lies insecure of all her treasures, like the richest man who
told his friend of his riches, but says his friend a little iron could
take it all from you, so I value iron most, so it was, it was all taken
from him, but we have the iron, & minerals more useful & more
safe besides our defences r in these munitions of rocks, here we r
safe with all the riches we may possess, & we have the best defence
the most rocks, the best women, most beautiful children & more of
them than any ppl on the earth in proportion to our number, therefore boys the Great Basin for me. cannon fired amid three cheers—
long & loud by the Fifty WW. Phelps, said he rejoiced at what was
said, this glorious country with its mineral wealth, whose history is
written upon its ruins, complimented the company highly on the
unity and good feeling they had ever preserved, said they were the
best boys you could scare up among any fifty, had endured more
hardships, than any other Fifty & preserved better feelings than he
had ever before seen. Parley our head has been vigilant & persever-
ing neither the snow, the rain, the bad road, the thunder nor the
lightning had prevented him from going a head & finded passes &
so it was with the whole company. said hed offer the following toast.
"The city of the L S Lake may her men never be wanting in union
industry & virtuous wives, To fill the Country & kingdom with eternal lives." Cannon fired, amid three cheers, D Fullmer said, he glad
to hear what been said & as to this valley said nothing was lacking
but inhabitants to fill it up & as has been observed we have the best
women, & the most beautiful children, & the most of them, we have
the tools that can populate this desirable country, with the help of
God. cannon fired three cheers. Dan Jones spoke of his feelings his
respect for his nation [Wales], groaning under the tyranny and
bondage of the old world, his heart felt keen in their behalf if had
the ability would carry this goodly land of liberty to them, spoke of
being among the nations, feelings produced thereby, his desire to
see the good of the nations gathered where they could enjoy liberty,
recalled to his mind the Saints, his labours & toils with them, said he
had always been among the foremost in discharge of duties among
the Saints, knowing those who were most diligent earned the greatest reward he had outdone himself, was sorry he was not able to do
more on this journey, that he might earn the great reward, thanked
all for their kindness and courtesy shown to him & prayed God to
help us all. Cannon fired, amid 3 cheers. Captn Brown called for by

the Coy said he not much to say but would give 3 cheers for the Presidency, the church, the Company, & the Saints, which was responded to by 3 hearty cheers, amid the cannons deafening roar, Parley then called upon the Coy to sing when, was sung "O come come away from Northern blasts retiring" & ["]Come listen to my story while Winter lingers bye" which was also responded to by 3 deafening cheers & the cannons roar, when the cannon has roared & three cheers been given, small arms were fired by those who felt disposed, which was many. Parley said enough ammunition wasted for to day. Captn Brown, recapitulated the order, when firing ceased a round or two of the Boxing gloves was tried, & ten pin alley was visited, some go for the horses, & others tend to the Plates, Dishes, &c used at the feast, jolly time. "Am glad I had time to write it, & that C West, got a candle & held it for while I did it" After dark prayers & singing & Dancing mild pleasant night. Some wrestling.

HAIGHT: All was busy to prepare a dinner for the reception of the company which did not get in last night we raised a liberty pole and at one oclock the company hove in view and as they came up we fired a salute of 5 guns and small arms. The dinner being ready the fifty sat down in order, Br Pratt and his counsellors at the head Capts Brown Jones & myself next and the rest filled up the table which was formed by spreading a waggon cover on the ground and all sat on the ground to eat D. Fullmer ask a blessing. It was truly an interesting scene in the wilderness where white mans foot had never trod before, to see a table spread with Roast Beef Mince & Pumpkin pies Apple pies Sauce Coffee &c After the report was finished Br Pratt addressed the company contrasting the difference between the situation of the Saints in the Great Basin and the rest of the World where the Air, Earth and water are not free but here all are free &c also that this day should be celebrated as the anniversary of the city of L. S. Lake as long as the sun shone upon it.

BROWN: We reached our camp on the 8th. Bro Pratt got in the evening before, when we got in sight of camp we saw a flag hoisted upon a pole high above the wagons; and soon the little brass piece gave us a salute. The boys were very glad to see us and we to see them, great preparations were making for a dinner a table was spread large enough to seat 50 men, there being no ladies present, and a bounteous feast of roast beef, pumpkin sauce, apple pies, mince pies &c was enjoyed at dinner a toast was offered by bro Pratt to this amount, May this the 8th of January be kept as the anniversary of the founding of the city of the Little Salt Lake which will hereafter be built After dinner we had several patriotic speeches, fireing of canon and lastly a song, "Come a way," followed by a gun

Campbell's account of this extraordinary celebration in the wilderness is itself remarkable, considering the primitive conditions under which it was written by candlelight. The exuberance the company expressed for the area and the nation and for each other and what they had accomplished reflects no awareness of or concern for the difficulties and suffering they will soon experience on the journey homeward. The city they knew would be established here—Little Salt Lake or Parowan—became known as the "mother city" of southern Utah, because most of the early settlements in the region, including Cedar City, were pioneered by the Parowan settlers. But Parley's exhortation that "while the sun & moon should endure, & so long as a Settlement was here, they should perpetuate this 8th of Jany as the day we celebrate . . . the first anniversary of the Settlement of this place" has been ignored; Parowan celebrates its founding on January 13, the day in 1851 when George A. Smith and his 120 settlers arrived.

Parley's statement that the expedition members "were the best boys you could scare up among any fifty, had endured more hardships, than any other Fifty" refers to a Mormon pattern of organization that began in 1844 with creation of the Council of Fifty in Nauvoo. This administrative body helped in organizing the Mormon exodus from Nauvoo and the western migration. The Council functioned in the early years in the Great Basin,[118] and early colonizing efforts were often organized by fifties.

The song "Oh Come, Come Away" sung on this occasion was composed by Parley during the expedition, though just when he found time and energy during their arduous travels is hard to say. The text is fascinating with its reference to teaching the gospel to "Joseph's sons"—the Indians—and particularly to the possibility of finding a "remnant" of Dan Jones's ancestry. This refers to a belief among Mormons that somewhere in the region was a tribe of Welsh-speaking Indians, which was apparently the reason for including Welsh-speaking Dan Jones in the exploration.

"Song of the Southern Pioneers"

O come, come away, from Northern blasts retiring,
These wintry times to milder climes, O come, come away

---

118.   Kenneth W. Godfrey, "Council of Fifty," in Ludlow, *Enclopedia of Mormonism*, 1:326.

Where Gentile foot has never been
    The clear blue sky is always seen
    And Spring is ever green, O come, come away
    O come, come away, where hope is still inspiring
    Where flow'rets bloom in rich perfume, O come, come away

There 'mid the mountains towering dome
    The Colorado's waters foam
    And freedom finds a home, O come, come away
    O find, find a way, the Gentile saints are coming
    In Zion's car, from realms afar, O come, come away.

Come, come in might and majesty,
    Extend the reign of liberty
    Sound, sound the Jubilee, O come, come away

O come, come away, where Joseph's sons are roaming
    In solitude and manners rude, O come, come away
    We'll teach them there the Gospel true
    Their ancient covenants to renew
    As angels brought to view, O come, come away.

O come from realms where tyrants still are reigning
    From poverty and cholera and war come away
    Imperial Zion rise in might
    Increase thy towers, extend thy light
    And reign it is thy right, at home and far away.

O come, come away, the mountains still exploring
    Turn every crook search every nook, O come, come away.
    The secret treasures of the hills
    The rivers, lakes, and murmuring rills
    Are ours boys by Heaven's will, So come, come away.
    We'll search mid the glens where cataracts are roaring
    The mountains steep, the caverns deep, O come, come away

Perhaps these solitudes contain
    A remnant who In Maddocks reign
    From Wales came o'er the main, so far, far away
    O come Captn Jones your kindly heart is yearning
    O'er kindred dear, let's find them here, O come, come away.
    Six hundred years they've dwelt alone
    To friends and kith and kin unknown

Arise your kindred own, and bring them away.

And when from these toils, we're merrily returning
Warm hearts shall meet, each other greet, O come, come away
Come, come our social joys renew
Where wives and children welcome you
Sweethearts warm and true, O come, come away.[119]

Wednesday, January 9
ARMSTRONG: [There are no further entries in this journal, substantial parts of which have been lost.]
CAMPBELL: T . . . Pleasant day. Bre fixing up to start, writing, mending, washing, wrestling &c. T noon 59 Camp prayers singing & Dancing T 38. Wagons in our absence went on to 283 1/2 miles
HAIGHT: Preparing to start for home tomorrow I shall leave this place with regret. It is one of the most lovely places in the Great Basin On the East high towering Mountains covered with Evergreen forests and one of the most Beautiful creeks running from them. On the West and South a large Valley of the most beautiful lands. Little Salt Lake bordering the valley on the west and beyond a range of hills covered with verdure and backed with high towering Mountains covered with Eternal snows all of which contribute to beautify the scenery and while the clouds hang heavily on the Mountains and the storms and tempests are roaring the valley enjoys a beautiful serenity.
BROWN: day was spent making preparations to start home.

Campbell's note that the wagon odometer now registered 283 1/2 includes the four miles added by moving from the site of Paragonah to that of Parowan. Haight's "high towering Mountains covered with Evergreen forests" are the rugged uplands of the Markagunt Plateau.

---

119.   Campbell, *Southern Exploring Expedition Papers.*

The Long, Cold Trip Home

Thursday, January 10, 1850

CAMPBELL: T 34 Pleasant morning, started 10 A M come to Red earth creek 297 [287] miles, when we started the morning cached 5 tire & other wagon irons about 10 paces West of Liberty pole, burnt ashes, coal & pieces of wood & put on the top of the cache, we struck up the creek 1/2 mile to crossing this morning, the lame ox of Parleys which was left at Red earth creek, find, but it was unable to come on. Pass Sage & Greasewood, & Camp on Grass plot, near Spring 120 yards from road, at the right fuel scant, Sun setting 297 miles, T in shade at noon 55 T at night 38, Camp prayers & singing, Parley gets round fire, talks good things to the Brethren, gave his ideas, his experience & answered questions.

HAIGHT: We left Big Creek and start for home our cattle tender on their feet came 14 miles and camped where we came to the road we made when we came out

BROWN: [From this point, Brown's journal is a continuous narrative with no indication of dates. The editors have attempted to insert his entries at what seem to be appropriate dates as his accounts coincide with those of Campbell and Haight.] We started taking the California Road back.

"Red earth creek" is Red Creek at the site of Paragonah, their campsite of December 23. The "sage and greasewood" lands through which they passed this day are now covered with fields of alfalfa. Camp was at Buckhorn Spring in the northern part of Parowan Valley about four miles south of the junction of SR 20 with I-15.

Friday, January 11

CAMPBELL: T 40 Cloudy morning, Cattle hard to get up this A.M. Went ahead about 8 miles, many of the Breth in Camp keep journals. 11h 20m start Pass on to Kanyon, mouth. Begin to ascend hill 313 [303], steep and rocky. Sideling descent to cedar valley 314 miles, Pass on 10, cedars by wayside & Camp among them, thought from the Way Bill of distances given to Parley by Captn Fly's camp that we would find water here, but Camp among Plenty snow, Good

Mt feed (bunch grass) 100 yards to the right, an ox of Hopkins'
being hunted after by many of the Bre—ascertained he had taken
the track backwards. John D. Holliday & Isaac Brown take their
horses & track him back to the Liberty pole bring him to Camp.
They got in, a little after 11 P.M. Snowed all night, nearly 4 in of new
snow all over. Roadometer stands at 206 [306] 3/4 T 38 Phelps gets
R.C. to write his song completed to day. "A life on the Desert plain"
HAIGHT: Weather mild and cloudy road soft travelling had
comenced raining in the afternoon came 9 miles camped at the
foot of a Mountain without water
BROWN: The second day it snowed on us

Following Fremont Wash just west of present I-15 along the
"California Road" cut the previous fall by the Jefferson Hunt and
other California-bound wagon trains, they arrived in six miles at
the mouth of Dennis Hollow. Here the road turned left to ascend
what are known as the South Hills dividing Parowan and Beaver
Valleys. After nearly four miles of difficult travel—"steep and
rocky" ascent, "sideling descent" are typical—they camped in the
snow, without water, in the north end of Little Valley at about 6,500
feet elevation. A rough jeep road now generally follows this route.

Saturday, January 12
CAMPBELL: T 22 clear beautiful morning. Start at [illegible]. Go on
1/2 mile then ascend very steep long hill, Go down sideling, & over
(& thro) a narrow passage cut thro cedars, short turns and sideling,
a foot in places of drifted snow. Snow 2 & 3 in deep, strike down &
onto Kanyon leading out of the Mts few hundred yards past foot of
hill where a road comes in from the right 309 miles, tolerable good
road bench land, thro some cedars & then thro sage for about 6
miles till you strike Meadow valley bottom. Then for 3/4 mile, very
wet & miry, wagons go in clear to the hub in places & cattle mire
down, rich bottom soil, snow just melted & melting, come to crossing of Meadow valley [Beaver] creek 315 3/4, 6 yards wide, & 8 in
deep at crossing Willows plenty see cotton woods 5 or 6 miles North
at the mouth of Kanyon Fir in places some of the Bre reckon as
much water as Big Cotton wood clear stream Rocky bottom, Bro G.
Nebeker finds some coal stone on this bottom, beautiful day (T in
Phelps bosom,) Pass on 1/4 mile pass a small run of water & 1/2
mile further a small stream. Very Deep steep bank, rich land in this
bottom. Pass over 5 miles sage hill & camp by 4 1/2 P.M. At 320 3/4
in little Clay Basin T at night 20—good run of water in narrow sage
creek about 1 yard Wide, which we get by digging hole thro the ice,

Pass many dead cattle. Parley said he could look with the glass up to Meadow creek kanyon, discovered much Pine Fir & good many cotton woods, he says its firstrate soil singing in Camp—Judge Phelps— "Life on the Desert Plains" revised & clean copied by R.C. Much Jawing in Camp.

HAIGHT: Snow 4 inches passed over a Mountain came 8 miles to Beaver creek here is a rich valley that is fit for a settlement came 5 3/4 miles over a sage ridge and camped on Sage creek verry little feed for cattle.

After climbing the "steep long hill," where today's jeep road turns into an almost impassable jeep trail, the road descends "California Hollow" to Greenville Bench and on to the Beaver River bottoms near the present town of Greenville. Campbell describes "a narrow passage cut thro cedars, short turns and sideling." John D. Lee, clerk of the company that would travel the same road almost exactly a year later on its way to establish the Iron Mission, was more specific. He wrote that they "passed through heavy bodies of dwarf pine (pinyon pine) and ceder (juniper)—in fact the whole face of the country is covered with timber for 10 ms at least."[120]

In the "Meadow [Beaver] valley bottom" the party discovered what other explorers had learned about the Beaver River: it is inconstant. After it emerges from the Tushar Mountains and flows through the south end of the town of Beaver, it splits into small streams and sloughs; the marshes that bogged down Parley's wagons still exist. At the west side of Beaver Valley the waters consolidate, and the river flows through a gap between the Mineral and Black Mountains and out into the Escalante Desert—where its inconstancy was more deadly. In 1776, hoping it would lead them west toward California, Escalante's explorers found waterless wastes instead and soon abandoned their goal of Monterey. In 1826, on his first exploration to California, Jedediah Smith made the same mistake. Trying to follow the river west, he learned something about the Great Basin: its rivers don't go anywhere. He named it Lost River. And in 1849, Jefferson Hunt left the company of gold-seekers he was guiding to California and rode alone forty miles into the Escalante Desert, seeking a rumored shortcut the Beaver River seemed to promise. James S. Brown, a California-mission-bound

---

120. John D. Lee, "Journal of the Iron County Mission," *Utah Historical Quarterly* 20 (July 1952): 254.

Mormon with Hunt's company, wrote of his return: "Sometime in the night Captain Hunt came into camp, so near choked from lack of water that his tongue was swollen till it protruded from his mouth; his eyes were so sunken in his head that he could scarcely be recognized. His horse, too, for the need of water, was blind, and staggered as he was urged on. Their stay had been thirty-six hours, on the sands, without water."[121]

Founding of the town of Beaver came five years after Parowan to the south and Fillmore to the north. Twenty men from Parowan arrived in February 1856 and built a twenty-by-twenty-foot cabin in which they lived while laying out the town. Settlers from the north soon arrived and built a prosperous sheep economy. With discovery of minerals in the Mineral and San Francisco Mountains in 1870, miners streamed into the area. As friction developed between Mormons and the newcomers, federal troops were sent to keep order, building Fort Cameron in 1874. Another federal presence was the establishment of the Second Judicial District Court of the Territory of Utah in 1870, with the specific charge to identify and prosecute those responsible for the Mountain Meadows massacre in 1857. In this court, John D. Lee was twice tried for his part in the massacre and finally convicted. He was taken to the site of the massacre and, on March 23, 1877, executed.

Sunday, January 13

CAMPBELL: T 29 Poor place to camp, this white Desert weed, which looks like feed at a distance plentiful, but Mt feed by driving some 2 miles off cold location, Cut holes in ice & water cattle & horses with Pails— leave 10h 10m.A.M. Cross Deep ravine—Go up it 100 yds—323 miles. Good level road to day—commences snowing, comes larger & faster—foremost teams camp about 1 1/2 P.M. at forks of Kanyon— 329 m other teams come up in 3/4 hour—Plenty feed on the side hills to day & camp amongst plenty feed & cedars—many of which r dry & make hot fires—some good bottom grass which the cattle seem to relish to day, tho the other day they rambled 10 miles when turned out on bottom feed—but cattle very hungry got little to eat last night—Parley this morning called Camp together to see who would let one of their yokes of cattle haul the Cannon when Nathan Tanner volunteered to haul it to day Snows hard to night—large Flakes, Road icy & slippy to day Frosty night T 29 snowy—Camp singing

---

121.   Hafen and Hafen, *Journals of Forty-Niners*, 118.

HAIGHT: Quite cool comenced snowing at 10 o'clock A.M. Snowed the rest of the day Snow fell one foot Came 8 3/4 miles camped in the hills plenty feed.

The inedible "white Desert weed" according to Southern Utah University range ecologist James E. Bown, was probably silver lupine, a legume found over a wide range of habitat, from high mountain slopes to the Mojave Desert. In springtime its pods are poisonous to sheep and produce malformed calves when eaten by pregnant cows. Its leaves and stems turn white in winter.

Camp this night was at the fork of Wildcat Creek and its tributary, Fortuna Creek, about two miles after exiting the north end of Beaver Valley.

Monday, January 14

CAMPBELL: T 14 Snow 1 foot deep About camp, snows 2 or 3 in deep last night. Start at 11 A.M. Take up the right hand Fork of Kanyon travel up 1/2 mile & cross ravine, then take up small kanyon to your left, travel in 10 in snow, hard to see the track, sometimes snow a foot deep, clear blue sky, clouds fly swiftly thro the air, Piercing breeze Northerly wind, after crossing ravine & going up small kanyon to the left for 1/4 mile, Pass on Mountain land thro deep snow, to 334 1/2, the road hard to find, sometimes had to wait till find the track we went after we got to 332 1/2 down a hill sideling then turn to left 50 yards & take short turn to the right then ascend, go between two cedar Groves, 100 yds farther these Summit of Mountain 334 1/2—Pass down, Cattle lick the Snow—dry deep snow in the hollows over a foot—clear blue sky, beautiful day, reach Willow Stream—Plenty water, bad crossing 338, cedar half mile to the right. Plentiful, sage Plenty near crossing Willows. Cattle march of to the bottom 1/2 mile where the feed can be seen above the snow—cold night T 18 (35 Horses and Mules in Camp—when we started, 38—Vances left—Mathews & Jennings took 2 back)

HAIGHT: Comenced to ascend the Mountain it raised gradually at first through a dense forest of Cedar it was very steep toward the top 5 1/2 miles to the summit then descended 23 1/2 miles to Reed Creek

BROWN: the snow was so deep we could not find the road half the time . . .

Travel today was through dense pinyon-juniper forest generally following I-15 as it ascends to the 6,500-foot pass in the foothills of the Tushar Mountains. Camp, where they will also spend the next miserable snowbound day, was on Pine Creek, 3 1/2 miles over the summit.

Tuesday, January 15

CAMPBELL: T 24 S Wind, snow storm all night & continues storming this morning. 10 A.M. nearly all Camp in bed, not a fire light 12 noon continues, some few get up to cook. Captn Brown round seeing if men enough up to go after the Cattle W Wadsworth & R.C. go & find the Cattle & horses bring them up to water some of them 3 miles a head beautiful Wheat Grass ahead along this bottom ceases snowing—Sun breaks out about night 7 P.M.—Wind comes from the North, & snow or sleets till bed time 9 P.M. T 28

HAIGHT: Remained in camp snowed and blowed all day and night. Br Pratt quite unwell.

Wednesday, January 16

CAMPBELL: T 23 Still snowing & storming Southerly breeze. Moderates a little but still continues snowing. Butcher a Beef, get up cattle, stringing out to start at 10 1/2 A.M. Pass down thro a bottom of beautiful Wheat grass 4 & 5 in above the snow. Come to Cedar creek right of road, Willows on banks. 343 1/4 Roll down hollows & over rocky road to Rocky bluff ascend 347. Rough road snows nearly all day. 8 & 9 in deep. Cloudy, & disagreeable day, W Wind, Camp at 4 P.M. at Wayside 349 3/4, ceases snowing as we Camp we did not pass within half or Quarter of a mile of creek. we struck to our left round the hill, that is cedar creek, T 27 Good bunch grass on the Mts round

HAIGHT: More mild but snowed part of the day came over a sage plain 5 miles to cedar creek, then 6 3/4 miles and camped in the sage in the hills no water had to melt snow road very crooked.

"Cedar creek" is Cove Creek, which emerges down a pass between the Tushar and Pavant Mountains. Over this pass comes I-70 today after ascending Clear Creek Canyon from the Sevier. Near where the Pratt explorers crossed Cove Creek, the Mormons, in 1867, built Cove Fort, a massive structure with thirteen-foot walls of volcanic stone. Ira N. Hinckley built the fort at a cost of around $20,000. He was an ancestor of Mormon president Gordon B. Hinckley, who, in dedicating the restored fort as a museum and visitors center, commented he had been eager to see the most expensive barn the church ever built.

From Cove Creek, the explorers moved on six and one-half miles to Dog Valley. Camp was about at Dog Valley Creek, which they apparently did not discover under the snow.

Thursday, January 17
   CAMPBELL: T 2 below, but by 8 & 9 Warm the sun shining Cattle got up by 9 A.M. Pass small dry hollow & ascend hill 350 3/4. Pass nearly 1/4 mile on the East foot of Rocky bluff 352. Sun strong, 6 in snow all over, cedars & sage abundant. Warm, descend hill 356 3/4. Descend hill into Large valley 357 3/4 Desert weed bottom & rocky bluff to the left about 2 miles on Sage Ridge 362. Grove of cedar 3/4 mile to the left. Leave road & make track to the right to Camp by cedars. Cedar hollow 360—bunch grass, but mostly covered with snow. Wind blowing in hollow Camp by 5 P.M. From Descend hill into large valley, to where we camped no feed, but plenty snow. T 14 boisterous night
   HAIGHT: Snow one foot we came meandering through the hills some 8 [3?] miles then crossed a desert plain 8 1/4 miles farther and camped 1/2 mile south of the road by some cedars..

After "meandering" through Baker Canyon, the explorers emerge into the south end of the Black Rock Desert, named for its numerous volcanic craters and cinder cones. It is indeed, as Campbell wrote, a "large valley," stretching fifty miles north to the vicinity of Delta.

Friday, January 18
   CAMPBELL: T 30 Cattle got up & starting before 9 A.M. Strike over to the old track 3/4 mile passed over bunch grass considerable above the snow which is 8 in deep—Descend hill into extensive long bottom; Foot of hill 367. 1/4 m road turns left along bottom. Mt. range on the right (East) snowy: Greasewood all round, small bottom, no sage [3]70 3/4. Rush creek [3]72 3/4. Plenty feed, otherwise poor cold place to camp, Plenty water, Camp by 2 1/2 at Prairie Creek, Plenty water, Willows & sage.. Good feed ahead 1/4 mile—Snow 6 in deep 377 miles—bad crossing—Cloudy & dark, Hunters report another road nearer the Mts Snowy night, T 29
   HAIGHT: High winds and snow most of the day crossed the soft Saleratus plain and a salt creek came 11 miles camped on prairie creek

Camp on "Prairie Creek" this night was on Meadow Creek, about at the present town of Meadow. Nearby is Kanosh, named for the

chief of the Pahvant band of Indians who lived in the area. The
Pahvants were descendants of the bearded Indians the Escalante
expedition encountered on their attempt to blaze a trail to
California in 1776. Escalante wrote,

> The five of them who came first with their chief, were so fully bearded
> that they looked like Capuchin padres or Bethlemites. . . . We
> announced the Gospel to them as well as the interpreter could man-
> age it, explaining to them God's oneness, the punishment He
> reserves for the wicked, the reward He gives to the righteous. . . . We
> told them that if they wanted to attain the blessings proposed we
> would come back with more padres so that all could be instructed. . . .
> They all replied very joyfully that we must come back with the other
> padres, that they would do whatsoever we taught them. . . . Scarcely
> did they see us depart when all—following their chief, who started
> first—burst out crying copious tears, so that even when we were quite
> a distance away we kept hearing the tender laments of these unfortu-
> nate little sheep of Christ.[122]

The little sheep did not always remain tender. Though Kanosh was
friendly to the whites, and in fact joined the Mormon Church,
renegade members of his band killed Captain John W. Gunnison
and seven of his exploring party on the Sevier River in October
1853. Chief Kanosh died in 1881 and was buried in the Kanosh
cemetery after a Mormon funeral—unlike the other famous
Indian chief of pioneer times, Walker, who in 1855 also died on
Meadow Creek and was secretly buried, Indian style, in the Pavant
Mountains to the east.

Saturday, January 19
    CAMPBELL: T 18 Stormed and Snowed all night, 6 in new snow. R.C.
    after the cattle this morning. Snow on the level bottom 12 & 14 in
    deep. Snowy. Cattle got up & start about noon. Snowy & Cloudy,
    expect we r good ways to the left of the track, some believe they see
    the track or travelled road 1 or 2 miles nearer the Mts East. Strike
    angling towards the Mts. Snow about 2 feet 2 in on an average. Two
    steers give out & r left behind, 1 mule left behind—Get to Rock [sub-
    sequently called Chalk] creek by 6 1/2 P.M. Some of the hind teams
    later getting in 14 ft Wide 16 in deep. Cotton wood on banks where
    we strike it. small portion of the Sky to the West clears off T 18 we

---

122.   Warner, *Domínguez-Escalante Journal,* 66–67.

passed a Dry creek about 3 mile back where there was good feed, but snow covered.

HAIGHT: Snow fell last night 10 inches making 1 1/2 foot start on our journey at noon still snowing very difficult finding the road. Came 10 miles to Rock Creek which took us till 7 oclock we found plenty dry wood which was very acceptable for we were cold and weary Snow 2 feet deep some 2 of our animals gave out and left on the road.

BROWN: The snow continued to fall and when we got to Chalk Creek we could go no farther with the teams the day we got to this place we traveled in snow two feet deep. One ox gave out also a mule they were lost.

At this point, the party was in trouble. Animals were giving out. Snow kept piling up, too deep for wagons to travel. They struggled on to Chalk Creek, near the present site of Fillmore, and there half the party, with all the wagons, would spend the next three weeks, waiting for the weather to make travel possible. The camp they established, digging into the south bank of the creek and making other rude shelters, was 1 1/2 miles downstream from the fort the pioneers would build two years later in the middle of what is now Fillmore. A reminiscence by Volney King establishes the camp location. A child with the original settlers, he wrote fifty years after their arrival: "They were camped on the north side of the creek on the old road opposite some dugouts or cellars where previous travelers [the Pratt company] had camped during a storm. On Wednesday the twenty ninth of October after choosing the location for the settlement about one and one half miles above on the south side of the creek, they hitched up and drove to the site selected near which they crossed the creek."[123]

Brigham Young visited the area in 1851 and gave both the town and Millard County their names, in honor of the president who had signed the bill creating the Territory of Utah. His flattery didn't work; Utah would wait forty more years for statehood. It was Brigham's plan to make Fillmore the territorial capital, it being about in the center of a territory that then stretched from the Rocky Mountains to the Sierras. That didn't work very well, either. The settlers who arrived late in 1851 worked four years to build a

---

123.   Volney King, "Twenty Five Years in Millard County," typescript, Territorial Capitol Museum, Fillmore, Utah, 1910.

capitol building of the red sandstone quarried in the Pavant
foothills. The legislature met there for one full session, in 1855. In
1856 and 1858, it met there only long enough to pass a resolution
to adjourn to Salt Lake City. After that, the idea was abandoned.

The State House, originally intended to include four wings in
form of a cross, was never finished. Congress provided an initial
appropriation of $20,000, but, despite repeated petitions, no more
money was provided; only one wing was built. After the legislature
made Salt Lake City the territorial capital, ownership of the building passed to Fillmore City, and it became, in turn, a school, jail,
office building, and church. In 1927, the state regained ownership
and restored the building as a museum.[124]

Sunday, January 20
   CAMPBELL: T 13 Beautiful clear morning—remained in Camp all
   day. Snow bound—R.C. Writing under Parleys dictation Report of
   Journey for Legislative Council
   HAIGHT: Weather more mild remained in camp

Monday, January 21
   CAMPBELL: T 16 Snowy, Northerly Wind, Cattle seen to & counted
   Capt Brown & Bro Potter, go a head 5 miles, report snow deeper
   there than here, by 6 inches, 2 feet deep, small creek a head & but
   little fuel. R.C. Writing under Parleys dictation continuation of
   report, afterwards Breth all called together Parley spoke on the
   expediency & necessity of part of the Camp going ahead, & reporting our situation, & if necessary sending us teams back, that they
   might see to their families & not stay here & all eat up the Provision.
   Considered it advisable to take this step after hearing the Report of
   those who had went a few miles a head and ascertained the snow
   was still deeper. Moved by Wadsworth and seconded by [left blank]
   that a part of the Camp go home—Parley spoke as to when should
   start. WWPhelps proposed we start day after to morrow. Many being
   in favor of starting to morrow, it was carried—Parley gives instructions about taking 7 lbs Bread & meat to make 14 lbs &c How the
   Cooks fly about is a caution—Bro Mathews goes back left
   Wadsworth's mule laying in the snow stretched and dying—T 25
   Snowy night—R.C. making clean copy of report.
   HAIGHT: As it was impossible for the waggons to proceed any farther until the snow went off it was agreed that part of the company

---

124.   Everett L. Cooley, "Utah's Capitols," *Utah Historical Quarterly* 27 (July 1959): 260–62.

take the horses & mules and go home and the rest take up winter quarters and come on as soon as the weather will permit. Voted. We start tomorrow

BROWN: It was evident that the wagons would have to be left here till the snow melted and how long that would be we knew not. It was finally thought best that a portion of the men take some of the best animals and try to make Utah fort a distance of 107 miles and an unknown route to all of us. We were forced to do this for the want of provisions.

Even under the extremity that dictated the decision to separate the party, they did not lose sight of the purpose of the exploration. Campbell spent the better part of two days writing the report Parley Pratt would make to the Territorial Assembly when he reached home February 1. The report, printed in the final chapter of this volume, is remarkable, considering the conditions Campbell described under which he wrote: "laying on my belly & a hundred other positions, cold Snowy night open wagon."

Those assigned to speed home on horseback, mostly family men, included, besides Pratt, John C. Armstrong, Josiah Arnold, John H. Bankhead, Andrew Blodgett, Isaac H. Brown, John Brown, William Brown, Homer Duncan, Ephraim Green, Isaac Haight, Isaac B. Hatch, John D. Holladay, Joseph Horne, Dimick Huntington, Dan Jones, Jonathan Packer, William W. Phelps, Robert M. Smith, Benjamin F. Stuart, Nathan Tanner, Stephen Taylor, William Wadsworth, and Chauncey West.

Left behind with the wagons were David Fullmer (president), Rufus Allen, Robert Campbell, Sterling G. Driggs, Peter Dustin, Edward Everett, James Farrer, Hail K. Gay, Samuel Gould, Madison Hambleton, Henry Heath, William Henrie, Sylvester Hewlitt, Charles Hopkins, Alexander Lemon, John Lowry, Jr., George B. Matson, William Matthews, George Nebeker, Gardner G. Potter, Thomas E. Ricks, Seth B. Tanner, William P. Vance, Christopher Williams, William S. Sidney Willis, and Alexander Wright.

ACCOUNTS OF THE HOMEBOUND PARTY

Monday, January 21

PARLEY P. PRATT [whose account begins this same day because his recorder, Campbell, is to be left behind]: Cloudy and again snowing remained in camp. This day I was taken very sick, of a bilious

attack, and was confined to my bed. We held a council and finding
that our provisions would only sustain half of the company till
spring and travelling with the wagons being impossible was decided
to leave half the company to winter there with the wagons and cattle and the other half with some of the strongest mules and horses
should attempt to reach Provo. The Southern frontier Distance
upwards of one hundred miles. A part of the company that
remained was mostly young men without families. My councillor
David Fullmer being placed in command. Th[is] was in a country
of shrub Cedars which would afford some shelter for the animals
and richly clothed in bunch grass, and some portion of the hill
sides when the snow had blown off being nearly bare, the cattle
could live.

Tuesday, January 22

PRATT: In the morning I was still very sick, but about noon bid
farewell to those who stayed, mounted a mule, and, with upwards of
twenty men [actually twenty-four men including Parley] and animals, we commenced our wallowing in the snow. We made about
nine miles, and camped in a cedar thicket. Being unable longer to
sit on my mule or stand on my feet the snow was shoveled away
some blankets spread and I lay down— I had not eaten one mouth-
ful for a day or two, but vomited many times very severely.

HAIGHT: Still snowing at 11 1/2 oclock Prest Pratt and a company of
24 men and 26 horses & mules started home it stormed so, we had
to travel by a compass. came about 9 miles and camped in some
cedars Br Pratt sick

BROWN: 24 of us including bro. Pratt started with 26 horses and
mules and a few days rations, leaving bro. Fullmer in charge of
camp. We traveled about 9 miles the first day and camped in some
cedars, it snowed all day and we could not see our course only at
intervals, we aimed for a gap in the mountain where we supposed
the road passed through it being impossible to follow the road. We
carried a shovel with us to clear the snow to make fires and to make
our beds.

Camp would have been in the vicinity of present Holden. In 1855
settlers from Fillmore moved here and built what they called
"Buttermilk Fort" because of refreshments served to travelers
there. Later the name was changed to Holden in memory of Elijah
E. Holden, Mormon Battalion veteran who froze to death in the
mountains nearby. Brown's "gap in the mountain" is Scipio Pass,

where I-15 now goes between Canyon Mountains and the Pavant Range.

Wednesday, January 23

PRATT: This morning I was better and we again started the snow being from three to four feet deep on a level the men went ahead on foot, the entire company men and animals making but one track, the person breaking the track would tire out in a few moments, and, giving place to another would fall into the rear—this day we made 9 or 10 miles and camped in a mountain pass, 13 miles South of the Sevier River. It was long after night when we wallowed into camp, waist deep in snow, and shovelling away the snow, we made fires, spread our blankets, and sank down to rest, being entirely exhausted; our animals either tied to cedar bushes without food, or wallowing up the hill in search of bare spots of bunch grass.

HAIGHT: Weather clear Br Pratt better Start on our way as we approach the Mountain the snow grows deeper from 2 1/2 to 8 or 10 feet have to break the snow before our animals. Came over the Mountain and camped on the side in some cedars two of our animals gave out and we left them. It was dark before we camped faint and weary and no feed for our horses We shovelled away the snow and built a fire and melted snow and made our coffee eat our supper dug a hole in the snow spread down our blankets and laid down to rest our weary limbs came 12 miles

BROWN: Next day we found the snow very deep as we neared the gap in the mountain two animals gave out and were left; our animals were so worried [wearied?] that they could not break the road through the snow and the men had to go before and break a track for the animals. This was severe work one man could not go more than [illegible] or 10 rods before he would give out and have to fall back and let another take his place. The snow was frequently waist deep every man and every animal stepped in the same track, we reached the summit the second day, went down about a mile on the other side camped to the right among some cedars near a spot of grass on the point of the mountain. It was dark before we camped and our animals were so tired they could not hunt the grass that night but stood among the cedars and ate bark, a thing I never saw before. The snow was about three feet deep at camp and it was very cold two men got their feet frostbitten.

The labors of this long and very difficult day took them over Scipio Pass and down to near the edge of Round Valley. Starving deer will

browse on juniper, but for horses to do so shows their desperate
condition.

Thursday, January 24

> PRATT: We were obliged to leave several f our animals which gave
> out. We passed thro' M [Round] valley—made about 10 miles—
> camped on the heights some 4 miles South of the Sevier. It was still
> snowing our animals found some bunch grass onthe hillsides.
>
> HAIGHT: at daylight we took our horses up to the top of the
> Mountain where the wind had blowed the snow of to feed. At noon
> we start again leave 2 animals that have given out snow badly drifted
> decend from the Mountain cross a valley covered with sage two
> more animals gave out we camped in some hills no water melt snow
> come 10 miles Snowed in the evening
>
> BROWN: Next morning we drove our animals up to the grass and let
> them remain till 10 A.M. when we drove them to camp and packed
> up; one horse and one mule were unable to go and were left in
> camp. We descended into a little valley from the Sevier River we
> shoveled off the snow to a depth of two feet to make down our beds,
> it snowed and drifted all night and we were completely covered
> about a foot deep.

Camp this night, at what Parley will call "ressurection camp," was at
the north end of Round Valley, about at the Juab-Millard county
line.

Friday, January 25

> PRATT: This morng we found ourselves so completely buried in snow
> that no one could distinguish the place where we lay. Some ones ris-
> ing began shovelling the others out. This being found too tedious a
> business, I raised my voice like a trumpet and commanded them to
> arise, when all at once there was a shaking among the snow piles, the
> graves were opened, and all came forth—we called this resurrection
> camp—passing on we forded the Sevier and camped in the heights 6
> or 8 miles North of the same—the snow this day being much less..
>
> HAIGHT: Awake in the morning covered with snow two feet deep
> proceed on our journey came 5 miles and cross the Sevier River
> came 7 miles farther and camp without water
>
> BROWN: Next morning it was still snowing we packed and went on in
> the storm, all walking that cold and driving our animals one of
> which turned aside and I went to drive it into the trail, it kicked me
> on the knee and knocked me over in the snow. The horse was shod,
> it gave me great pain so much so I could not stand the brethren ran

to my assistance I asked them to lay hands on me they did so and I was healed instantly by the prayer of faith in the name of Jesus. I went on my way and never felt the pain after, giving God the glory. About noon we reached the Sevier. It has quit storming, we crossed the river and traveled about five miles, when we camped in some cedars. It was very cold but we had plenty of good wood.

The crossing of the Sevier River was just before that north-flowing stream makes its swing to the west and then south to lose itself in what was then Sevier Lake.

Laying on of hands and prayer for healing the sick or injured has been from the beginning a tenet of Mormon faith.[125] Camp this night was in the hills above Chicken Creek Reservoir, near the south end of Juab Valley.

Saturday, January 26
PRATT: This day we travelled 16 or 18 miles. Camped in a pouch of cedars 3 miles South of Salt Creek snow again about 2 feet deep.
HAIGHT: came 18 [13?] miles snow two feet deep our provisions almost exhausted some entirely out 50 miles from any settlement
BROWN: Next day we entered Juab Valley where we found the snow over two feet deep. We camped on the cedar point three miles south of salt Creek. Soon after we got into camp it began snowing again.

Cedar Point, as it is still named today, is in the foothills of the San Pitch Mountains, three miles south of Nephi.

Sunday, January 27
PRATT: Our provisions being nearly exhausted, Chancy West, Dimick Huntington and myself volunteered to take some of the strongest animals and try to penetrate to Provo, which was still some fifty miles distant, in order to send back provisions to the remainder, who were to follow slowly. We started at daylight. D. Huntington soon gave out and fell back into the rear company West and myself breaking the way on foot and leading the mules in our track, and sometimes riding them, travelled all day, averaging about knee deep in snow. Camped at 11 at night on Summit Creek extremely hungry and feet badly frozen, we built a small fire, it being the coldest night we had ever experienced, and after trying in vain to thaw out, our frozen

---

125. Doctrine and Covenants, section 42:44, 66:9, among other references.

shoes stocking and the bottoms of our drawers &pants, we rolled
~~ourselves in our blankets, and lay trembling with cold a few hours.~~
HAIGHT: Br Pratt left us to go to Fort Utah to send us provision
came 12 miles camp on sick creek weather very cold snow deep little
feed for our animals.
BROWN: This morning bro. Pratt and one other man took two of the
best mules and started on to Provo leaving the remainder to travel
on as fast as we could, which was not very fast. Our animals were
near giving out and we had three men who could not walk two were
frosted and one snow blind; our provisions were running very short.
Bro Pratt was to send us assistance from Provo. We camped at a little
creek where we had nothing but a small willows half dried to burn,
which gave us a very poor fire for one of the coldest nights we had
on the whole trip.

On this bitter cold day, followed by an even more miserable night,
Parley Pratt and Chauncey West rode twenty miles, camping long
after dark on the low divide between Juab and Utah Valleys. The
remainder of the mounted party followed, managing despite
hunger, frostbite, and snow blindness to make twelve miles to
camp near Mona.

Monday, January 28
PRATT: Arose long before day; but a few mouthfuls out off the last
black frozen biscuit remaining saddled up our animals, and after
another laborious day in which living on a piece of biscuit not so
large as our fist we entered Provo at dusk—raised a posse of men
and animals with provisions, and sent back same night. These
picked up one of our men whose name was Taylor, who had wandered off ahead of the rest and had reached within some 8 miles of
Provo—they found him sunk down in the snow in a helpless condition his horse standing by him nearly frozen to death—he lived, but
in a measure lost the use of his limbs.

The relief company met those we had left somewhere in the
southern end of Utah Valley and brought them in safely.

I rested a day or two, and arrived home about the 1st of Feby—
found my family all well.

This terminated an expedition which explored the best portions of the country from Salt Lake to the mouth of Santa Clara on
the Rio Virgin. Distance in going and returning about 800 miles.[126]

126. Campbell, Southern Exploring Expedition Papers. This account is not in Pratt's
       handwriting. Apparently it was dictated shortly after his return. An edited, less
       complete version, with some inaccurate dates, appears in Pratt, *Autobiography*.

HAIGHT: Themometer 30 below zero. Are almost perished with cold came 12 miles camped on Summit Creek had a little flour stired in boiling water

BROWN: Next morning the thermometer was 30 below zero. It was the severest night I ever experienced. Next night we camped on Summit creek. Had plenty of wood. Here we eat the last of our provisions we had been on short rations for several days.

The dispatching of a provision-laden relief party within an hour or two of Pratt's arrival after a thirty-mile ride is a dramatic example of Mormon cooperation and saved at least one life. The near-frozen man was British-born forty-three-year-old Stephen Taylor. His frozen limbs recovered sufficiently that he was able to pursue the arduous trade of blacksmithing.

Summit Creek was in the vicinity of present Santaquin, still twenty-five miles from Fort Utah and safety.

Tuesday, January 29

HAIGHT: Same for breakfast and not half enough came 8 miles to petetenete [Payson] and to our great joy Br P Conover & Stoddard came to us with provisions for which we feel to thank them and our God[,] came to Spanish Fork and camped came 12 miles

BROWN: Next day bout 12 o'clock we met relief at Pateatneat creek which was welcomed by us and was received with thankful hearts to God and our brethren, viz: Peter Conover and two others. We camped on Spanish fork

Wednesday, January 30

HAIGHT: came 12 miles to Fort Utau and were very hospitably received by the Breathren and our hearts burned with gratitude to God for delivering us from starvation and death

BROWN: the day following we reached the fort at Provo. We found the people under considerable excitement on account of the Indians who had become hostile and were killing cattle and shooting at the whites. Bro Pratt had gone on to the city.

Indian troubles had begun in September 1849 when an Indian called "Old Bishop" was killed in a scuffle over ownership of a shirt he was wearing. Unrest, including shooting arrows into horses and cows, continued for several months, during which time Brigham Young urged the settlers to avoid violence but to be vigilant and to keep the Indians at a distance. Replying to a letter of January 9 reporting the Indians were stealing livestock and threatening attack on Fort Utah, Brigham repeated this advice, warning that the settlers would have to answer for killing Indians who were stealing.[127]

On January 31 another letter from Isaac Higbee reported that Indians had killed fifty to sixty head of cattle and were threatening to kill the Utah Valley settlers. Finally, Brigham approved the settlers' plea to be allowed to defend themselves. On February 8, a body of militia sent from Salt Lake City with a cannon attacked the Indian camp a mile upriver from Fort Utah. Some forty Indians and one settler were killed, and uneasy peace was restored until outbreak of the Walker War in 1853.

Thursday, January 31
> HAIGHT: left Fort Utau came 15 miles camped on dry creek Breathren sent us some horses
> BROWN: Next morning we started about 9 oclock and traveled as far as Dry Creek here we were met with some fresh animals sent by bro Pratt from Cottonwood

Dry Creek flows out of the Lone Peak Wilderness through Alpine and enters the north end of Utah Lake.

Friday, February 1
> HAIGHT: Very cold come 21 miles to Cotton Wood I staid with Brothr Homr Duncan
> BROWN: Next morning we had horses enough to mount every man we moved merrily on and all reached home that night. . .Found my family well they had enjoyed good health during my absence.

Saturday, February 2
> HAIGHT: Arrived safely at home found my family all alive and well except Mary her health very poor So the Lord has brought us safely home after suffring much hardships

CAMPBELL'S ACCOUNT OF THE SNOWBOUND WAGON PARTY AT FILLMORE

Tuesday, Jan 22
> Has snowed nearly 5 inches of new snow—Snowy morning T 25 Parley sick and vomiting. R.C. completed clean copy of Report had

---

127. Journal History, January 9, 1850. Quoted in *Inventory of the County Archives*, 10.

to write it laying on my belly & a hundred other positions, cold Snowy night open wagon without a stove cover not fastened down with tacks. stitched it being 11 Pages, & handed it to Parley while the company just starting [Parley] spoke to them & said God bless you Brethren, you have my good feelings & I leave Bro Fullmer who I believe is able and competent to lead you if you will hearken to his council, don't be idle because you have nothing to do, but inform yourselves & see to the cattle and do as you are told, & I believe I'll soon see you all in safety at home. We have chosen those who have families to go home, but we will have the worst of it. God bless you and about 10 1/2 A.M. Coy starting—they were 24 in number, had 26 horses & mules, Leaving 8 in the Camp No of men left 26. about 3 P.M. commenced heavy snow storm, large flakes of snow falling T 26

Wednesday, Jan 23

T 2 below zero. Hard frost, meeting of Brethren left here called by Prest Fullmer, voted that William Matthews be Capt of this Coy, that Sterling Driggs, Sidney Willis and Gardner G. Potter be Captn of Tens, all carried unanimously Bro: Potter will not have Ten but he will be Captn the Sandpitch Brethren. off steer of Bishop Lowrys dead. T at noon 30 beautiful Sunny day. Breth called together at evg Bro: Fulmer cahorting us and reminding of what Parley said, not to [be] neglectful of the Lord and he would not be of us—Camp prayers and singing—said if the Breth wished to have dancing nights he had no objections, if it could be got along with in decency & order—& to their profit & benefit. Voted that Robert Campbell take charge of the Dancing & see that its done in order, & so far as he knows figures & steps instruct the Brethren. Breth go & see to the cattle round halo or circle round the moon. T 18

Potter was among the five men who joined the expedition in Manti, the others being Madison Hambleton, Edward Everett, John Lowry, Jr., and Sylvester Hewlitt.

Thursday, Jan 24

T 30 moderate morning—Breth sent off to herd & water the cattle, report band of Indians down the creek, Cattle go farther down the creek where the snow some less T 24 sky look clear mixed with clouds, Sun sets clear, afterwards comes up a South wind, Camp prayer & singing—Ute Indian school commenced—T 30 R.C. making out Emigrants Guide

In the back of Campbell's journal, in his handwriting, are $2^1/_2$ pages, two columns each, listing some 260 Ute Indian words with their pronunciation marks and English meaning. Probably this list was used in the Ute Indian school Campbell says was started on this day. However, the most capable interpreter, Dimick Huntington, had left with Pratt three days earlier. Huntington may have helped Campbell compile the list earlier, though this is hard to imagine, given the rigors of the trip and Campbell's journal-keeping duties. Perhaps the combined knowledge of those remaining in the wagon camp was sufficient to compile the list during the days of study in the Indian school. The first few lines of his first columns and the accompanying photos illustrate. The vocabulary is printed in full in an appendix of this volume.

Ash'enty.	I want.	Kish	be still.
Ābbat	Large.	Kick'āmush,	more
An'ka	Red:	Kamush'	another
Annaniah,	What you call it.	Kī'ba	Mountain
Āt	Good.	Kāv'owuts	a colt
Annebin	How many.	Kut'ōshy	done.
Āp	Day or hour	Kunōk'ship,	burnt
Ā'dick	Stop.	Kishōp'	Lasso
Ash'py,	to ride.	Kōkweep'	charcoal
Āt'pāgā	a trout.	Kābuah	you're a fool
Bā'ragy	to wash	Kāranoop'	saddle

Also at the back of Campbell's journal is a single page of what he calls a "Copy of Way Bill from 'Southern rim of Great Basin to Utah' by James Hecox." Whether this is the beginning of the "Emigrants Guide" Campbell says he was making is unclear. The complete, remarkably detailed and accurate guide he ultimately prepared, perhaps the finest waybill ever made of the route from Great Salt Lake City to the Santa Clara, is printed in the last appendix of this volume. Also included there is Campbell's waybill from Great Salt Lake City to Sampitch.

Friday, Jan 25
T 28 Bre report some of the cattle doing firstrate, a few only 3 or 4 miles from here look poorly, living on browze, drove them down about 8 miles from here an extensive bottom, abundance of grass above the snow which is only at that place 8 in deep. one of the Utes

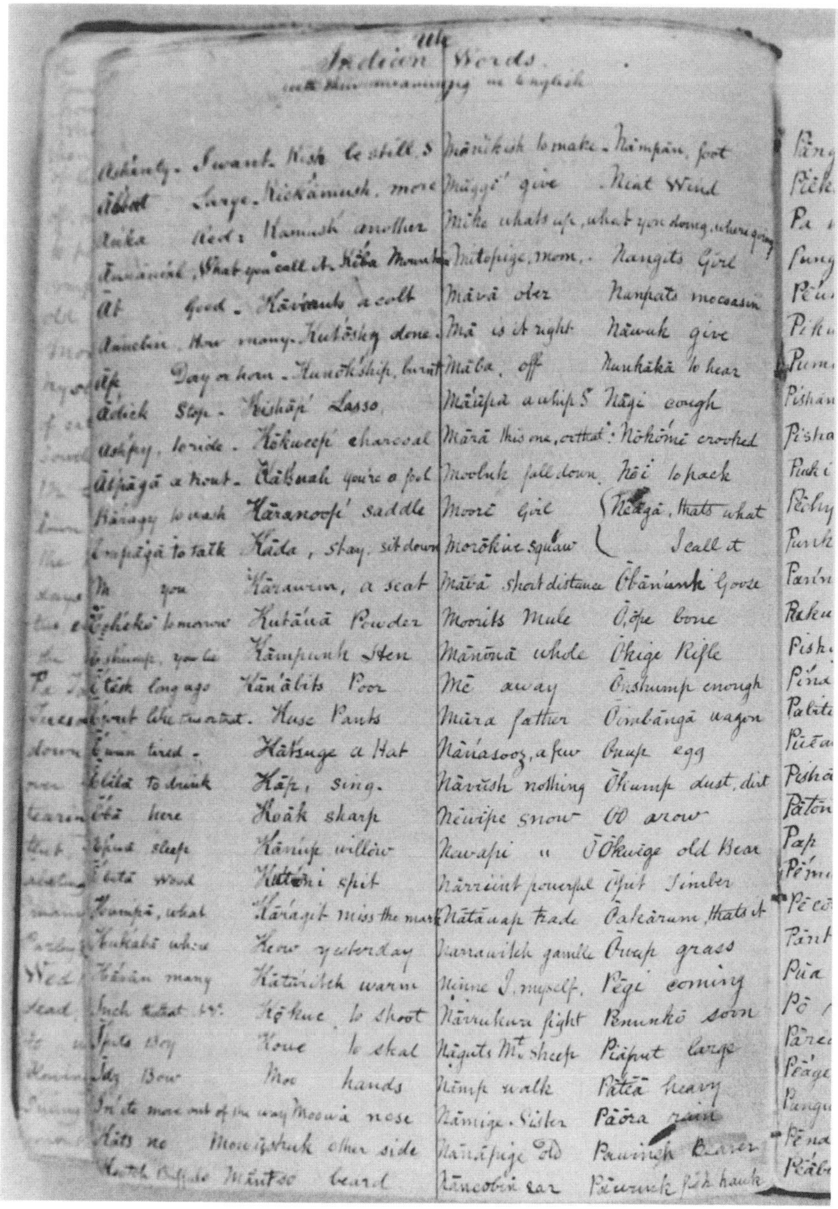

Ute Indian Words.
with their meanings in English

Achenty - I want. Kish be still. S
Abbot Large. Kickamush. more
Aaka Red. Kamush another
Ambanick, What you call it. Kiba Mountain
At Good. Kavaunts a colt
Aunchee, How many. Kutosky done.
Ap Day or horn. Kauckship, burnt
Adick Stop. Kishap Lasso
Ashpy, to ride. Kokweep charcoal
Atpaga a hunt. Katbuah you're a fool
Banagy to wash. Karanoop saddle
Impaga to talk. Kada, stay, sit down
M you. Karaurin, a seat
Ephako tomorrow. Kutaua Powder
shump, you lie. Kampunk Hen
Etek long ago. Kan'abits Poor
like that. Kuse Pants
tired. Katsuge a Hat
Etila to drink. Kap, sing.
Eta here. Koak sharp
Epud sleep. Kanup willow
Etata wood. Kattoni spit
Jompa, what. Karagit miss the mark
Jukabs where. Kew yesterday
Kasan many. Katunitch warm
Such that. Kokue to shoot
Ipits Boy. Koue to steal
Idz Bow. Moe hands
In'ite move out of the way. Moowa nose
Aits no. Moungwuk other side
Hatch Buffalo. Mantso beard

Manikush to make. Nampan, foot
Maggi give. Neat Wind
Mike what's up, what you doing, where going
Mitopige, mom. Nangits Girl
Mava old. Nanpats moccasin
Ma is it right. Nawuk give
Maba, off. Nuukaka to hear
Maupa a whip S. Nagi cough
Mara this one, or that. Nokomi crooked
Moolut fall down. Noi to pack
Moore Girl. Neaga, thats what I call it
Morokue squaw
Mava short distance. Obanunk Goose
Moorits Mule. Ope bone
Manona whole. Okige Rifle
Me away. Onshump enough
Mara father. Oombanga wagon
Nanasooz, a few. Onupe egg
Navush nothing. Okump dust, dirt
Neuipe snow. Oo arrow
Newapi " . Okuige old Bear
Narrient powerful. Ojut Timber
Nataua trade. Oakarum, thats it
Narrawitch gamble. Owap grass
Minne I, myself. Pege coming
Narrukura fight. Penunko soon
Niguts Mt. sheep. Piaput large
Nimp walk. Patea heavy
Namige Sister. Paora rain
Nanapige old. Pauinch Beaver
Nanecobin ear. Paurunk fish hawk

Ute dictionary from Robert Campbell's journal.

Second page of Ute dictionary from Robert Campbell's journal.

came into Camp, been after a deer, broke its leg, but got away from him, tenpenny Utes Snow about 4 hours to day. 5 in new snow—gets to be clear sky towards night—T 30 R.C. continuing Guide

The "extensive bottom" to which the cattle were driven was probably the area of springs and intermittent streams southwest of Fillmore and just east of the cinder cone called "Tabernacle Hill."

Saturday, Jan 26
T 28—mild S Wind. snow passing away the tops of the Sage bush become bare, T midday 36Thawing fast—Indians bring 6 or 7 Buckskin which the Bre traded for. R C. copying Hieroglyphics, Distances of the rout. R.C. making table of. T 28

Campbell's copy of the "Hieroglyphics" or petroglyphs found earlier in Parowan Gap is also in the back of his journal. His drawing as well as the panel as it appears today are shown in the accompanying photographs.

Sunday, Jan 27
T 14 Breth in Willis ten finish their cellar house to day with roof & chimney—cover it with Dirt—7 or 8 Indians come into camp with Buckskins which the Bre traded for the ten penny Utes. Warm day. T at noon 36 in shade in the sun 56 at night T 10

This dugout and the one finished a few days later by Driggs's ten will soon be abandoned as the company, unwisely as it turns out, decides to move on.

Monday, Jan 28
T 2 below Zero, Bre who have been with the cattle for three days report them in firstrate feed, in a valley 10 miles West, where 3 creeks sink & make rich dense feed T 39 some read, write, sing Wrestle &c T at night 16

The cattle had to be to the southwest. Ten miles west would have put them in the broad lava flow called the Cinders.

Tuesday, Jan 29
T 24 R.C. Washes. Noon T 36 snow disappears some There was a large halo round the moon last night. Wolves howl T 28

Wednesday, Jan 30
T 29 Boys who come from the cattle report they have considerable to eat—Wolves at one of them, Butcher a Beeve—noon T 50 in the sun 86 T 29

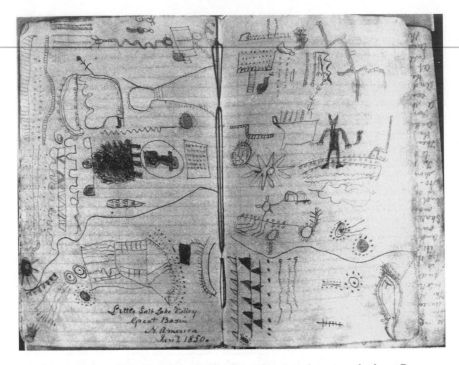

Two facing pages of Robert Campbell's diary showing the petroglyphs at Parowan Gap. Note that the right page is vertical and the left horizontal, with its top at the binding edge of the page. Campbell was with Pratt on the Virgin River and so did not see the petroglyphs himself. Presumably he copied into his journal sketches made by others who were part of the wagon party's exploration of Little Salt Lake and Cedar Valleys. If his drawings are compared with the modern photos of the glyphs on the following pages, the top part of his left page appears to represent what is shown in petroglyphs 1, the middle part of his right page includes images from the top left of petroglyphs 2 (which overlaps with petroglyphs 1), and the top of that page corresponds with carvings in petroglyphs 3. Courtesy LDS Church Archives, copy photograph by J M. Heslop.

Thursday, Jan 31
> 2 Drigg's ten finish their cellar kitchen 9 by 8 ft cloudy T at noon
> 32—in the sun 56 clear afternoon. Lyceum or school established Fa
> Williams gets sack full of chalk Rock from banks of creek, good

According to Campbell's February 5 entry, this school was held every evening while in this camp. Presumably it continued in the second snowbound camp established later, but certainly not during the strenuous days of travel to come. It would be interesting to

Parowan Gap petroglyphs 1. Courtesy Cedar City District, Bureau of Land Management.

Parowan Gap petroglyphs 2. Courtesy Cedar City District, Bureau of Land Management.

Parowan Gap petroglyphs 3. Courtesy Cedar City District, Bureau of Land Management.

know what subjects were discussed and by whom discussions were led.

Friday, Feb 1
   T 2Capt Matthews believes there could be good Settlement for few families on the extensive bottom where our cattle feed T 32 T at night 14

Except for a couple of farms, none was ever established there.

Saturday, Feb 2
   T 5 Little wind this 2 days, but sunny & clear T 31 T at night 10

Sunday, Feb 3
   T 3 clear cold day Sunny T [daytime] 31 clouds gather in the S.W. T 14 [night]

Monday, Feb 4
   T 21 Pleasant morning. Gardner G. Potter, Madison D. Hambleton & John Lowry, pack on their backs and start for home [to the new Sanpete Valley settlement]. Thawing T 41 T 32 [night?]

These are three of the five men who joined the expedition at
Manti. Their home in the Sanpete Valley was forty-five airline miles
away, but to reach it meant either climbing over the Pavant Range,
whose peaks are over ten thousand feet high, or swinging north
around these mountains and crossing the lower Valley Mountains
to reach the Sevier.

Tuesday, Feb 5
   T 32 beautiful morning. Griggs & Willis go ahead, few miles road
   impassable. S. Tanner kills a Deer. T 52 Thawing fast—surely Israel
   remembers us to their God. Lyceum held every evg, some debate. T
   32 R.C. making [illegible]

Wednesday, Feb 6
   T 29 at noon T 58 Thawing fast. Sun shines strong. Potter &
   Hambleton & Lowry return, report snow very deep for few miles
   but afterwards passable. Meeting, voted we start to morrow. 200
   Men sent after cattle, some fix food, the carriage &c &c T 34

Instead of striking east into the Pavant Range, the Sanpete men
must have gone north, over Scipio Pass, where the snow was deep,
then into Round Valley, where they felt it was passable. The decision
of the camp to move forward was a mistake, as they will shortly learn.

Thursday, Feb 7
   T 24 Cattle all got up by 11 A.M. T 50 fine day 387 miles Start at 12
   1/2 P.M. travel to Thorn Plum creek 393 1/4 m. About a foot snow
   in deepest places. Camped after dark 6 1/4 miles, 8 in deep, 6 feet
   Wide. Sage plenty, feed on hills to the right T 26

"Thorn Plum creek" is probably Pioneer Creek, two miles south of
the present site of Holden. Here they will spend the next three
days while exploring the best route.

Friday, Feb 8
   T 20 Drive cattle up on the hills for feed.. Plenty bunch grass. T 34
   noon 58 T at night 34 beautiful day.

Saturday, Feb 9
   T 32 Boys been a head 10 miles on snow shoes. Snow 2 & 3 ft deep
   going over the divide. T 44 Coy voted to go round the Mt West &
   explore

The "divide" is Scipio Pass, where Parley's horseback group had found the going so difficult. The "Mt West" is the well-known volcanic Pavant Butte. Going that way, while much longer, might have been wise. It would have meant travel through the mostly level Sevier Desert to the area of Delta. From there they could have gone up the by then south-flowing Sevier River and reached Juab Valley without crossing another mountain pass. But the exploration didn't go far enough to discover this route.

Sunday, Feb 10
Fine day T 28 T 43 cloudy. Fitting up snow shoes all round

Monday, Feb 11
T 10 little snow during the night cloudy. Hamilton Potter & Lowry start, also Coy to explore round the Mt move up with wagons 3/4 mile to cedars 394 miles

John Lowry's daughter years later recorded his reminiscences, including an account of the trip home by the three men. While it lacks specifics, perhaps overstates Lowry's role, and has an incorrect date of arrival in Sanpete, it graphically describes the hardship of winter travel in that country:

Two of the men, Porter and Hamilton, who enlisted when father did, decided that they would like to return home and insisted that father go with them. These two men calculated that by traveling on snow shoes they could reach home in two days. Father hesitated about undertaking the trip; he felt that he was lacking in experience, and he had never walked on snow shoes. However, he finally consented. One of the men had a good pair of snow shoes, the other made himself a pair out of thin boards. With the use of a saw, father made a pair out of an ox bow and tied rawhide strings on them. They traveled up the canyon [probably Pioneer Creek, because they were headed into the Pavant Range] about six miles from where the city of Fillmore now stands. They continued their journey all day. Before reaching the summit, they came to a point where the creek forked, and left a narrow ledge. They traveled up that ledge, and twice came to a place that they could not go around very well. On the south side was dense bushes and on the far north side it was so very steep. They helped each other by first lifting one man up to where they could in turn help the other one.

They traveled until nearly dark looking for a place to stop, and finally found a place where a big pine tree grew, and its limbs came way down to the snow, and just close to this tree were two smaller ones. They trimmed the limbs of the big tree which they used for fire wood, and the limbs from the small trees they placed on the snow, and spread their blankets on them for a bed. When they had a good fire, they began to think of something to eat, for they had traveled since early morning, not stopping to partake of food.

Mr. Hamilton was the man who prepared the food for the journey, and when he brought it forth, they found that he had nothing but twenty small biscuits. Father said he did not try to sleep that night, but gave the older men the benefit of the bed, and he kept the fire up.

The next morning they started early, after partaking of their scant rations, and climbed about a mile and a half, and then reached the summit, and looked off north into Sanpete Valley. While they were standing there a gust of wind came and took their hats off. Father was dressed in buckskin, and his moccasin got wet, and he had the misfortune of freezing his toe. From their point of view they looked down the mountain and saw a pine tree [and] agreed to meet at that tree, for they were sure they would be separated from each other in going through the timber down the mountain side. Father had not traveled very far when his toe began burning terribly, but he pressed on; went as fast as he could down the mountain side, through the brush, and over into the snow. He got to the pine tree quite a while before night; the wind had blown away the snow and he soon had a fire. He gathered up wood enough to last the night, although he was suffering much from the effects of a frozen toe.

Mr. Hamilton soon put in an appearance, but it was dark when Mr. Porter arrived. The second night closed down upon the three travelers, and they were still far from home.

They each ate their last biscuit, and the two older men [Hamilton and Potter were thirty-nine years old, Lowry twenty-one] slept as much as they could, but father said he could not sleep. Early the next morning they started out on their snow shoes. They were traveling almost east, and came out of the hills and into the valley where Salina is now located. They had not traveled very far that morning when their friend Hamilton said he could not see, he was snow blind. Father took him by the hand and led him along, notifying him of the rough places in their way. In the vicinity where they were there were some springs, and they followed on the west side of the stream of water from these springs which ran to the north.

They realized afterwards that they made a mistake in following the stream, for they came to the place where the stream emptied into the Sevier River, and in order to continue their journey they must cross the river. They removed their clothing, rolled them up with their blankets, and with the straps they used to tie their snow shoes on they strapped the bundle to their shoulders to keep them dry.

Father said he would always remember one thing Mr. Hamilton said to him: 'John, you try crossing the river first; you have no family to take care of,' but father thought he did not want to drown in that icy water. However, he crossed to the opposite shore in safety, and the two men followed. He then began tramping down the snow, which came above his knees, that they might have a smooth place on which to dress.

While they were crossing the stream the sun disappeared behind the west mountains. Can we imagine what the thoughts of those men were, what emotions stirred their souls, that winter night, in that lonely spot, far away from the abode of man, having had nothing to eat all day and no food for an evening meal, and nothing with which to make a fire but green willows, which were in abundance around them.

They proceeded to break the willows, and with their jack knives scraped the bark until they had quite a bunch of scrapings, then with flint and steel struck fire into it, and soon had a good blaze. They broke willows and placed on the snow before spreading their blankets for a bed. The two older men were groaning very badly because of their sore eyes, lay down and got a little sleep, father breaking willows and keeping the fire going. When the first streak of light appeared in the eastern horizon he spoke to the men, telling them it was time to make another start on their journey. Mr. Hamilton, who had been so sure they could make the trip in two days, was now in such a weakened condition that he refused to get up, saying: 'I can't possibly go on.' But father, brave, strong, and courageous, insisted on him getting up. He finally got him onto his feet, tied his snow shoes on, rolled his blankets with his own, and they started very slowly at first, then after a while he could walk a little faster.

They finally struck on an Indian trail, which they followed, and it led them to the head of Twelve Mile Creek Canyon; then they went down to the Sevier River, then Mr. Hamilton gave out and could go no farther. The wind had blown the snow off a little ledge, and they had no trouble in making a fire and prepared to spend the fourth night in the wilds.

The following morning they had the same trouble getting Mr. Hamilton up and moving. They arrived in the camp of their loved ones about four o'clock that afternoon, about February 1st, 1850 [actually February 25 if they made the trip in four days], in a sad condition, but with gratitude in their souls that they had been protected and brought safely to their home.[128]

Thursday, Feb 14
Breth have returned from exploring round the West foot of Mt report no snow scarcely 30 miles ahead on the Sevier which turns Southward & forms its lakes West of our encampment about 20 miles see Indians, Pivants fishing at the Lake have lots of large fish. Bre go down to see the Lake, & others to explore round, some going a head to explore further on the road to morrow. Bright Sunny days T ranging mornings about 25 noon 40 nights 30 Prest Fulmer thinks good settlement could be made in this valley Breth nights preach & pray, & day times read write, herd to cattle &c:

The fish-filled lake was Sevier Lake, now for most of the year a dry playa. On the map of the 1776 Domínguez-Escalante expedition the lake is named "Laguna de Miera" for the group's cartographer Bernardo de Miera y Pacheco.[129] Had the scouts explored north along the Sevier River instead of south to the lake, they might have recommended this much more level and snow-free route.

Sunday, Feb 17
T ranging as above, tho' last night it did not fall below 40. Pleasant Sunny days, with little frost nights. Little SE. Wind all night & during day which takes the snow off fast. Breth go 13 miles a head on the road report snow very deep others come in from exploring West. See many Lakes, & the course of the Sevier, but did not get to see the Pi Vants. Excellent prayer meeting to night. Breth united & in firstrate Spirits cattle however very poor. Fa Williams caches some articles, couples his wagon shorter, cuts off some of the box &c

Sunday, Feb 24 [after a seven-day gap]
Fa Matthews & R.C. went a head over the Mountain gone 4 days last week, snow over 18 in deep, hard snow crust, but see feed all along. snowed on Thursday & Friday last 4 in each night & T on Saturday morning stood as low as 14 good meeting to night.

---

128. Anderson, "Sketch of the Life of John Lowry Jr.," 6–8.
129. Warner, *The Domínguez-Escalante Journal*, p. 131

Monday, Feb 25
 T 28 South Wind, blowy all day. John Lowry Sylvester Wilcox &
 George Petty come into camp from Sand pitch with letter from
 Isaac Morley informing us of Utah battle &c. T noon 40 at night 32
 mild Wind blowyng south

It is not certain whether this is John Lowry, Jr., returning after his
arduous trip home, or his father, John Lowry, Sr., who was also in
the Manti settlement. Probably it was young Lowry, since he would
be able to guide the messengers to the snowbound camp. The letter follows:

Sandpitch Feb. 21st 1850

David Fulmer Little Salt Lake Valley
         Br David I am requested to inform you a little adetive to the pre-
sent situation of things that are going on in the Utah Valley. President
Young has sent one hundred and fifty men in to that Valley to subdue
the Indeans. mesengers from that Valley have ben sent here to
inform us what is going on there General Daniel H Wells has the
command of the party when the mesengers left the Utah there was
twenty two or three Indeans killed—and the main boddy of Indeans
that was left had retreated to a Canien in the east mountains supposed to be som fifty or sixty of them a few had mad their esscape otherwise. Br Isaac Higbey had one son killed in the battle and quite a
number of the brethren wounded some of them had quite a number
of our horses were shot. the mesengers inform us that it was believed
the wounded would recover we are anctiously waiting to hear the
final issue. the mesengers have started for camp this morning.
         The mesengers wanted me to inform you of the present situa-
tion of things and request you not to let the indeans have any of
your guns or amunition when you return we wish you to send the
Brass Gunn to this valley if you think you can spare it if you have
more bread stuf than you want we should like to exchange and let
you have in salt lake to the same amount. it is a general time of
health hear Walker and his band are quite friendly as yet
         with resspect yours as ever
Isaac Morley[130]

The "Utah battle" the letter reports, in which forty Indians were
killed, is the one that was impending when the advance party

---

130. Campbell, *Southern Exploring Expedition Papers.*

arrived at Fort Utah January 30. In view of this report, the company was much more security conscious the rest of the trip. Fullmer's reply to Morley's appeal for food, arms and ammunition, and the brass cannon will be delayed almost three weeks because of the company's snowbound predicament.

Tuesday, Feb 26
> T 40 Windy from all quarters camp moves together, fixes brush all round our wagons, forming a circle with a gate outlet on the East side T 42 A good deal of foolishness in Camp. Bro Fulmers reproofs it. T 38 Windy

Dissuaded from moving forward in the deep snow, the company rearranges its wagons for greater protection from the weather and for greater security against possible Indian attacks. They will remain here, near present Holden, another week.

Wednesday, Feb 27
> T 34 Windy. Blows up a Snow Storm from the South, pretty severe, all day. T noon 27 at night 26

Thursday, Feb 28
> T 26 Frosty last night. Snowy. T 24 stormy day T 22

Friday, March 1
> T 14 Beautiful day. T 28 cattle put up to near the Springs on excelent feed. T 22

Saturday, March 2
> T 18 Pleasant day. T 40 considerable dancing, Wooden shoemaking cleaning guns, Tailoring. Ringingking, reading, writing & singing.T 24

What "ringingking" was we have been unable to learn.

Sunday, Feby [March] 3
> T 27 2 Utahs came into Camp. Smoke the pipe of peace with them, give them Tobacco & pipe to smoke it with. the Pah-vants they left about noon. Snowing a little T 38 at night 26

Wednesday, March 6
> T ranging about 26 morning 44 noon & 28 night. Cloudy morning but pleasant days. Sunny. Start to day about 8 1/2 A.M. First small spring running cross the road 395 3/4 Plenty feed, right of road, many springs. Spring stream 396 1/2. Cedars & plenty feed. Went

on to brow of hill right of road & camped about noon 399 miles. 5 miles to day. Beautiful day. First cattle & wagons go on the top of the snow. Butterfly passes camp. Snow in deepest places averages 7 inches, many places no snow scarcely. T noon 48 S Wind, which is the only wind there can blow here

They here begin their approach to Scipio Pass, but stop just short of beginning the ascent.

Thursday, March 7
Travelled early in morning on the snow crust, but after going 3 mile had to strike up on the sides of the Mts as the cattle went in snow being about 2 foot deep. Camped on side hill having come 4 miles 403. Plenty feed. Snow off on the South side of hills, but deep drifts on the N Side beautiful sunny day

Camp is a little more than three miles short of the summit.

Friday, March 8:
All go a head shovelling snow, then part come back, get up the Cattle & start. It snowed 2 or 3 inches last night. Shovel snow upwards of a mile, in one place 1/2 mile snow being 2 feet deep. Wind round the Mts going up very steep places & down steep Mts to avoid the snow & avail ourselves of the South sides of the Mountain heights where the snow blown away by the winds. Travelled 3 miles & camped nearly opposite to Summit of dividing Ridge on the Mts Plenty feed. Melt snow for oxen 406 miles. Camp prayers & singing every night when weather admits. Beautiful Sunny day, clear sky.

Saturday, March 9
All go a head shovel snow, cut brush & cedar & then some return. Yoke up & start climbing over rocky Mts thro dense cedars, over hollows or ravines of the Mts where snow drifted 3 & 4 feet in places, down almost perpendicular descents, beautiful day come 1 1/2 miles 407 1/2 Camp about 250 yds on the North side of divide, on side hill left of road. Breth making sleds for to run wagons on. Willis and Heath, go on to within 4 miles of Sevier, report it best to take the left hand side of the valley on the benches. little snow there & plenty of feed all along. Hard Frost nights Hewlitt has T put past [illegible]

Winding one and one-half miles over, down, and around hills, cutting through pinyon-juniper forests much of the way, in order to advance less than a quarter mile down the north side says much about the difficulty of their ordeal.

Sunday, March 10

Bre put sleds under the wheels of his wagons & 20 men in two trips
take 2 wagons, which they call the Mountain maid & Mountain
Clipper to port necessity down this kanyon about 1 mile to mouth,
the snow from 8 inches to 3 & 4 feet deep, we keeping along the
Mountain side to our left near the foot of Mountain then striking
left over to Mountain foot on the West of the valley called Port
necessity where the snow is nearly off. about 3 miles the snow from
the mouth of the Kanyon to Port Necessity avering [averaging] 1
1/2 feet deep, which is hard & compact. Beautiful day. Freezing in
shade all day. Old men who stay in Camp melt snow for cattle.

This day and the next three, except for one day spent confined to
camp by a violent storm, were spent shoveling snow, doubling
teams and shuttling wagons off the mountain to a relatively snow-
free campsite they called Port Necessity in the southwest corner of
Round Valley. With that kind of effort they managed to advance
the company, a few wagons at a time, three miles in four days.
Replacing wagon wheels with sled runners worked for a day when
the snow was crusted, but failed the next day, even with eight or
ten oxen and nearly all the men working to pull each wagon, when
the snow softened. The oldest men in the expedition were Samuel
Gould, seventy-one; Christopher Williams, sixty-one; and William
Henrie, fifty. All remained with the wintering-over wagon company
and, presumably, were the "old men" who stayed in camp melting
snow for the cattle.

Monday, March 11

a cloudy morning, cold Wind blowing down Kanyon heavy smoke
seen for 2 days on Sevier a head.. try sliding the wagons again to
day, & have teams 4 & 5 yoke of cattle to draw them. snow gets so
soft find it impractical. South Wind, shovel road for better than 1/2
miles snow from 1 1/2 to 4 feet deep, then double teams & take all
the wagons down to foot of the Kanyon by sundown, camp on the
West side of Mts near mouth of Kanyon, hard days work on men &
cattle. Breth come back from the two wagons a head & help us. Mild
evg. Plenty feed on the S E sides of the Mts where snow is entirely
blown off. Fa Taylors ox found dead this morning.

Tuesday, March 12

about day break, violent gale of Wind blowing down Kanyon &
increases to a perfect tempest blowing over Parleys large wagon

which was left out of line tearing the cover off Hamiltons wagon, blowing down the tent &c. nearly 4 inches of snow fell from 7 to 11 O'C. storm abating & renewing all day, just as it had a mind to. many not out of bed till nearly night, some few cooked breakfast Parley's wagon fixed when wind abated so they could.

Wednesday, March 13

hard frost last night. Fa Williams ox "Brandy" found dead. About 10 A.M. oxen got up & nearly all yoked to wagons. Men go ahead & shovel. Quite a stiff breeze blowing from the South, clouds sail swiftly thro the skies. Sunny. Take the wagons with little shovelling from the mouth of Kanyon 1 1/2 miles over to Port Necessity, foot of Mts on the West, teams go back to mouth of hollow & bring the balance of Wagons then all hitch up & go on 2 1/2 miles & camp near cedars on beautiful bench feed which extends 6 or 7 miles on. Very Windy from the South, nearly blowing our covers off. Melt snow & water the cattle, which many have done all along. Fine day Thawing. 410 miles. Indian camp

They have now conquered the last difficult mountain pass. Though they will see more storms and will have to melt snow for cattle a few more days, there will be no more shoveling, and snow will no longer be a major difficulty. Progress toward home will be slow but steady from this point on. In Round Valley where they are camped, the town of Scipio was established in 1859.

Thursday, March 14

2 more Indians come into Camp. water cattle by melting snow, hitch up & go on 3 1/4 miles, pass over beautiful feed. An Indian with several squaws and children, come & camp with us. Lake Utes, have only heard of the war, don't know anything about it, friendly, trade for a few skins with them. Clouds heavy & black pass swiftly over our heads. Sunny. 413 1/4 we do not trade Guns or ammunition with the Indians. Snowy. Good meeting, Bro Fulmer speaks first rate and others. Windy. Indians camp with us.

Travel and camp are on the bench on the west side of Round Valley.

Friday, March 15

South Wind, mild evening. Clouds pass swiftly over us sometimes discharge the snow & hail up on us. sometimes clear day take up hollow & over ridge to the right of the road. Fa: Williams team slow, turns out & baits every day. Go 4 1/4 miles, encamp at N foot of ridge beautiful camping place. Abundant, good feed & dry fuel melt snow & water all the oxen. Indians follow us up & camp with us firstrate meeting Bro Fulmer talks emphatically on the propriety of keeping together, strong helping the weak &c. Indians camp with us wish to sell one of their squaws for (Tuitsimbungo) cow or ox 417 1/2

Camp this night is at the north end of Round Valley. Campbell here displays his growing understanding of Ute language. On the list he compiled of Ute Indian words, *Quitsimbungo* is the word for cow or ox.

Saturday, March 16
mild night Windy, strike road 1/2 mile from encampment Good going, down hill, little snow in the road, & some drifts, started about 9 A.M. Wind turned Hail storm for 2 hours. Indians follow us & Camp with us nights. Reach Sevier 420 1/2. Willows on banks, & feed mostly eat off at crossing, no cedars near, some sage, & greasewood. Sevier muddy, with banks like Missouri river, 30 yards Wide 2 feet deep, good ford. Go on 1 1/2 miles & encamp on Sevier beautiful feed, good bottom of feed 1/2 mile North. Indians camp with us. Beautiful afternoon, estimate of provisions taken 700 lbs in Camp, 422 miles Write letter to Prest I Morley, see copy of do on file. Willows for fuel. Hard Frost, snow all off on bottom.

Fullmer's letter to Morley in Sanpete follows:

Sevier 16th March 1850

Prest Isaac Morley
Sandpitch Settlement
Dear Bro:
     Yours of the 21st Febry last has been duly received by your faithful messengers, who arrived in our camp at Thorn plum creek on the 25th and we were truly thankful at your kindness in sending us the intelligence therein contained. all the Camp felt to bless you for doing this for a word from head Quarters was sweet to us, altho' we were sorry that some of our Brethren were wounded & one slain. our prayers have been that God would bless our Brethren, & overrule all these things for the good of his people. We send you the Brass cannon with 9 Bullets &other implements belonging to the same also Balance of Keg of Powder We have not President Youngs authority for doing this, but presuming your request in this thing

was reasonable &having all the load we can deal with, we willingly give it up to you, on the condition that it will be subject to the Prests order also brought to Salt Lake valley or any where else he might wish. As to Provisions, we have made a dividend of the amount of bread stuff in Camp to each person &we find that there is only 1 1/2 lbs per day for 20 days, without meat nearly. it would therefore be injudicious &unsafe for us to part with that, which in all probability will barely supply our own wants—It would have been a satisfaction to our Camp did their circumstances allow them to spare you some provisions

We started from our last encampment on the 6th &have reached here to night, 11 days travel, making 30 miles if we had come by the road, but the snow being so deep in Kanyons on the travelled road, we left the road, &made our way round the benches & places where the snow was nearly off, altho' we had much snow to encounter on the side hills, in one place shovelling snow 1/2 mile which would average 2 feet deep, &shovelling thro' many deep drifts in other places, same day, & for 2 days succeeding we shovelled nearly a mile each day, then we shod our wagons & by hand run 2 of them 3 miles, taking about 20 hands to a wagon, the snow melting however by warm day with South winds the Cattle were able to travel sometimes on the snow & other times breaking thro' & in this way, we got over into the little valley before coming over the divide into the Sevier valley, The Breth returning to your place will be able to give you more minute details, &to them we would respectfully refer you for all particulars.

We here observed the Council you gave us concerning trade with the Indians in guns or ammunition, a few Lake Utes have travelled & encamped with us these three days &are desirous of obtaining ammunition. They act quite friendly.

We have come on so far with peace union and prosperity, for which we all feel thankful, &have generally at our little meetings firstrate times, altho we are Mountaineers &Pioneers still we feel a good deal like being in the service of him who has set his hand in the last days to restore the earth, the air, the elements, &all things which has been cursed because of mans degeneracy, and with the blessing of God upon us we hope to be preserved with our cattle &property to go safely home in union & peace &meet with our Brethren on the 6th April at Conference

The Camp join in sending their love &blessings to the Sandpitch Brethren &remains yours in the N. & E Govt truly.

P S. We return the ox belonging to Bro: Shoemaker and was astonished to hear that Bro: Shoemaker had not received the one put into his charge we left in lieu of the same belong to Prest Young, ~~would you be pleased Bro: Morley to have some inquiry made con-~~ cerning this ox of the Prests he is a 6 year old ox, crooked horns, he has Red spots with Brindle streaks in them, &White spotted with Red sp with crooked hind legs, Branded on the nigh horn "B Y" & C or G on hips ~~We presume he may be dead, but we do not know, as we have heard of oxen dying in your valley in much better condition than he was, but~~ if he is in your vicinity in all probability some of the Brethren know of it[131]

Sunday, March 17

exchanging loading. taking from out of wagons with weak teams, & fa Henry [Henrie] leaves his weak ox with the Indians, gives it to them. Shoemaker's ox sent to Sandpitch by the Breth going there, 5 of them who start about 11 A.M. as we leave Sandpitch Breth give us a hearty farewell & the Indians come & shake hands with us all. Move on thro a bottom clayey Soil, excelent feed, 1 mile square, then strike over a succession of small ridges. Barren, Sage & Greasewood, see Sevier to our left & considerable smoke coming from its bottom. no snow on road except drifts. one Indian boy comes along, says its the Sandpitch's who r camped there. camp on ridge. Beautiful day. Cedars by wayside, & plenty feed on the hills. 428

The "Sandpitch Breth" would be Edward Everett and Sylvester Hewlitt, the two men remaining of the five who joined the expedition at Manti, and John Lowry, Sylvester Wilcox, and George Petty, the three men who on February 25 had brought from Manti Isaac Morley's letter informing them of the Indian troubles in Utah Valley and requesting any arms and ammunition as well as provisions the expedition could spare. Camp this night was at the south end of Juab Valley, near present Chicken Creek reservoir, six miles south of Levan.

Monday, March 18

stray ox gone. Find his track & 2 Indian tracks after him. beautiful day. Crossing of Slough creek 429 3/4 Plenty feed, 3 yards Wide 16 in deep, muddy, miry crossing, cedars on Mt sides some ways off. Pass up to 433 1/4 & camp on Slough creek bottom. nearly a mile wide excellent feed. We have come within 1/2 mile of Slough since

---

131.   Campbell, Southern Exploring Expedition Papers.

crossing. Indians who come into camp this morning follow us & understanding we were mad brought their chief to smoke with our chief which they did. Indian solemn, they leave us about 1 P.M. 1 of them, the young man, who followed us yesterday & went to the Sandpitches one f them. Beautiful day, little snow in places on the road, it is an adhesive clayey soil, much soil remaining on our wagon wheels. Tie up cattle at dark. 6 men on guard during the night, very cold wind, little Greasewood & Sage for fuel

Camp is probably on Chicken Creek, near Levan, a small farming community that was the childhood home of Matt Warner, one of the few members of Butch Cassidy's outlaw Wild Bunch who was able, eventually, to go straight and die in bed.

Tuesday, March 19
cold North Wind, cloudy, cattle soon fill themselves, cattle & horses improve, some, little lame however & poor. Start about 8 P.M.[A.M.]. Go thro sage bottom. After leaving Slough bottom, find 2 & 3 & 4 inches snow. At 437 1/4 strike up to the left towards hills & camp at 439 1/4 Come 6 miles, snow 5 & 6 inches deep, cedar & feed. Plenty fuel. Cold day. come thro clayey poor soil, sage Plentiful. N Wind. Guards stationed.

Wednesday, March 20
cold N Wind, cloudy, start about 11 A.M. & roll on to 443 1/4, keeping by the foot of the hills, west side of valley. Snow drifted deep on the North side of hills, beautiful feed all along on the hills & plenty cedars. The valley covered with snow—East

Thursday, March 21
beautiful morning. Sunny, clear sky, strike on to bottom & cross Onappah Kanyon creek at 446 1/4 beautiful feed. where the creek overflows Pass on down along the creek which runs North in a deep ravine, sage & Greasewood bottom many sloughs water brackish, snow about 1 foot deep but very soft. Camp about 4 P.M. at 452 1/4 near Watadge creek, having come 9 miles. see smoke a head 4 or 5 miles off. Cloudy

"Onappah Kanyon creek" is Salt Creek, which the expedition had ascended from the site of Nephi almost four months ago to reach the Manti settlement in Sanpete Valley. "Watadge creek" is North Creek, which comes out of the Mount Nebo Wilderness and joins

Salt Creek to flow north into what is now Mona Reservoir. Camp
was about a mile south of the reservoir.

Friday, March 22

beautiful morning. Strike up bottom, frosty night, amidst many
sloughs, strike east to road, at 453 3/4 turn out & bate at noon snow
about 6 in deep, soft, Watadge creek 457. Snow now 2 & 3 in deep;
feed abundant all along. Watadge creek flows down onto bottom &
joins Onappa kanyon creek, which is now a pretty large creek, flowing thro the middle of this valley North. See Indian fires this side
the creek on the bottom, their Wika ups on the other side of the
creek. Camp on Warm Spring creek 460 1/4 Good feed towards
mountains. Cattle tied up to night & Guard stationed. Pleasant mild
evg but cloudy.

Saturday, March 23

Boys go over and see Indians, ask for teacup, very hungry. Go on to
Summit creek, thro some snow about 1 foot deep. Camp between
the branches snow all off. Cloudy day. Good feed & fuel 468. Ox in
Sterling Driggs team lay down the end of Yohab

They are now on the low divide between Juab and Utah Valleys, as
their oxen continue to fail.

Sunday, March 24

beautiful morning, start about 9 A.M. Snow off from road soil dry
warm, little dusty. Atmosphere warm & Sultry meet Ammomah.
Give him provisions & letter to take to Isaac Morley telling him of
our success. Pateatneat creek here bate our teams 2 hours. 474 1/4.
start on & go to Spanish fork & camp, one of Walker's Indians with
us. Good road to day. Fa: Gould goes back & brings Driggs ox to
Pateatneat

Ammomah was Chief Wakara's brother, who was supposed to
guide the expedition up the Sevier and into Parowan Valley but got
sick and left them after only a few days. Apparently he was now
recovered. "Pateatneat creek" is at the site of Payson. With oxen so
worn, this day's travel of seventeen or eighteen miles to Spanish
Fork was remarkable. But they were in familiar country on an
established road. More important, they must have been energized
by the nearness of home.

Monday, March 25

12 Indians come into Camp, boys trade for skins & Hopkins for a horse gives his lame ox. move on to Hobble creek, pretty high water. bate at Spring creek water brackish. Good roads, dry and dusty. Camp N bank of Provo, rainey afternoon 493 miles. Gould goes for ox and could not find him. some snow as we approach Fort. leave wagon of Parleys & one yoke of cattle.

Ten miles today brings them to the first settlement they have seen in three and a half months.

Tuesday, March 26

Pleasant morning. Brethren from Fort come out & tell us the news. Start & go on to American Fork & camp. Some muddy road. Hopkins team gives out. Cotton woods on banks, Green Grass 2 & 3 inches high, acres of it where Prairie burnt. Showery afternoon, but clouds roll round west, clear moonlight night. 504 1/4 little rain.

Wednesday, March 27

Pleasant morning. 7 boys leave us for town this A.M. Dry creek 4 yards Wide 10 in deep, said to be dry in summer. Find a mile with 7 & 8 in snow in the road noon 1 1/2 hours, then move on over mountain some of the cattle lay down, 3 oxen left. All the Balance go over & camp at Hot Springs 11 1/2 miles, 415 [515] 3/4 Good feed, water hot, but does to cook with. Camp prayers & Bro Fulmer exhorts a little

"Over mountain" refers to Traverse Mountain, known locally as "Point of the Mountain," the low divide between Utah and Salt Lake Valleys where the foothills of the Wasatch Mountains slope down to the bottoms of the Jordan River.

Thursday, March 28

early start. Roll on to Cotton wood settlement to Captn Matthews by 2 P.M. Sunny day. Green Grass abundant. 426 [526] 3/4

THE OFFICIAL REPORT

Pratt's Report to the Legislative Council

On February 5, just eight days after his return from this arduous journey, Parley presented his official report to the Legislative Council, or Assembly. Basically it was the report he and Robert Campbell composed together in the snowbound camp near Fillmore, Campbell writing it, as his journal records, "laying on my belly & a hundred other positions, cold Snowy night open wagon." The report is based almost entirely on Campbell's remarkable journal in which he wrote virtually every day before going to bed.

With the weary and famished oxen able to go no farther, and with provisions alarmingly low, Parley and half the company mounted the strongest horses and mules and rode for home; that strategy would get the report back to headquarters quicker, would conserve the dwindling provisions, and would give the oxen a chance to rest and regain their strength. Campbell stayed with the wagons, so the balance of the official report, giving the sketchiest account of the mounted party's return, was written by Parley after he reached home.

Aside from its general description of the country, the journal's chief value to Brigham Young in his colonization efforts was its identification of likely sites for Mormon settlements—which was, of course, the expedition's basic purpose. At least twenty-five present Utah towns are located where the report indicated favorable conditions. The report follows, with the names and settlement dates of those towns inserted:

Great Salt Lake City Feb,y 5th 1850
To The Legislative Council of Deseret,

Mr. President & Gentlemen~

Being appointed by your honorable body to take charge of an Exploring expedition Southward took leave of my family from Great Salt Lake City on *Thursday 22nd November 1849*, reached Captain Browns the same evening, where many of the Company had already arrived.

Frid 23ᵈ Completed the organization of the Company consisting of 47 men, whose names and outfit has already reported in a communication dated the 24th from Captn Brown's. The number of horses &mules was not then ascertained, but we now report 38.

Sat 24ᵗʰ Company start from Captn Browns and encamped on Willow creek 20 1/2 miles from Great Salt Lake City. Here we were overtaken by a severe snow storm which lasted till noon next day, and fell some 10 inches of snow.

Sab 25ᵗʰ Started at noon, and wading thro' snow, crossed the summit of the Mountain bounding our valley on the South and, descending into the Utah encamped after dark on Dry creek, snow 1 foot deep.

On *Tuesday [November 27]* following reached Utah Fort, Distance 46 miles and passed on 4 1/2 miles to Hobble creek, here we found a desirable place for a Settlement [**Springville**, 1850]. Good soil, and plenty water.

On *Wednesday [November 28]* passed Spanish Fork 59 1/2 miles, where there is some good land [**Palmyra**, 1852, later absorbed by **Spanish Fork**], 14 yards wide, 14 in deep, Rocky bottom, steep banks, Cotton wood timber appears in small clusters along banks, and an open Kanyon in the Mountains East, intimating, plenty of timber. Camped Pateatneat creek same evening 64 3/4 m, 9 feet wide, 17 in deep, and like City creek running on the highest levels of land, here is fine soil, beautiful grass, and desirable place for a Settlement [**Payson**, 1850] here Marshall Scott called on us for some help to pursue horse theives supposed to have passed Southward, furnished him 10 Mounted Volunteers, who gave chase as far as Sevier river and returned fruitless.

On *Thursday [November 29]* passed Summit creek, divided into 2 branches, the one 3 feet Wide, the other 30 feet Wide, Rushing stream 1 foot deep, Cotton woods on banks 1 1/2 miles from mouth of Kanyon, which is apparently open and easy of access, rich feed all round, fine soil [**Summit City**, 1851, later named **Santaquin**]. The creek is on the dividing ridge between Utah &Yohab vallies, and runs nearly on the level of the highest lands. Dense cedar grove 2 1/2 miles SS.W. on a small hill. this is a pleasant situation overlooking the Utah Lake, and its valley on the North, Yohab with its rich vallies, and is a spot every way calculated for a city and Settlement [**Clover Creek**, 1852, later named **Mona**], rather limited in its resources. Passing on thro rich feed in the fine valley of Yohab we encamped at a Spring 78 3/4 miles.

On *Friday [November 30]* continuing thro' fine feed, and a beautiful landscape &rich soil [**Salt Creek**, 1851, later named

Nephi], we entered the Kanyon which leads into Sandpitch valley & encamped 2 miles above its mouth, steep and difficult crossings. This creek bears West then North into the Utah, affording as much water as Big Kanyon creek.

Next morning *[December 1]* leaving the wagons to follow myself and Bro: Huntington started on horseback for the Sandpitch Settlement where we arrived same evening after sunset, distance abut 35 miles or 130 1/4 from GSL City; found Fa Morley and the Brethren well, and generally in good Spirits. beautiful location fine stone quarry, Plenty fuel, soil not pleasant, being composed of adhesive clay~

Next day *[December 2]* being Sabbath gave some instructions to the Brethren in public meeting assembled had a good time.

On *Monday 3ᵈ December* I was taken very sick, confined to bed all day, vomited every few minutes. 1 P.M. the report of the Brass piece followed by a beautiful song, announced the arrival of the company who passed over the creek and encamped.

Next day *[December 4]* recovered my health, visited Camp & received 5 additional volunteers making our whole number 52 with 2 additional wagons, and teams. Whole No of Wagons 15.

On *Wed 5ᵗʰ* started in good Spirits down the valley towards the Sevier which we reached on Thursday evg and encamped on its banks. This is a noble river, sluggish current several feet deep, and apparently navigable, for small steamers, and having somewhat the appearance of the Western Jordan, but much larger: but its valley, and the country we had passed since leaving Sandpitch was mostly a Desert with the exceptions of small bottoms of grass and willows. Here we met C Shumway, J Allred &B Ward who had been out to trade and explore; and who brought us a sample of good stone coal found a short distance up the river. Here also we met Captn Walker and a portion of his band. We remained in Camp with them on Friday all day and that night. Much sickness prevailed among them which we found to be meazles. We prayed, and administered to them by the laying on of hands, nursed the sick with tea, coffee, sugar, Bread & Meat, gave them medical advice, and divided to Walker, and his brother Arripin, (who was sick) the bag of Flour sent to him by President Young. We, in turn received much information of the country South & East from Walker, &Ward, and were furnished by Walker with an Indian guide (called Ammomah) who left us the 3ᵈ day following having been sickly since he started with us. We took leave of our White and Indian friends on Saturday &continued our journey up the Sevier for several days crossing it frequently at good fords, and once on the ice with our wagons; it snowed a little every day, but was never to exceed a few inches deep in the valley, and finally we had three bright days with severe cold, and Thermometer at one time 21 below Zero Faht. The character of the valley was still a desert except here and there a few hundred acres of rich bottom [**Salina**, 1863; and **Richfield**, 1864], supplying sufficient feed for any amount of trave; Cedar fuel was every where plenty on the neighboring hills and mountains.

On *Wed 12ᵗʰ* the river being enclosed on both sides by a Mountainous range, and running thro a close Kanyon were forced to leave it, and make over a spur of the Mountains to the left for several miles, pass rather difficult for wagons having to double teams for 200 yards mid rocks and snow, and forests of cedars and shrub Pine, having gained the summit, after some delay and toil, we had a beautiful descent thro' the forests above mentioned for several miles and finally encamped at night fall in a beautiful rich valley on the Sevier [**Marysvale**, 1863], clothed richly and densely with grass, rushes and willows and some tall pines, shewing themselves in the distance in the open valley, and abundance of them on the sides of the Mountains and in the Kanyon of a small stream flowing in from the West. On past reaching the boarders of this grassy vale, we erected a mile board, marked 200 miles from G.S.L. City. This valley is watered by two streams besides the Sevier, containing from one to Two thousand acres perhaps more of excellent land, and is connected with more good land a few miles farther up the valley, which is from 1/4 to 1 1/4 miles wide. This location tho' limited in soil has an abundant supply of fuel, and building timber convenient, and its creeks tho' small have sufficient fall for overshot water power to any extent. Continuing up the river from this place for 2 days we encamped on the Fork to our right, 3/4 miles above the junction. The two Forks r nearly equal: right hand rather the largest. One comes in from the South West, the other from an Easterly course thro' a Kanyon, and the two divided by a lofty range of Mountains.

Next day *[December 15]* continuing up the Fork to our right we were stopped before night [just south of **Circleville**, 1864], the valley terminating in an impassable Kanyon, an abrupt chain of Mountains sweeping round us before and on each hand, the river rushing like a torrent between Perpendicular rocks. Snow at our encampment 4 in deep. Weather still cold. same evening after going into camp, Brother Driggs and myself on horseback, rode about 8 miles to find a pass to the left, of which we had been informed by Walker &Ward. Country very rough, clothed with shrub cedar

&Pine, marred by huge piles of stone washed down from the Mountains and full of gulleys. The dry beds of streams caused by torrents from the mountains, and the hills too abrupt for a passage with wagons, & the snow having increased to 2 feet deep as we ascended. We returned long after night &were joyfully received by our Brethren, who had begun to be anxious about our safety.

Next day [December 16] remained in camp while Captn Brown and others, attempted to search a pass on horseback over the great Wasatch range, to the right, in order to find our way if possible to the valley of Little Salt Lake. They rode all day, mid deep snows ascending and descending, rugged and stony precipices, and returned after dark to the great joy of the Camp. They reported a pass very difficult but not impassable.

On *Monday 17th* Camp rose at an early hour and prepared to ascend the Mountain. Myself, Captn Jones, Bro: Phelps, Bro: Fulmer, and fa Dustin, with some 20 others, waded on foot among the snows, axes, spades & picks in hand, preparing the way for the wagons which followed. night found us encamped in two bodies several miles apart in the midst of the Mountains having doubled on some of the teams and helped them up and down with ropes almost perpendicular rocks & precipices in sometimes shovelling the snow which was deeper than our heads hanging over us like the cornishes of a cavern. At night while thus encamped a heavy snow storm fell on us, accompanied by high winds, dispersed our cattle, put out our fires, and confined us closely till noon next day: at which time, clearing up a little, we gathered the cattle with some difficulty and hauled the rear wagons for 1 1/2 miles past the advance camp of the former day. Camping in a rocky sage hollow snow very deep, cattle little or nothing to eat, and the winds howling thro' the night like distant heavy thunder—towards morning more calm—cattle gathered—the rear wagons brought up. Company all together once more, shovel on thru' snow about 2 feet deep, and encamped at evening, several hundred feet below the heights we had passed. The next day descending thro' a smooth Kanyon, several miles very gradual encamped in far less snow, and tolerable feed. Captn Brown and myself had rode several miles down the kanyon, passed thro' a gate of perpendicular rock, which we called Summer gate and entered the neck of a valley snow not more than 2 or 3 in deep, returning after dark, with the news, diffused joy thro the camp and the next day the 21st all descended thro' Summer Gate and encamped on the Northern extreme to Little Salt Lake valley. [They emerged from the mountains down Fremont Wash, about ten miles south of Beaver.] Cedar for fuel. Plenty feed, nice water.

Sat 22nd Continued our journey thro' Sage Desert, and
camped among the Sage using it for fuel and snow for water. Our
cattle found abundant grass some of which was green & free from
snow.

Sab 23rd Passing thro' country mostly Desert, arrived on some
broad rich meadows dotted with willows, the effects of a stream
coming out from the Eastern Mountains which had spread and
sunk. Passing this in about 2 miles we came to Red creek
[**Paragonah**, 1851], having struck the road made by Captn Hunts
train of wagons, & subsequently followed up by the California emigrants. Distance from GSL City 272 miles. From this place we sent
dispatches to your honorable body, and our families &friends by
Joseph Mathews & Schuyler Jennings, by which you will have
learned partially our views of that part of the Country and its
resources.

On *Wed 26th* same hour that our express started for the valley,
Twenty of us started with Pack animals Southward, leaving Thirty
men under the Presidency of Br: Fulmer, in charge of the wagons
and cattle, to explore more fully the vicinity. We soon found that
our express had run before the tidings were one quarter known of
the rich resources in the immediate vicinity, besides Red creek, with
its thousands of acres of rich soil convenient for water, well supplied
with fuel pasturage and meadow, we found 4 miles Southward a
large stream flowing westward from a Kanyon in the Wasatch range,
having a rapid current, running on the highest lands and enriching
thousand of acres which descended from it South West &North, this
stream affords twice the water of city creek.

Six miles Southward is another stream flowing out of the same
range nearly as large as city creek which we called South creek, and
which like the other two streams in the valley, flows rapidly on the
highest lands, and affords alluvial fertility in its red wash for thousands of acres surrounding, and on which the richest kind of feed
[**Parowan**, 1851]. The principal soil of these streams consists of a
Redish Sandy loam washing from the decomposing Mountains on
its East and terminating in rich meadows and black soil with heavy
wire grass, willows & weeds. Away on the West towards the Little Salt
Lake which like a mirror shews itself some six or eight miles distant.
All these farming lands lay at the immediate Western base of the
Wasatch range which serves for a Fort or fence on their Eastern border, while their foot hills, nooks and kanyons and some places on
the plains are clothed with inexhaustible supply of shrub pine and
cedar fuel. Most of the hills and lands beyond the reach of water are
richly clothed in pasturage while the Kanyon of Centre Creek opens

an easy highway into the very bosom of the Mountains, where are inexhaustible stores of lofty Pine from the size of a fence Pole to every desirable size for logs, for Sawing, hewing, shingles &c. Stone quarries of Sand &Free stone and Lime, abound in the neighborhood. All these streams afford most convenient mill sites.

Passing on from there Southward the land continues rich and grassy for several miles—then few miles of Sage intervenes which is the Southern boundary of Little Salt Lake Valley.

Five miles from South creek brought us to the brow of a hill which descended into a fine large valley lying to the South West. On this hill comes out large Springs making several acres of very rich bench land on its immediate sides [**Enoch**, 1851]. Black soil, clothed with grass & canes. These streams descending Westward make a rich grassy meadow perhaps half a mile Wide and two or three long. Continuing on Southward we passed over several miles of second rate land consisting partly of mud plains and sage, and partly of lively Sandy soil &grass. Thousands of acres of which may be watered. Some five or six miles brings us to a large stream called the Muddy clothed with hundreds of acres of scattering Cotton woods some if which were large. Below these is a handsome expansive plain of very rich land, consisting partly of overflowed wire grass meadows, all of which might be drained and cultivated using the waters on the higher lands. Other portions of this plain were dry, level and delightful for the Plough clothed with rich meadow grass Rabbit weed &c— soil mostly black loam very rich. These meadows about 2 or 3 miles Wide appeared thro our telescope to extend from 10 to 20 miles up and down. The stream that waters this where we crossed it going South consisted of two branches 10 feet wide, & 1 foot deep, running swiftly. this supply would be greatly increased by the June floods. This stream comes out of the Mountains high and runs nearly level with the surface of the ground, the waters are easily managed, can be used up on the dry and thirsty lands on either side thus rendering its swampy parts tillable. But the best of all remains to be told, near the large body of good land on the Southwestern borders are thousands of acres of cedar contributing an almost inexhaustible supply of fuel which makes excellent coal. In the centre of these forests rises a hill of the richest Iron ore, specimens of which are herewith produced. This valley of water, soil cotton wood ~~and cedar~~ taken in connection with the cedar, and mineral wealth and the resources of Little Salt Lake valley constitutes a field of rich resources capable of sustaining and employing 50,000 inhabitants at present, and 100,000 eventually. All of which inhabitants would have soil, water, pasturage, plenty building timber and mineral wealth

more conveniently situated, than any other portion we have seen
West of the states. The climate of this country seems to us very
delightful compared with other places in the Basin. It was frosty but
not extreme. It was snowy but not much. Its days in the latter part of
Decemr and forepart of January were pleasant and sometimes
oppressively warm. the sunset hues and atmosphere resembled the
West Indies, a little modified by cool breezes. The nights were decid-
edly colder. The Thermometer ranging at the above dates at noon
from 60 in the shade to 32 at evening and at sunrise and taken as a
whole we were soon convinced this was the 'firstrate good' place we
were sent to find as a location for our next Southern colony [**Cedar
City**, 1851].

From this creek called the muddy [now Coal Creek] the
wagon road which we had been in since reaching the centre of the
[Little] Salt Lake valley bore off to the West, some 20 miles around
the point of a Mountain, we therefore left it and continued
Southward along the immediate foot of the Wasatch range of 17
miles, it still being an open valley where the map shews a Mountain.
This brought us to the Summit of the Basin rim, where we
encamped for the night in a fertile valley on the best kind of feed &
good soil [**Kanarraville**, early 1860s]. Plenty fuel, several small
streams coming out from the Wasatch with rapid currents, and running on the highest points of land in the valley till lost in a lake near
the Summit, or in alluvial meadow bottoms. The valley was never
less than from one to Three miles wide, and even the very rim of the
Basin seemed to invite Settlement, altho somewhat exposed to cold
and storms in Winter [**Harmony**, 1852, and **New Harmony**, 1854].
Cedar fuel every where abundant—the Mountain range nearly perpendicular and in many parts composed of Red sand stone in
progress of dissolution. One dome or tower of Red Sand stone,
seemed to rise like the dome of a church a mile above the level of
the mountain.—the clouds played swiftly round its head while all
else was clear. Four or five very lofty Pines showed themselves in the
mouth of kanyon: (so much for Fremonts far famed Basin rim, its
more like a platter & would certainly spill mush & milk if filled to
the rim and jogged by an earthquake.)

Sat 29th Descending Southward down an open valley we soon
came to a living stream [Ash Creek] which ran Southward thro a
Kanyon, a spur of the Mountain from the right closing in close to
the Wasatch, here we were forced to leave the stream and lake to
our right over the hills for many miles. Country rough and marred
with huge stones, the North side a foot deep with snow, on the
Summit and South side very miry. This range of hills distinctly

marked a change of climate. Night found us encamped on a stream in a rough broken country. Cotton wood, ash and some oak thickly studded along its banks. Here some Vi Ute Indians visited our camp, stayed with us over night and piloted us for a day or two, increasing in numbers as we penetrated their country. Appeared well pleased and very talkative. Next morning [December 30] soon after starting came to a few acres of fertile bottom [**Toquerville**, 1858], covered with old corn stalks and Squashes~ These were several years old their present farms being farther down. A short distance brought us to the Main Virgin, which here runs a Westerly course gathering the waters thro small tributaries from the North or Basin rim. It was here 18 yds wide 1 foot deep, swift current, Rocky bottom, flowing mostly thro' Kanyons which forced us from it over a high Sandy hilly country to the left and camping again on the river at night, on a small fertile bottom. Distance from GSL City to the rim of the Basin b our route 311 miles. From the rim 13 miles rapid descent brought us to milder climate, &first cultivation. A mile or so further brought us to the bank of the virgin before mentioned. The great Wasatch range along which we had travelled during our whole journey here terminates in several abrupt Promontorys. The Country Southward opening to the view as it were a wide expanse of chaotic matter huge hills, Sandy deserts, cheerless, grassless, waterless plains, perpendicular rocks, loose barren clay, dissolving beds of Sandstone &various other elements, lying in inconceivable confusion, in short a country in ruins, dissolved by the peltings of the storms of ages, or turned inside out, upside down by terrible convulsions in some former age. southward the view was open for at least 80 miles, shewing no signs of water or fertility and the Indians tell us there was noon told us there was none Eastward—the view was bounded by vast tables of Mountains one rising above the other and presenting a level summit at the horizon, as if the whole country had occupied a certain level several thousand feet higher than its present, and had washed away, dissolved, or sunken, leaving the monuments of its once exalted level, smooth and fertile surface. Poor &worthless as was the country it seemed everywhere strewed with broken Pottery well glazed & striped with unfading colors, it may have been the choicest portion of Gods vineyard.

Jany 1st 1850 Rainey day—Passed on down the Virgin were soon met by more Indians,. the bottoms now expanded about a mile in width and several miles in length, loose Sandy Soil, very pleasant for farming, extremely fertile, easily watered & sometimes subject to overflows. No timber in the country save cotton woods, large, along the streams, sufficient for temporary building and fuel.

As we passed downward, a range of hills divided this fertile valley [**Washington**, 1857], from another of perhaps equal extent [**St. George**, 1861], the two containing Perhaps 3 or 4000 acres of very desirable land. At the lower termination of the second valley a fork from the North called the Santa Clara entered the Virgin. The river below the junction running in rough kanyons, amid a rugged worthless country. The view at some 20 miles distance to the South West bounded by a rugged Mountain chain, some snow on its summit. Junction of these two streams was 80 miles from where we met left the wagons and 352 from GSL City by our new pass over the rim of the Basin, about 20 miles further by the usual wagon pass down the Santa Clara~

The climate in which we were now located appeared to be that of early Spring the new grass was Springing up, some Plants were green. The buds of the trees were swelling, the days almost oppressively warm, nights moderately cold, sometimes freezing a little, rain at intervals all day and thro' the night. On the 1st of Jany Thermometer ranging about 64 in the shade at noon, 34 at night &morning.

The Country below being of the most unpromising character, according to appearance, and the information we received from the Indians, corroborating us in the same, and our animals almost unable to travel and daily growing weaker, having frequently and daily to be unpacked, and lifted out of the mire, it was thought imprudent to venture further. We therefore turned to the North, up the Santa Clara and encamped on New Years evening on a wet miry bottom in the midst of heavy rain about 2 miles above the junction on our homeward journey. The Indians were with us till a late hour, being robust men, well armed with bows and poison arrows, and nearly equaling us n numbers, we fed them, sung for them, they joining with much glee in the chorus of our new hymn "O come, come away["] The chief made us a speech bidding us welcome to his country, wishing to be on friendly terms with the Mormons, the Utahs especially Walkers band, the Americans, and all good people, he invited and stronged [strongly] urged our people to settle with them and raise cornee. They left us about 10 P.M. and returned again next morning, piloted us all day. We saw no appearance of women or children among them, they cultivate in small patches only, raise good crops by irrigation. We gave them some Peas for seed together with presents of Dried meat the Flour which we could not well pack to the wagons.

Jany 2nd Passed up the Santa Clara 13 miles, and encamped in a good grove of cotton wood and ash mingled with grape vines having passed many hundred acres of firstrate bottom land easily watered and liberally timbered [**Santa Clara**, 1854].

Jany 3ʳᵈ Continued still up the river thro' some fertile and good bottoms well timbered with Cotton wood [**Gunlock**, 1857] and over some barren hills &Plains striking the new wagon road made by Captn Hunt. Travelled on it some distance—&camped among the Cotton woods, some good grass on the Mountain sides the first we have had for several days.

Friday 4ᵗʰ Passed over a hilly country, and rather rough roads, passing the rim of the Basin. Camped near it in some cedars 4 in of old snow, and considerable snow fell during the night. Animals fared well on the mountain grass which was green.

Sat 5ᵗʰ Passed down a few miles thro a fertile valley [Newcastle], still snowing. Came to running water and the Camp of Purblo and a few wagons, about 12 miles farther we reached Captn Fly's Camp of perhaps fifty wagons, men, women and children who have lain by on a fine stream to shoe their cattle and recruit. Of them we purchased some Whiskey, drinked tolerably free, some of us lodged in their tents and had the luxury of sitting in a chair. Here was seen some of the richest specimens of iron ore, which was scattered over the hills and said to exist in inexhaustible quantities two miles up the kanyon, which Kanyon thus opened out, as we were informed into a fertile meadow [**Pinto**, 1856], this small stream would water some fertile land, and cedar fuel is abundant, and easy of access. Pasturage inexhaustible. The country West &North West expanding into a vast plain or valley unexplored, with Mountain ranges interspersed lost from our view in unexplored immensity [this is the Escalante Desert].

Sab 6ᵗʰ Travelled 25 miles, and camped on a small stream at the foot of the iron hills and cedar groves, a few miles from the Muddy mentioned in our outward passage.

Mond 7ᵗʰ Travelled across the Muddy and its bottoms and encamped at the Springs on the hill—Captn Jones and myself left the camp, and walking and riding till dark 11 miles farther reached the camp of Captn Fullmer & our wagons, who had removed during our absence from Red creek to Centre creek found all well, Counted up and compared our discoveries. His party had during our absence searched out much country to the West and visited a small Lake [Rush Lake] and some good lands [no settlement was established here, only scattered farms and ranches] separated from Little Salt Lake by a little mountain range. They had also visited Little Salt Lake and found what Walker calls "Gods own house," consisting of a Kanyon and Perpindicular rock penetrated by a

branch of Little Salt Lake and covered with Hieroglyphics, and
strange figures chiseled on the rocks, some of which they had
copied [Parowan Gap petroglyphs]. They had also explored a portion of the valley of the Muddy &found the Iron mine, which we
also found, they had also penetrated various branches of the
Kanyons—found inexhaustible supplies of Pine timber and some
other valuable timber, also quarries of Free stone, Plaster a Paris,
and water lime, ~~specimens of which are herewith presented~~.

Tuesd Jany 8th Brethren erected a Liberty pole hoisted a flag
marked with one Star and Great Basin, and a Free Soil banner, prepared a public Dinner, had the cannon well charged, & all things
ready for the reception of the Pack Company we had left under
Captn Brown. They arrived soon after noon amid the discharge of
Kannon and small arms. All sat down to a most substantial public
Dinner being the first celebration of the peopling of Little Salt Lake
valley, which we hope will be celebrated annually around that spot
till a hundred thousand merry hearts can join the festival.

Wed Jany 9th Rested ourselves and animals~

Thurs Jany 10th Recommenced our return journey. Camped at
evening in the open plain towards the North end of the valley.

Friday Jany 11th Travelled about 9 miles over a range of mountains. camped in a snow storm among the cedars.

12th Travelled 9 miles to Beaver creek. here were broad expansive meadows; good soil, some of it much like the church Farm of
Great Salt Lake Valley, and watered by one creek as large as Big cotton wood in our valley, and several smaller streams, all coming out
of the Wasatch, and shewing Kanyons and Mountain sides of timber,
large groves of Cotton wood appeared at some distance above us
and some tall Pines distinguished by telescope at the mouth of the
Kanyons. Cedar groves as usual, at some miles distant from the
farming lands. This is an excellent place for an extensive Settlement
[**Beaver**, 1856]. Passing this place, encamped 5 miles further on a
small sage creek.

13th Travelled 11 1/4 miles over a hilly country & encamped
without water

14th Travelled 9 miles and descended into a small valley &
encamped at night on Reed creek

15th Laid in Camp during a heavy snow storm

16th Travelled 11 3/4 miles over a hilly country, and encamped
without water

17th " 16 3/4 miles camped in a cedar hollow—without
water—country worthless, save for pasturage fuel. snow nearly 1
foot deep

Frid 18th Travelled 11 miles and descended into a low well watered valley of meadows and soil [**Meadow**], and encamped on Prairie creek, small stream, somewhat brackish, snow fell during the night about 1 foot additional

Sat Jany 19th Hitched up at noon, and wallowing in snow, sometimes upwards of two feet deep, arrived long after night at Rock creek [now known as Chalk Creek; this is the site of **Fillmore**, 1851], 10 miles distant &encamped—snow 18 in deep—Plenty of cotton wood fuel. Cattle nothing to eat, but little Browze & Willows

Sab Jany 20th Remained in camp, snow too deep to travel, and sustain the cattle Weather clear and cold:

21st Cloudy again. Snowing, remained in Camp.

Here the writing changes to that of Parley P. Pratt.

Here by unanimous will of the company it was decided to leave the waggons and cattle in charge of Bro. David Fulmer and 26 men with provisions suficient to last them till spring and the Remainder 24 men with myself attempt with pack animals to fource our way home.

We took leave of the camp on *22d Jan,* and after fourcing our way one hundred and ten miles, through snow from one to four feet deep for about 8 days arived safe in Utau fort with the loss of about six animals. the delays and toils caused by snow exhausted our provisions two or three days before reaching Utau. at this crisis Chauncy West and myself forced our way to Utau and sent out provisions to the company who were then 24 ms. distant.

Great credit is due to the people of Utau for their liberal and prompt action on this matter. horses and provisions were started before midnight in the evening of our ~~arival~~ arrival, although hendred [hindered] and even fired on by the Ute Indians while gathering their animals. A Br. who left the Camp without leave and contrary to advise was picked up by our Utah Relief express 6 ms. Beyond the fort, being nearly frozen to death. He now lies at Utau, cripled in his feet by frost.

I arived home on *wennsday evening the 30th of Jan* having been absent ten weeks. The Pack company arrived soon after, some with frozen limbs but I believe generally in good health and Spirits.

I now wish to bear witness of the fifty who accompanyed me on this expedition, and to have them in honorable remembrance. With scarce an exception they were patient and cheerful under all circumstances. Willing to be guided and controlled, and I can truely say that, in twenty years experience in the toils and hardships of the Church I have never seen men placed in circumstances better calculated to try their utmost strenth and patience. And at one time another half mile of deep snow intervening between them and camp would have caused every man to sink exausted without being able to fource their way any longer.

They are first Rate men, and I have promised to remember them for the very next undertaking which requires toil, Labour and sacrifice.

I have the Honr to subscribe myself
Your Obedient servant Parley P. Pratt[133]

---

133. There are two copies of this report, both mainly in Campbell's handwriting. They are virtually identical except for the final two paragraphs, added by Parley in his own handwriting, paying tribute to the men of the expedition.

EPILOGUE

Whether the men of Parley's expedition appreciated his remembering them for more toil, labor, and sacrifice is hard to say. For most if not all of them, with or without the recommendation, labor and sacrifice there would be. For Parley himself there was no rest; within a month of his return he was back at work on the toll road he had begun building through Parleys Canyon. The road earned $1,500 in tolls in the summer of 1850. By the following March, Parley, with his earnings, was en route to Chile to open South America for Mormon missionary work. That was his tenth full-time mission. His eleventh, in 1854, took him back to Chile. On his twelfth, in 1857, he was murdered in Arkansas.

Some of the expedition veterans became Mormon bishops, stake presidents, and mission presidents. Some were mayors or other civic officials. Several served in the territorial legislature. Many served LDS missions, some of them several, many overseas. One of them, Chauncey West, served as far from home as Ceylon and India. George Nebeker colonized the Moab area, then Carson Valley—both failures—then spent thirteen years in charge of building the Mormon Church in Hawaii, acquiring the property on which the church's temple, the Polynesian Culture Center and Brigham Young University Hawaii now stand. Some, besides Parley, died early, violently. Isaac Brown was killed by Indians, Josiah Arnold murdered in a break-in attempt, Sterling Driggs killed in a threshing machine, William Willes in a sawmill.

But what mostly characterizes the later lives of the Southern Expedition veterans was the willingness with which so many of them answered the calls to colonize—and to accept the hardship and sacrifice that colonizing demands. Brigham Young's goal was to establish a Mormon empire stretching from the Rockies to the Sierras and beyond. The expedition itself was an early step in that effort, but only a step. Its veterans took many other steps, colonizing from San Bernardino to the Carson Valley to the Salmon River to the Elk Mountain and dozens of communities in between. Many

of them returned to establish or build the Iron Mission and the
Cotton Mission and other places they had explored with Parley.
One was Isaac Haight, called to manage the new iron works in
Cedar City. He served there as mayor and stake president until the
Mountain Meadows massacre. He was cut off from the church for
his part in that tragedy. Though his membership was later restored
and he continued to serve the Mormon Church, the last third of
his life was spent in hiding or at least exile from the scenes of his
major labors. By contrast, there was doughty, old Samuel Gould,
the expedition's seventy-one-year-old patriarch, who, ignoring
Indian threats that drove everyone else off, lived into his late eight-
ies alone on his ranch on Hurricane Mesa.

What motivated the courage, commitment, and sacrifice of so
many? Perhaps Isaac Haight expresses it best. Barely two months
after he returned home with Parley, he learned in the April general conference of the church that his stay at home would be brief.
His journal reports that "I with six other Elders were appointed to
go to England on a Mission and leave our Families which seems
rather hard after enduring the fatigues of the winter. Yet I am willing to go and forsake all [for] the Gospel Sake and go to work to
prepare for the journey."

Which seems as appropriate an expression as any of the spirit
behind the Southern Exploring Expedition.

Appendices

Related Papers

PLEDGES OF SUPPORT

1849 Nov 17

We the undersigned agree to pay immediately the sums set to our names for the purpose of assisting and furnishing the exploring company to start on their journey forthwith, believing, that is highly important the company should prosecute their journey as speedily as possible.

H. C. Kimball		25.00	Paid 24	
Daniel Spencer	not paid			
John Smith	not paid	5	Paid to W W Phelps	
Newel K. Whitney	not paid	an ox	Polly Stringham [?] 1	
Horace S. Eldridge	Recd	an ox	Jan [?] P. Park	1
John D. Lee	not Recd	A Beef		
A.P. Rockw	5 Paid			
B.F. Johnson	not paid	5	Bradford Leonard	5
W. Draper		1	F.D.Wade	2.42
W. Lewis		1	Anna Pullen	.45
Mary Wodey		50	M. Riche	25
Edwin Bingham		1		
O. T. Whitn		1	_____	
D hnso		1		82.52
Jo		1	[scratched out, illegible]	L. C. Rich
Willam Macleary		.50		
David Pettigrew		1	5 pds of Coffee W. Muir	

RECEIPTS AND EXPENDITURES

Cottonwood Ward,— Nov 23d, 49

Pres,t Young and the Council:
Gentlemen:

We submit to your honorable body the following Report of Cash and property Recd on our subscription List; and also our expenditures of the same

H. C. Kimball	24.00	Carried up	55.40
A P Rockwood	5.00	Bradford Leonard	5.00
W. Draper	1.00	E. D. Wade	2.42

Wm Lewis	1.00	Ann Pullen	0.45
Mary Wooley	0.50	Mr Riche	0.25
Edwin Bingham	1.00	Hiram Jackman	0.50
F. T. Whitney	1.00	E F Sheets	0.75
David Fairbank	0.95	Old Subscription	9.25
John Quail	0.50	B. Nevy	1.90
M. Clayton	0.95	G. B. Fairbanks	2.00
A Butterfield	0.50	C H Foster	2.00
Daniel Miller	1.00	L Sympson	0.50
Henry Royle	1.00	A Russel	0.50
Ruben Perkins	1.00	Levi Savage	0.50
J N Perkins	1.00	J Harrison	1.00
Andrew Perkin	1.00	W. C. Mitchel	1.00
Henry Johnson	2.0	D Wood	1.00
J. H. Mitchel	0.50	S K Marble	2.50
Erastus Bingham	2.50	William Hamblin	0.50
Robt Miller	0.50	Pugmire	1.25
E Snider	1.00	C. Dalton	0.25
Widow Smith	1.00	Jim Andrews	1.00
J N Johnson	1.00	Jas Holbrook	2.00
John Vance	1.00	Daniel Nevey	5.00
Milan Macelroy	0.50	James Beck	0.50
David Petegrew	1.00	A. G. Fellows	1.00
Polly Stringham	1.00	A B Cherry	5.00
Iam P. Pack	1.00	E Hanks	10.00
Wm Miller	1.00	W. G. Backins	5.00
	55.40		118.42
Brought forward	118.42	Brought forward	179.07
E. T. Clark	1.00	E W More	2.00
B Beck	1.00	C. U. Spencer	5.00
Parrey	1.00	W H Dame	0.50
E Newman	0.25	J M Crosley	0.70
F Herryman	1.00	S T Knowlton	10.00
A P Stewart	1.00	Saul Richards	0.50
C Haight	0.50	Eli David	2.00
W. B. Jones	0.50	Horace Libbies	3.80
Jackson Pendleton	1.00	Mr Gibbs	1.00
E Wooley	0.50	J G Hovey	0.50
S Chipman	1.45	G. C. Murdock	1.00
Colby	0.95	J P Squares	0.50
Dame	0.50	Peters	0.50

Deirvy	1.45	Christian Per	0.60
James Caff	1.00	Weer	0.50
I Knapp	2.50	Oheesemanger	2.35
J. S. Washarman	1.00	Burr frost	1.00
Moses Daily	0.50	Joseph Harker	1.00
Lemmon	1.00	R. C. Woosey	0.50
M. II. Peck	1.95	Jesse Fox	0.50
P Nebeker	0.50	Daniel McCoy	1.00
P B Lewis	1.00	Jared Ward	0.35
C Mullen	0.50	G. Brown	1.00
R Wins	0.50	David Frederick	0.50
T prory	0.50	Alex Leman	0.50
W M. Hide	0.95	M H daws	1.00
R. M Allen	0.25	Alex Stephens	4.00
J Turner	1.00	Joseph Murdock	1.00
Rhodes	5.00		
N Collins	0.40		225.07
Geo Winder	1.00		
R C Allen	0.50		
J. Fulmer	1.00		
M. D. Balis	1.50		
Wm McBride	1.50		
P Asby	0.50		
I Turlap	1.00		
D Russell	5.00		
Hickinlooper	1.00		
T Standing	1.00		
W Glover	16.00		
	179.07		

We have 225.07 is as the subscription appears upon the face of it. But the Amount actually Recd is $223.50 I enclose the Original papers that Br Bullock May if necessary decipher any errors in names

I Remain your Br. In the mane co [?]

P. P. Pratt

Private James Ure $5—for R C from Glover coffee 2 lbs. Ten few peaches

Expenditures of the Public funds for the exploring expedition south as follows:

Willard Snauen for Rodeameter	0.25
To James Furgisan to buy paper	0.25
10 lbs Rice at 25	2.50
9 lbs Butter 25	2.25
3 " " "	0.75
6 Tallow 20	1.20
Beaf	1.00
50 lbs flour at 8 ½	4.25

4 lbs dried fruit 25	1.00
100 lbs sugar 33 1/3	33.33
100 lbs coffee 33 1/3	33.33
1 Beef Cow 30	30.00
1 Beef Ox o.35 H Duncan	35.00
1 Beaf ox 34	34,00
1 Bear Cow 28	28.00
1 Ox	32.00
	239.11

Sum Total of Receipts by Subscriptions

As per Lists	223.50
Suplement Wm Henry	5.00
W. W. Phelps	10.00
	238.50

Total Expenditures—	239.11
Total Receipts—	238.50
Balance	000.61

T Bullock
R. C.

David Fairbank	35		
John Quail	50	Hiram Cook	0.5
Moses Clayson	50	Ed Marks	0.75
Ad Butterfield	50		
David A Mitt	1		
Hinz Royal	1		
Ruebin Perkin	1	Received on the with Subscriptions
I. N. Perkins	1	$213.50 two hundred and thirteen
Andrew Perkins	1	dollars and fifty cts
Henry Johnson	2	on hand from the subscrip 213.50
I. H. Mikial	50	nine dol 9 00
Erastus Binepher	2.50	
Robert Miller	50	
E. Snider	1	
W.Ian Smith	1	
F. H. Jo		

LETTERS SENT FROM SANPITCH SETTLEMENT

Sandpitch Settlement
Wed 5 Dec 1849

Prest. Y K &Richards

Enclosed we send herewith sketch of Camp Journal &c up to yester-days date. We have been successful &prosperous so far in all our under-takings & Journeyings. The Providential hand of the Almighty has been over us for good since we left and to him we give the honor & humbly entreat of him to guide us by day &by night, that we may do much good for Israel.—

We start this morning & may reach the Sevier to night, perhaps not till to morrow but we crave an interest in your faith & prayers, as our Camp continually pray for you and all the household of faith

All is well, all is well

Rob Campbell Clerk   Parley PPratt

[On bottom part of three-fold letter] 5 December 1849 Exploring Coy To Prests Y K & Richards Enclosing copy of Journal to yesterdays date
[On a scrap of paper] Parley told me to take down this R. C.
Cleon Ellmer—Sandpitch Settlement—5 December 1849
Dark cherry Red ox 6 years old in Spring, white belly, darker legs, with white spots, white spot on middle of back & white on his rump or cross the line, inside of trt [?] white—Black head, long bushy tail

The following is Campbell's journal sent to the First Presidency from the Sanpitch settlement. It covers the first five days after departure, and differs only slightly from that portion of his complete journal.

F23ᵈ Nov [1849] Left C H at 11 A M. cold day—muddy many water furrows in the city bad to cross, poorly hedged. Kanyon creek bridge 4 3/8 ^miles^ (4 1/4) Pleasant ~~hav~~ Mill crik —Bridge over —at Gardner mill. 6 3/4 ^m^ Good road, Cotton wood creek crossing 8 3/4 ^m^ cold Camp at C John Browns—Brethren rendezvous 10 1/2 ^m^

S24ᵗʰ D Fulmer weighing out the Bl of groceries &flour some 60 lbs ^more or less^ of coffee to return to city. cold morning P P P writes letter to B Y

R. C. copies Do enclosing Returns &c—aggregate in Camp 12 wag-ons 1 carraje—2 yokes of cattle Buros—

No of horses &mules not yet assertained—One Brass field piece— guns innumerable ammunition in proportion

Start out by 11 1/2 A. M. Bishop Crosy's place where irrigation enters—&road leaves—Big field 11 3/4—Further Cotton Wood crossing

12 3/4 ten to 1 P. M. reach first knoll beyond Cotton wood—Forks of road, take the right—14 ^miles^—Pleasant but cool—sun to be seen thru the haze good light Sandy gravilly soil—dry feed abundant, on the right &left—where the grass burnt—Prairie covered with green grass 1 to 2 inches high Dry creek 17 1/2 feed Plenty—no water—Some fuel—Fork of road 1/4 miles. Good roads. Camp at Willow Creek ^soft and swampy^ Good water—no fuel—Plenty feed. 20 1/4 ~~Thermom~~ Killed a yearling—fat and good—Cattle tied up about 8 P. M. as the snow falls fast. Camp gathers around five many jokes &stories told—singing song & afterwards ^a hymn^ come, come ye Saints. Prayer by P. P. Pratt—then retire to bed

Sab. 25ᵗʰ Snowy morning 1/1/2 deep all over—Thermomer 31 Breakfast cooking—Parley keeps to bed—Singing in wagons—W. Wind —11 A.M. clearing up FT 33 Snow 7 deep Ceases snowing—Dan Jones arrives. Camp goes for cattle—Hitching up—Start at 12 1/2 P. reach Hollow—steep ascent 21 3/4, Good road to Hot Springs, 23 Miles. 136 heat.—These Springs are to the right of the road a few yards. (6 or 7 rods) then begin to ascend—freezing. Snowing a little—road turns to the left &ascends steep Kanyon 24 1/2 double teams ~~3 to 4~~ 300 yards Summit 25 miles ^Views of valley & Lake &c—turn to the left few hundred yards then descend long hill steep descent—sun sets—Freezing hard snowing a little Northerly wind reach Dry Creek—6 ^h^ 25 ^m^—camp South side. 31 1/4 miles *Mond 26ᵗʰ* Ther 25 degrees Snowing—freezing good water. cotton wood timber—10 A.M. start. Small winding hollow 33 miles— (Dirty Shirts.) can't tell road ^or feed^ so much snow on ground. 9 inches deep—Small hollow (sideling). 33 3/4—American Fork 34 1/2 10 in deep ^clear water Rocky bottom trees^ Small cotton wood near 10 in snow, in places 1 ft ^Snow ceases at noon^ *Oct. 26ᵗʰ.* 38 1/4 to ~~Muddy~~ Swamp creek, ~~swampy~~ ^muddy^ & soft for ^n^100 yards 18 in deep ^unable to see the mts^ 39 Pond at the right of road—~~Sandy~~—Sage & Greasewood, abundant ^trees^, Cedar groves. Utah Lake to the right a few miles, ^cloudy.^ Camp by 5 P. M. at cedar Grove 20 yards to the left of road, 43 1/2 John Scott, reaches camp—after Purbelow mountaineer ^for stealing horses^ R. C. accompanies him to the Fort where Parley was preaching—afterwards Judge Phelps spoke by the spirit also D. Fulmer— good meeting—yoke of cattle subscribed. also help in vegetables, milk baking p &c R . C. had his washing done here by Capt Hunts Lady, Sister Hunt—The Fort enclosure of about 1 1/4 acres and 57 horses Is Higbee Prest. Indians round the Fort. R. C. Armstrong stays at Rob Egberts— Guards stationed at Camp to night

Tues 27ᵗʰ, Ther. 43. Thawing—clear amosphere, able to see M^tns^ Lake &c. Camp reaches Provo ^river^ by 11 A.M. 46 miles.18 in deep, clear water Rocky bottom (103 ft wide) 34 yds wide Before reaching Provo ^few yards^ pass over 2 small branches or sloughs in the timber E Wind. Muddy

^wet soft^ roads. Fort built on the south bank of Provo, 100 yards from river. Camp waits ^halt^ 2 1/2 hours. R. C. starts after Roadometer wagon started 1 hour—Parley and Jones wants bill. Soft swampy springs, 2 of them 50 1/2 miles—~~Nearly~~ about 3/4 miles past Fort pass over a branch of Provo, also irrigation furrow. noon Ther 45—Rocky rough road to Rock right side of the road & slough caused by springs few yards East running out of the Mt very bad to cross—51 3/4—~~Large Stream clear water~~ Spring creek—clear water—Rocky bottom 10 in deep —14 ^ft^ 9 ^in^, x 4 59 ft Broad (or 19 yds) 52 1/2 —1/4 mile to small slough—these ^sloughs^ originate from springs ^little^ East at the Mts. 53 1/2 Hobble Creek 28 ft broad 2 ft deep Camp South side up creek 150 yards—Plenty Cottonwood fuel—firstrate feed—Thawing all day—so the cattle can feed well to night—Parley reaches camp 6 P.M. F Ther 40 Yoke of cattle today and chain from [left blank] Rains nearly 2 hours

Wed 28th. Beautiful morning. Sun rises a little after 7 Freezing The 31 John Scott with nine men—leave 22 min past 9 OC. Armstrong plays a tune about every morning at starting time, Leave Hobble creek &bear South West level Prairie Small Hollow 55 1/2 steep banks Ther at noon in the sun 57 cold N Wind Thawing, wet roads, snow only 2 in. deep—dry feed plenty all along. 59 1/2. Spanish Fork 14 yds. broad 14 in deep— Rocky bottom, steep banks, & steep descent 100 yds from creek & steep ascent 150 yards past it. Cotton wood timber & plenty willows. Good camping place—Grease wood &sage studded thickly all over the Prairie to the right &left—62 1/2 Low swamp this Swamp continues for 3/4 ^mile^ by hawing a little you can go thru better, Some good black soil soft Travelling Thawing 64 3/4 Pateetneat—creek wide 9 ft. deep 17 in—Col. Scott & party stay here till we came up Hears word from Indians that Purbelow here 3 days ago &that he camps at the Hot Springs to night— reach here at 3 P.M. Camp Cotton woods and willows.

P. P. PRATT LETTERS TO FAMILY

Severe River
Dec 8th

Dear Wives and children

I am well & so are all the compy, 52 children & one Indian[134] On *Monday 3rd* I was very sick. I vomited all day without taking anything and puked up about 2 quarts of Bile without mixture of anything else. I was kindly taken care of by Br Washburn who also washes and bakes for me. On *Tuesday [December 4]* rested at Sanpitch and were joined by five Brethren and 2 waggons.

---

134.   This apparently refers to Ammomah, who had been asked by Chief Walker, his brother, to accompany the expedition as guide.

On *Wednesday 5th* 9 miles south through a desert of Sage

Thursday 6th 12 miles through a Desert and encamped on the Severe

River South of Latitude 39

Friday 7th were met by Walker the Chief of the Utaws who rode up on horseback just as we had left our camp. We turned about and encamped with him for the day Toward evening his camp came up consisting of theiir women and children, cattle Horses and dogs. Many of them and of the Indians South are sick and dying of Measles. We visited several lodges this morn and laid hands on them;, after kneeling down with them and praying. We also sent some of them coffee and provisions. Walker sends with us a Man called Ammon as a guide and interpreter.

Last eve Bro Shumway and Barney [Ward] and others came up and camped with us, they having been South with 2 wagons to trade. Form them and Walker we learn much of the country south etc. We have some fine specimens of stove coal, and Salt obtained by them near here. This River is a beautiful navigable stream and Rich in Timber, Salt, Coal, Salmon Trout and [illegible] above, though here it is Desert.

To the Mrs. PPPratt
Salt Lake City
Deseret
Dear Family, The Camp is now moving out. Our course is Southward up the Severe R, thence to the Little Salt Lake and over the Basin. The snow is about 1/2 inch deep and rather cold.

When I think of my family it shores me up with the hopes of immortal and never-ending Joys. I love them more than [?] thousand lives. I feel that I am beloved, and thoughts of my lovely family circle makes me happy. I shall soon return and be in your midst. Oh Lord, in the Name of Jesus Christ keep My family and bless them.

> Pray for us
> Your husband and father
> Parley P. Pratt~

PRATT'S ACCOUNT OF THE EXPLORATION OF THE VIRGIN RIVER

The following account of the mounted exploration of the Virgin River basin was written by Pratt some time after the event.

> Extract from P. P. Pratts Explorations.
> December 1849

Sat 29th. Descending Southwrd down an open valley we soon came to a living stream [Ash Creek], which ran Southward thro a Kanyon, a spur of the mountain from the right [Black Ridge extending from Pine Valley Mountains] closing in close to the Wahsatch here we were forced to leave the stream and take to our right over the hills for many miles, country rough, and marred with huge stones, the North side foot deep in snow, the Summit and south side very miry. This range of hills distinctly marked a change of clime, encamped on this stream, in a rough broken country, cotten wood, ash, and some oak thickly studded along the banks.

Next morning soon after starting, we came to a few acres of fertile bottom, covered with old corn stalks & squashes: these were several years old their present farms being farther down, a short distance brought us to the main Virgin, which here runs a Westerly course gathering its waters, thro small tributaries from the North or Basin rim, it was here 18 yards wide & 1 foot deep, swift current rocky bottom, flowing mostly thro' kanyons which forced us from it over a high sandy hilly country to the left, encamping again on the river at night, on a small fertile bottom Distance from G. S. L. City to rim of the Basin by our route 311 miles.

From the rim of the Basin 13 miles rapid descent brought us to a milder climate and firs mile in Width and several miles in length, loose sandy soil, very pleasant for farming, very fertile and easily watered sometimes subject to overflow no timber in the country except large cotton woods along the stream, sufficient for temporary building and fuel as we passed downward, a range of hills divided this fertile valley from another of perhaps equal extent. The two containing perhaps 3 or 4000 acres of very desirable land [the valleys now containing Washington and St. George], at the lower termination of this second valley a fork from the North called the Santa Clara entered the Virgin. The river below the junction running in rough kanyons, amid a rugged worthless country— The view at some 20 miles distance in the South West bounded by a rugged mountain chain, some snow on the summit. junction of these two streams was 20 [about 80] miles from where we left the wagons & 352 from G. S. L. City by our new pass over the rim of the Basin but 20 miles further by the usual wagon pass down the Santa Clara

The climate in which we were now located appeared to be that of early Spring, the new grass was springing up some plants were green, the buds of the trees were swelling, days oppressively warm nights moderately cold sometimes freezing a little, rain at intervals, all day and thro' the night on the *1st of January [1850]*. T ranging about 64 degrees in the shade at noon, 34 degrees at night & morning

Jany—2— ^Turned homewards &^ Passed up the Santa Clara 13 miles and encamped on a good grove of cotton wood & ash, mingled with Grape vines having passed during the day many hundred acres of firstrate bottom land, easily watered and moderately timbered.

Biographies of Expedition Members

Rufus Chester Allen, First Ten[135]

Rufus C. Allen, member of the First Ten, was, at age twenty-two already well tested for the rigors to be faced by the Southern Exploring Expedition. Born in Delaware County, New York, October 22, 1827, he was baptized in 1838 and ordained a teacher in Nauvoo about 1842. He labored to ferry across the Mississippi the Mormons driven from Nauvoo in February 1846, struggled across Iowa that winter and spring, then joined the Mormon Battalion and walked from Council Bluffs to San Diego before doubling back to reach Salt Lake Valley in 1847. In 1848 he returned to Winter Quarters to bring his family to the valley.

With all these miles under his feet, he was called to join Parley P. Pratt's exploring expedition, during which he remained with the wagons in Parowan Valley while Parley's group explored the Virgin, then, on the homeward journey, remained with the snowbound wagons in Pahvant Valley before finally reaching home in April.

The traveling was not over. In 1851 he joined Apostle Pratt to open South America to missionary work, landing in Valparaiso, Chile. Unsuccessful, they returned in 1852. In 1853 he married Lavenia H. Yeardsley, but the same year was sent with the first missionaries to the Indians in the Virgin and Santa Clara country who had pleaded with Parley to send Mormons to live among them. During that mission he married a second wife, Margaret McConnell, and, in 1856, built a log cabin in Tonaquint, which was promptly destroyed by one of many floods of the Virgin River.

Returning to Ogden in 1857, he was made senior president of the newly organized Fifty-third Quorum of Seventy. During the Utah War scare that year, he was sent into Echo Canyon to build fortifications and spent much of the winter of 1857–58 there, guarding the canyon against passage of Johnston's Army. Then he was sent south again, settling first at Paragonah, Iron County, then, in turn, on Cottonwood Creek,

---

135. Information on Allen was found in Susan Easton Black, *Membership of the Church of Jesus Christ of Latter-day Saints*, hereafter called *Members* (Provo, Utah: Brigham Young University Press, 1977; reprint, Provo, Utah: Brigham Young University Studies Center, 1984); also in Kate B. Carter, comp., *Our Pioneer Heritage* (Salt Lake City: Daughters of Utah Pioneers, 1959), 2:561–62; Jenson, *Bio. Enc.*, 1:535; Whitney, *History of Utah*, 4:436–38.

Washington County (1861), La Verkin Creek (1862), North Creek near the town of Virgin (1863), Kanarra (1866), and finally St. George, where he served fourteen years in the recently completed temple. He finally returned to Ogden, where he served in the Ogden First Ward bishopric and died during the winter of 1888–89.

JOHN CHRISTOPHER ARMSTRONG,
FIFTH TEN[136]

John C. Armstrong. Courtesy LDS Church Archives, copy photograph by J M. Heslop.

John C. Armstrong was a man of parts—musician, dancing master, professional tailor. He used all these skills on the Southern Exploring Expedition—acting as bugler for the company, teaching the men quadrilles and other dancing steps, making boxing gloves and, as his journal records "[I] mended two pairs of trousers for the boys." Later, in Salt Lake City, he remade one of his large broadcloth cloaks into trousers for Brigham Young. A sketch of his life by his granddaughter describes him as "full of life"; certainly his journal of the expedition, though incomplete, is by far the liveliest.

Armstrong was born November 27, 1813, in Carlisle, Cumberland, England. On September 8, 1840, he married Mary Kirkbridge. Four years later, while serving a mission to England Parley P. Pratt taught the Armstrongs the gospel and baptized them on July 21, 1844. During this time, a mob burst into the Armstrong home, demanding that they deliver the Mormon missionary—whom Mary had safely hidden under a bed.

The Armstrongs emigrated to America in 1845, settling in St. Louis. In the winter of 1845–46 they joined the Saints fleeing Nauvoo and endured the muddy ordeal of struggling across Iowa and months of cold and hunger at Winter Quarters. In Abraham O. Smoot's company they finally reached Salt Lake Valley September 26, 1847.

---

136. Davis Bitton, *Guide to Mormon Diaries and Autobiographies*, hereafter called *Guide* (Provo, Utah: Brigham Young University Press, 1977), has a short summary of Armstrong's journal on page 13. Black, *Members*, gives information, as well. The most useful information, however, was found in Marcia A. Jolley, "History of Pioneers John Christopher Armstrong and Mary Kirkbridge Armstrong." Mormon Biographical Sketches Collection, microfilm, LDS Church Archives.

Joining Pratt's expedition, he was assigned to the Fifth Ten and served as company bugler. He remained with the wagons at the site of Parowan while Parley's group explored the Virgin region on horseback. On the homeward journey, he joined the forward group, which was composed mostly of men with young families, arriving home in early February.

From 1852 to 1854 he served a mission to his native England, but on the way home fell ill and died in St. Louis, leaving a young family.

JOSIAH ARNOLD, CAPTAIN, FIFTH TEN[137]

With no known journal or reminiscences and no mention in any of the early church biographical volumes, little is known of the early life of Josiah Arnold, who became captain of the Fifth Ten on the Southern Exploring Expedition. But the tragic end to his life is recorded.

Genealogy records show that Arnold was born October 1, 1800, in Hoosick Falls, New York, baptized a Mormon by Orson Pratt November 12, 1837, and ordained a seventy in Nauvoo October 1, 1844, by Joseph Young. Arnold served as a policeman in Nauvoo, and reportedly prevented assassins from apprehending Joseph Smith in 1844. The Journal History of the church on March 28, 1846, mentions Josiah Arnold as being part of the exodus across Iowa, and that on January 20, 1848, he signed a petition for a post office on the Pottawattamie Indian reservation in Iowa; apparently he emigrated to Salt Lake Valley that year or the following.

He was married to Martha McDuffy, Elizabeth Bliss (four children), and Clarissa Jones. In November 1849 he was called to join the Parley P. Pratt expedition and elected captain of the Fifth Ten. When Parley's mounted group explored the Virgin River country, Arnold stayed with the wagons at Parowan and discovered limestone in the mountains to the east. He arrived home with the advance group in early February.

Other Journal History entries record, on May 7, 1850, that he left for a mission to the Society (Hawaiian) Islands, and, on December 1, 1853, that he went with Orson Hyde to establish Fort Supply. This was a fort built by the Mormons twelve miles south of Fort Bridger, Wyoming. Both forts were burned by the Mormons in 1857 to hinder the approach of the U.S. Army to Utah. A third entry, on June 22, 1854, records that Arnold was made one of the presidents of the 18th Quorum of Seventy.

The final Journal entry, August 28, 1859, concerns his death. He and Charles M. Drown, with their wives, were staying at the home of a Mr. Eddy when two or three men attempted to break in. Drown was shot while trying to hold the door and died the next day. Arnold, who had

---

137. Black, *Members*; Journal History, dates as indicated.

gone outside to protect his horses from being stolen, heard the shots and ran into the street for help. He was shot through the thigh and died September 2, 1859.

JOHN HENDERSON BANKHEAD, SECOND TEN[138]

John H. Bankhead, a member of the Second Ten, was chosen to join the Southern Exploring Expedition after close association with John Brown, the expedition's captain. Born in Rutherford County, Tennessee February 14, 1814, Bankhead was converted by Brown in 1844 and, after coming to Salt Lake Valley, became Brown's neighbor in Cottonwood.

Moving from Tennessee, Bankhead established a plantation in Alabama and there married Nancy Crosby in 1842. In 1844 he was baptized a Mormon, sold his estate, and moved to Nauvoo. Driven from there, he crossed Iowa to Winter Quarters, then in 1848 reached Salt Lake Valley in the Heber C. Kimball company.

John Bankhead. From *Our Pioneer Heritage,* vol. 2 (Salt Lake City: Daughters of Utah Pioneers, 1959), 474.

An entry in the LDS Journal History, December 24, 1949, lists him among 175 men, divided into two teams, who engaged in friendly competition to "carry on a war of extermination" of ravens, hawks, owls, wolves, foxes, and other perceived pests from the territory. Points were given for each killing—one for a raven; two for a hawk or owl; five for an eagle, mink, or polecat; ten for a wolf, fox, wildcat, or catamount; fifty for a bear or panther. According to the official set of rules, the losing team was to host a dinner for all participants and their ladies, and the most successful hunter was to receive a public vote of thanks. Thirteen men who would join the Parley P. Pratt exploration participated in the "war," including all three members of the expedition presidency—Pratt, W. W. Phelps, and David Fullmer—and John Brown, captain of fifty.

On the exploring expedition, Bankhead was part of the mounted company that explored the Virgin basin and of the mounted forward company that arrived home February 2.

---

138.   Carter, *Our Pioneer Heritage,* 2:561–62.

Other Journal History entries show, on March 10, 1852, he was in the 8th Quorum of Seventy; June 12, 1857, that he was named to a committee for the Box Elder County Deseret Agricultural and Manufacturing Society; August 1, 1863, that he headed a committee of the Cache County Agricultural Society to judge horses and cattle. A final entry, November 8, 1884, is an obituary in the *Utah Journal* reporting from Wellsville, Cache County, that he died November 1 at age seventy. It records that he lived in Utah Valley until 1860, then moved to Cache Valley. Also that he was the father of seventeen children, ten living, and twenty-one grandchildren.

ANDREW JACKSON BLODGETT, FOURTH TEN[139]

One of the youngest men to join the Southern Exploring Expedition, Andrew Blodgett was born September 11, 1827, in Monroe Center, Ashtabula, Ohio. The dates of his baptism and emigration to the Great Basin were not found, but he married Mary Lee in Salt Lake Valley in 1849, leaving her pregnant when he joined the expedition.

During the exploration he remained with the wagons in Little Salt Lake Valley. On the homeward journey, though, he rode ahead with Parley's mounted party to reach home six weeks before his young bride gave birth to their first child, Andrew, Jr., March 10, 1850.

He moved to Manti to establish a farm in 1850. By 1857 he was living in Tooele, where the Journal History on July 4 reported he was a member of the committee of arrangements for the July 4 celebration. On September 2, 1866, in Tooele he and his wife were baptized into the Reorganized LDS Church. He died in August 1883.

ISAAC BROWN, FOURTH TEN[140]

Isaac Brown was born July 28, 1818/19, in St. Clair, Minnesota, and was baptized February 2, 1846, in the Nauvoo Temple, just before the Mormons were driven from the

Isaac Brown. From Frank Ellwood Esshom, *Pioneers and Prominent Men of Utah* (Salt Lake City: Western Epics, 1966), 54.

---

139. Black, *Members*; Journal History, date as indicated.
140. Black, *Members*; Journal History, date indicated.

city. He married Hannah Jane Davies, and their first and apparently only child was born April 21, 1847.

On the Southern Exploring Expedition Brown was the subject of considerable merriment when, as John Armstrong wrote in his journal on December 2, "I set fire to a patch of grass to burn out a wolf [and] told the boys to watch the fire and see what would come out They watched the fire and presently Isaac Brown came out and they got a good laugh." Later, in Little Salt Lake Valley, Brown remained with the wagons while Parley's mounted party explored the Virgin River region. As a recent father, he was allowed to hurry home by horseback while the wagons remained snowbound near Fillmore.

His life with his wife and young son was brief; the Journal History on February 1, 1851, reports that "Isaac H. Brown who left California alone or without any company was killed by the Indians on the Muddy," apparently somewhere between Las Vegas and St. George.

John Brown, captain of fifty[141]

John Brown was captain of the Southern Exploring Expedition and discoverer of the critical pass over mountains that otherwise might have defeated the expedition. His leading role in that expedition was typical of his service to the church and territory during his seventy-seven-year lifetime.

Born October 23, 1820, in Sumner County, Tennessee, he was trained for the Baptist ministry during his youth but joined the LDS Church in 1841. He was called on a mission to the southern states in 1843 and there made many converts, most of whom he led west in 1846. Learning that Brigham Young's Pioneer Company would not reach Salt Lake Valley until the following year, Brown returned to

John Brown. Courtesy Daughters of Utah Pioneers, copy photograph by Nelson B Wadsworth.

join them, while his company of Mississippi converts spent the winter in

141. Bitton, *Guide*, 42–43; John Brown, *Autobiography*; Carter, *Our Pioneer Heritage*, 2:421–31, 458–59, 480–81, 619–20; Jenson, *Bio. Enc.*, 1:511–12; Frank Esshom, *Pioneers and Prominent Men of Utah*, hereafter called *Pio. and Pro. Men* (Salt Lake City: Utah Pioneers Book Publishing Co., 1913), 774; Whitney, *History of Utah*, 4:48.

Fort Pueblo, Colorado, before meeting the Pioneer Company in Wyoming and traveling to the valley with them. On July 21, Brown and Orson Pratt were the first pioneers to enter the valley, alternately riding a single horse to explore some ten miles before returning to report to the camp in Emigration Canyon.

Brown returned to Winter Quarters that fall, brought his family to the valley the following summer, and shortly moved with a number of his Mississippi converts to Cottonwood, building a home between Big and Little Cottonwood Creeks at about Second West. It was there that the Southern Utah Expedition assembled and elected its officers. Two of his Mississippi converts, John Bankhead and John Holladay, joined it.

On the expedition, Brown was captain of the fifty and an advance explorer. He was with the twenty-man party that rode horseback over the rim to explore the Virgin and Santa Clara regions. When heavy snows bogged down the homeward expedition near Fillmore, he joined the mounted party that rode ahead to save provisions for the men with the snowbound wagons.

Following the expedition, he was called as traveling agent for the Perpetual Emigration Fund and helped outfit thousands of converts emigrating to Salt Lake Valley. He was a member of an exploring expedition to the Salmon River in 1857, the first justice of the peace in Lehi, a missionary to England in 1860, and presided over the Southern States Mission after the Civil War. He was mayor of Pleasant Grove for ten years, bishop there twenty-nine years, was elected to the territorial legislature from Salt Lake County in 1852, and represented Utah County there from 1859 to 1878. He crossed the plains by team fifteen times.

Brown married Elizabeth Crosby May 21, 1844; Amy Snyder February 22, 1854; and Margarett Zimmerman March 2, 1857. By them he had twenty-six children, including Amy Brown Lyman, who in 1940 became the eighth general president of the Relief Society. He was ordained a patriarch in 1893 and died three years later, November 4, 1896.

William Brown, Third Ten[142]

William Brown was born in Ontario County, New York, January 3, 1816, and baptized February 5, 1843, by Archibald Montgomery. He moved that same year to Nauvoo and, with most church members, was driven out in the winter of 1845–46 to cross Iowa to Winter Quarters. He crossed the plains in Ira Eldredge's company and arrived in Salt Lake Valley September 22, 1847.

---

142.   Black, *Members*; Jenson, *Bio. Enc.*, 1:466–67.

His first wife was Phebe Narcissia Odell, whom he married in 1838 and with whom he had six children, and in 1852 he married Elizabeth Andrews.

Called to the Southern Exploring Expedition in 1849 at age thirty-three, he was assigned to the Third Ten. He accompanied Parley P. Pratt and the company that explored the Virgin River region on horseback and also rode with Parley and the group that pushed ahead to reach home in early February.

In 1851 he established a farm in Bountiful where he lived out his life except for a brief period in 1861 when he was part of the effort to establish St. George. He is reputed to have cultivated the first roses in Bountiful. In 1877 he became bishop in the newly created South Bountiful Ward and served in that position until his death October 28, 1892.

ROBERT LANG CAMPBELL, CLERK[143]

Robert Campbell, only twenty-three when he was elected secretary and clerk of the Southern Exploring Expedition, was already seasoned in the hardship and tragedy suffered by many early Mormons. His wife, Joan Scobie, whom he had married in Nauvoo in 1845, had died with her infant in childbirth a year later. The apparent cause: exposure suffered in the expulsion from Nauvoo. So Campbell was ranked with the young single men of the expedition. But his meticulously accurate and detailed journal, faithfully written day by day, often under extreme conditions, is the indispensable record of the expedition and the basis for Pratt's official report to the legislature—a report Campbell also wrote largely from his journal, but with Parley's supervision.

Robert Lang Campbell. Courtesy LDS Church Archives, copy photograph by J M. Heslop.

Campbell was born in Kilbarchan, Renfrewshire, Scotland, January 21, 1826. He joined the LDS Church in July 1842 and served as a local missionary until January 1845, when he emigrated to America. He was ordained a

143. Bitton, *Guide*, 54–55; Black, *Members*; Jenson, *Bio. Enc.*, 3:613.

seventy in Nauvoo in 1845 at age nineteen, and began immediately to engage in clerical work. He crossed the plains to Salt Lake Valley in 1848.

On the exploring expedition, he accompanied Pratt on the mounted exploration of the Virgin River basin, and on the homeward trip remained with the snowbound wagons while men with families pushed ahead on horseback.

Shortly after returning to the valley in late March, Campbell was called on a mission to Great Britain. There, in Glasgow, he met Mary Stewart and married her November 14, 1853. They emigrated to Great Salt Lake in 1854 in a company of which Campbell was captain. Robert and Mary had eleven children. In 1855, he married a third wife, Jeannie Miller, with whom he had ten children.

On November 20, he was given charge of the clerical work in the Church Historian's Office, a position he held until his death on April 11, 1872.

Campbell was much more than a clerk. He was secretary of the Deseret Agricultural and Manufacturing Society, a regent of the University of Deseret, and a member and clerk of the territorial legislature. As one of the first to promote free schools in Utah, he was elected superintendent of Salt Lake City schools and, in 1862, superintendent of schools for the Territory of Utah, a position he held until his death.

STERLING (OR STARLING) G. DRIGGS, SECOND TEN[144]

Sterling Driggs, member of the Second Ten in the Parley Pratt expedition, was born in Alleghany County, Pennsylvania, February 12, 1822. With his parents he moved to Ohio on the shore of Lake Erie, where they were baptized Mormons and settled in Kirtland. When financial and other troubles drove the Mormons from there in 1837, the family fled to Missouri and later, in 1840, to Nauvoo.

In February 1846, when mob violence drove the Mormons from

Starling G. Driggs. Courtesy LDS Church Archives, copy photograph by J M. Heslop.

144. Black, *Members; Church News,* May 28, 1955; Jenson, *Bio. Enc.,* 4:698–99.

Nauvoo, Sterling drove a wagon across the frozen Mississippi. After struggling across Iowa to the banks of the Missouri, Sterling returned to evacuate his parents, but a few days out of Nauvoo his father died as did his mother a few months later at Council Bluffs. In the spring of 1847 Driggs joined the Brigham Young Pioneer Company and arrived in the Salt Lake Valley July 22, 1847.

On the Southern Exploring Expedition of 1849–50, Driggs was among those who stayed with the wagons in Parowan Valley while Parley's mounted party explored the Virgin, and with the snowbound wagons at Fillmore on the homeward journey. At that time, he was not married. He married Sarah Rogers in 1855. They had three children.

In 1851 Driggs joined the pioneers sent under Charles C. Rich and Amasa Lyman to found a Mormon colony at San Bernardino. A freighter, he hauled many loads of lumber to ship from the port at San Pedro and made several trips across the desert to carry merchandise to Salt Lake City.

When the U.S. Army threatened invasion of Utah in 1857, outlying Mormon colonies were abandoned; Sterling and Sara with their infant daughter, Olivia, settled in Parowan. There in 1860 he was caught in a malfunctioning threshing machine. He did not recover from his injuries and died December 3, 1860.

HOMER DUNCAN, SECOND TEN[145]

Homer Duncan, member of the Second Ten in the Southern Exploring Expedition, was born in Barnet, Vermont, January 19, 1815, a great-grandson of the Revolutionary War hero General Israel Putnam. At age fifteen he heard part of the Book of Mormon read and, according to his written reminiscences, "was at once convinced of its truthfulness." He shortly had a vision that he would join the LDS Church but six years passed before he was baptized, at Adam-ondi-Ahman, in 1838.

The following year, at Far West, Missouri, he was ordained a seventy by Heber C. Kimball and left on a mission to Ontario, Canada. Here, and throughout his

Homer Duncan. Courtesy LDS Church Archives, copy photograph by J M. Heslop.

145. Bitton, *Guide*, 93; Black, *Members*; Esshom, *Pio. and Pro. Men*, 850; Jenson, *Bio. Enc.*, 1:622–27; obituary in *Deseret News*, March 23, 1906.

life, his reminiscences record, he had many visions foretelling his activities, and many experiences of faith healing.

After marrying Asenath Melvina or Malvana Banker in 1841 (ten
children), he moved to Nauvoo. On his trek to Salt Lake Valley in 1848 he
was saved from a grizzly attack by the intervention of a small dog. He
joined the Pratt expedition in 1849–50, where he was part of the
mounted group exploring the Virgin River country and of the advance
group arriving home in February.

At various times, between missions to Texas in 1855–57 (from which
he brought back 1,300 cattle) and England in 1860–61, he farmed
between Big and Little Cottonwood Creeks and ran cattle in Rush Valley.
He married Sarah Trippess in 1863 (eight children), and America Clark
in 1870. He was called in 1863 to settle St. George, then moved, in 1869,
to operate a ranch near Cedar City. During his lifetime he crossed the
plains with ox teams eleven times. In his latter years he was senior president of the Third Quorum of Seventy. He died in Salt Lake City March
23, 1906, at the age of ninety-one.

PETER DUSTIN, FOURTH TEN[146]

When he joined Parley P. Pratt's exploring expedition to southern
Utah, Peter Dustin had been a Mormon longer than any other man on
the expedition except Parley himself. In fact, he was baptized by Parley in
1831, only a year after the church was organized. At sixty-eight, he was the
second oldest man on the expedition.

Dustin was born April 19, 1781, at Grafton, New Hampshire. On
September 11, 1803, he married Azuba Tubbs. Joining the church in
1830, he was ordained an elder and a high priest October 5, 1832, by
Oliver Cowdery and served as a branch president of the Blue River
Branch, Missouri, and on the high council. Between 1832 and 1835 he
served missions in Missouri, Illinois, Indiana, and upper Canada. He
went through the Missouri persecutions, the exodus from Nauvoo to
Winter Quarters, and arrived in Salt Lake Valley by 1849.

Called to the Southern Exploring Expedition, he remained with the
wagons in Parowan Valley while Parley's mounted party explored to the
Virgin River. When teams were forced to recruit in the snow-filled
Pahvant Valley on the way home, he remained behind while Parley and
others rode home, and didn't reach his own home until the end of March
1850.

After the expedition he located in Payson in 1850. No record was
found of his death.

---

146. Black, *Members.*

EDWARD (OR EWARD) EVERETT (OR AVERETT), FIFTH TEN[147]

Edward Everett was one of the five men who joined the expedition at Manti, having arrived there just two weeks earlier to found the first settlement south of Provo. All were assigned to the expedition's Fifth Ten. His date and place of birth, his baptism as a Mormon, or the time of his emigration to Salt Lake Valley are unknown.

On the Parley P. Pratt expedition he remained with the wagons in Parowan Valley while Parley's mounted party explored the Virgin River country. The LDS Journal History, December 30, 1849, records that he was one of three men who accompanied David Haight to explore the mountains to the east, in the area of the present Cedar Breaks National Monument, where they reported great quantities of pine timber. He also stayed with the snowbound wagons near Fillmore while Parley and others pushed forward on horseback to save the company's provisions. From their camp on the Sevier River, Everett and the other Sanpete men left the homeward-bound company to return to Manti, taking with them, in view of Indian threats, the small brass cannon the company had hauled throughout their journey.

Subsequent Journal History entries hint at Everett's later life in Manti: On June 18, 1854, that he was a member of the high priest quorum; and on July 24, 1857, that he offered a toast to "the sons and daughters of Manti—May they live long on the earth to defend the rights of the priesthood, and become as numerous as the sands upon the sea shore." No record was found of his death date.

JAMES FARRER, THIRD TEN[148]

James Farrer was born in Westmoreland, England, on March 12, 1823. He was converted to Mormonism there, emigrated to Nauvoo, suffered the exodus across Iowa in 1846, and arrived in Salt Lake Valley in the fall of 1847.

On the Southern Utah Expedition, he remained with the

James Farrer. Courtesy Daughters of Utah Pioneers, copy photograph by Nelson B Wadsworth.

147. Journal History, dates as mentioned.
148. Black, *Members; Iron County Centennial, 1851–1951* (Salt Lake City: Daughters of Utah Pioneers, 1951), 42; Utah census, 1870.

wagons in Parowan Valley while the twenty of the group, on horseback, explored the Virgin River region. As a single man, he also stayed with the snowbound wagons near Fillmore while others, mostly family men, pushed ahead on horseback to arrive home earlier.

Within months of his return in late March 1850, he was called to join the George A. Smith company of pioneers to settle Parowan and establish the Iron Mission to mine and smelt the ore Farrer and others had explored west of Parowan and Cedar Valleys. From Parowan other colonies were sent throughout southern Utah, and Farrer was one of those sent to Beaver, where in the 1870 census he was listed as a farmer. He died in Beaver August 26, 1899. His wives were Phidelia Ester Dame (m. 1856) and Martha Jane McEwen.

DAVID FULLMER, SECOND COUNSELOR[149]

Joining Parley P. Pratt as second counselor on the Southern Exploring Expedition, David Fullmer was one of the older—and certainly more experienced—members of the company. An early convert to Mormonism, he had been driven with the church from Ohio to Missouri to Illinois to Winter Quarters and finally, at age forty-six, to the Great Basin.

He was a member of the important policy-making Council of Fifty, and when the Mormons were driven from Nauvoo in 1846 was appointed captain of one hundred for the struggles of the exiled church across Iowa to reach Winter Quarters. On the way he was left as a counselor to Samuel Bent in the Garden Grove (Iowa) Branch to raise grain to feed

David Fullmer. From Frank Ellwood Esshom, *Pioneers and Prominent Men of Utah* (Salt Lake City: Western Epics, 1966), 92.

the thousands of Mormons who would follow. When Bent died, he became branch president and organized missionaries to fan out to solicit help for the poor. He and his family finally reached Great Salt Lake Valley with the Willard Richards company in 1848.

Born in Chillisquaque, Northumberland, Pennsylvania, on July 7, 1803, Fullmer became a farmer and, for a short time, a schoolteacher. In

---

149. Black, *Members*; Lyndon W. Cook, *The Revelations of the Prophet Joseph Smith* (Salt Lake City: Deseret Book Co., 1985), 257; Esshom, *Pio. and Pro. Men*; Jenson, *Bio. Enc.*, 1:289–91.

September 1831 he married Rhoda Ann Marvin. They became parents to eleven children. He moved with her to Ohio in 1835, where he heard of the Mormons and was baptized September 16, 1836. He received a patriarchal blessing from Joseph Smith, Sr., became an elder in 1836, and in 1839 was ordained a high priest and appointed to the High Council in Hancock County, Missouri, from which he was expelled with other members of the church. Later he became a member of the Nauvoo City Council. As a missionary he stumped for Joseph Smith's short-lived campaign for president.

He also married Margaret Phillips (n.d.) and Sarah Sophronia Banks (m. 1845), by whom he fathered nine children. He was sealed to all three wives in January 1846 in the Nauvoo Temple.

In 1849, he was named first counselor to Daniel Spencer in the Salt Lake Stake presidency, a position he held when called to join the exploration. In Parowan Valley, when Parley and twenty horsemen left to explore the Virgin River country, Fullmer was made president of the group remaining with the wagons. He also was left behind as president of the snowbound wagon party when storms forced separation of the expedition on the way home.

Arriving home in late March 1850, he resumed his duties as first counselor in the Salt Lake Stake presidency, and served as president pro tem from 1852—56 while Daniel Spencer was on a mission. He served as a counselor ten more years after Spencer's return, until requesting release because of failing health.

During those years he became a member of the territorial legislature, treasurer pro tem of Salt Lake County and of Salt Lake City, director of the Agricultural Society, and a patriarch. He died October 21, 1879.

HIAL KILPATRICK GAY, FIRST TEN[150]

Hial K. Gay, member of the First Ten, was born in North Carolina January 12, 1826. The date and circumstances of his baptism and emigration to Salt Lake Valley are not known. In 1848 he married Elvira Jane Omen, by whom he had six children.

On the Southern Exploring Expedition he remained with the wagons in Parowan Valley while Parley Pratt and the mounted party explored the Virgin River country, and also remained with the wagons snowbound at Fillmore, finally returning home March 28.

The LDS Journal History on May 7, 1850, lists Gay among "a company of men bound for the California gold mines and also a number of missionaries called to the Society [Hawaiian] Islands" who left Great Salt Lake City that day. Whether Gay was one of the Hawaii-bound missionaries

---

150. Journal History, dates as indicated.

or among those sent to the gold fields is not clear. Hiram Clark, who joined the company en route to California wrote to Brigham Young on July 23: "We arrived on the 15th of July, all in good health and spirits, having had a good time and no accident befell us. Having acted according to your counsel, we were blessed in our traveling and got on better than any other company. We laid by on Sundays and had meetings and attended to prayers every day, while other companies traveled every day and made all the progress they could to get to the gold mines; but before we got to the foot of the mountains we had left them all behind. . . . We found that the Saints in general were in the mines, but not doing much and a very poor prospect of doing better. . . . We think that many of the boys here would give their old shoes to be back and we think it would be as well if many were back to learn 'Mormonism' from its beginning again."

Whether Gay remained in California to live out his life is not known, but he died in Red Bluff, Tehama, California, January 18, 1915.

SAMUEL GOULD, FIRST TEN[151]

Samuel Gould of the First Ten is thought to be the oldest member of the Mormon Battalion and was certainly the oldest member of the Parley P. Pratt exploring expedition.

Born August 15, 1778, in Litchfield County, Connecticut, he was an early convert to Mormonism, leaving his first family to gather with the Saints in Nauvoo. Driven from that city, he endured the winter crossing of Iowa in 1846 and, with his oldest son John, at age sixty-eight enlisted in the Mormon Battalion. He carried with him a certificate from Brigham Young authorizing him to preach the gospel and testifying to his "good moral character and his zeal for the course of righteousness." He spent

Samuel Gould. Courtesy LDS Church Archives, copy photograph by J M. Heslop.

the winter of 1846–47 with the battalion's Sick Detachment at Pueblo, Colorado, and came on to the valley of Great Salt Lake in July 1847.

Called at age seventy-one to join the Southern Exploring Expedition, he remained with the wagons in Parowan Valley while Parley explored the

---

151. *Deseret Evening News*, date indicated; Jenson, *Bio. Enc.*, 3:383–84; Journal History, dates indicated.

Virgin River region, and also stayed with the snowbound wagons while, to save provisions, the mounted group pushed ahead to Salt Lake Valley.

One wife, Sally, bore him seven children; another, Fanny Ward Lester (m. January 1, 1851), bore four; and another, Cynthia Wright, bore one. He moved with his family to southern Utah in 1861.

The *Deseret Evening News* on June 10, 1870, published a letter written from Toquerville by George A. Smith that speaks eloquently of Gould's last years and of the hazards of living in that area. He wrote of visiting several ranches that had been abandoned due to Indian hostilities. "The first of these," he wrote, "was the ranch occupied by Elder Samuel Gould, about eight miles from this about the same from Virgin City, about 2,000 feet above either place [on the Hurricane Mesa, probably on a branch of La Verkin Creek]. . . . The old gentleman, above eighty years of age, did not scruple to move his wife and a family of small children to this isolated locality where he built a house, walled in a field, put it into cultivation and herded his own stock and that of any others who dare entrust it to his care, for all knew he could not protect it from the Indians if they had a mind to take it. His friends remonstrated against his taking his family to such an exposed position, but all in vain His wife was fearful, but what did he fear, who had braved three wars in defense of his country's flag? He had fought against the corsairs of Barbary, for three years he had served in the army in the late war with Great Britain [the War of 1812], as a volunteer he had served one year in the war with Mexico, he had smelt powder and seen smoke and blood in many a hard fought battle, and why should he fear a few half naked Indians? He laughed at all remonstrances, but after the killing of Dr. Whitmore and brother McIntyre by the Navajos at the Pipe Springs, and of Robert Berry, his wife and brother at Sort Creek by about 30 Piedes, Mrs. Gould utterly refused to live at the ranch any longer. The disappointment, annoyance and worry of abandoning the ranch told heavily upon the old hero, who stuck to the ground some time after his family had left, but the infirmity of old age, which will come some time, compelled him to follow his family to Parowan, where he became paralyzed, and after lingering some time he died last winter [December 30, 1859] in the 92nd year of his age."

EPHRAIM GREEN, CAPTAIN, FOURTH TEN[152]

A veteran of the Mormon Battalion, Ephraim Green was a logical choice as a captain of ten and chief gunner in charge of the small brass cannon on the Southern Exploring Expedition. He was forty-two years old when the expedition began.

Green was born March 5, 1807, in Redman, Jefferson County, New York. He was baptized in 1839 and in the summer of 1843 went to Nauvoo

---

152. Bitton, *Guide*; Black, *Members*; obituary, *Deseret News*, October 6, 1874; Utah census, 1850 and 1860.

and met Joseph Smith and other leading men of the church before returning to New York. In 1845 he moved to Nauvoo, shortly before the Mormons were driven from that city. He left for the west with the first company in early 1846, but was assigned to stop at Garden Grove to raise crops to assist later emigrants.

While in Garden Grove he learned of the government's call for a Mormon Battalion of five hundred men to march to California to secure that area during the Mexican War. He enlisted, completed what has been described as the longest infantry march in history, and was discharged. On the way back to the Great Basin he was working at Sutter's gristmill when gold was discovered. He worked in the diggings there until 1848, then returned to Salt Lake Valley by way of the Humboldt River, helping establish the Salt Lake Cutoff of the California Trail.

On the Southern Exploring Expedition, Green accompanied Parley Pratt on the horseback exploration of the Virgin River country. Later, he was finally relieved of hauling the brass cannon when he was chosen to go with the group hurrying home on horseback, leaving the cannon behind with the snowbound wagons. On March 16, from Round Valley, the cannon and nine rounds of ammunition were sent to the infant Mormon settlement in Sanpete Valley in response to an appeal for weapons to resist an expected Indian uprising.

Green was a farmer, living the later years of his life in Rockport, a townsite now flooded by the Rockport Dam in Summit County. In 1852 and again in 1865, he was called on a mission to Hawaii. He died of inflammation of the kidneys on October 4, 1874.

ISAAC CHAUNCEY HAIGHT, CAPTAIN, FIRST TEN[153]

Isaac Haight, captain of the First Ten in the Southern Utah Expedition, was an important but tragic figure in Mormon history. An early convert to the church, he served valiantly through the persecutions, the exodus from Nauvoo to the Great Basin, during and after the Pratt expedition, and in the colonizing of southern Utah, until caught up in the Mountain Meadows massacre. His life was tragic after that, but he remained faithful to the church to the day of his death.

Haight was born into a farming family May 27, 1813, in Windham, Green County, New York. At age eighteen he joined the Baptist church and became a teacher. He was described as five feet eleven inches tall, 170 pounds, dark-complexioned with black hair. Through much of his life he was troubled by lung and other health problems.

He married Eliza Ann Snyder in 1836. They were parents of seven children. They met Mormon missionaries in Cayuga County, New York,

---

153. Bitton, *Guide;* Black, *Members;* Juanita Brooks, *The Mountain Meadows Massacre* (Norman: University of Oklahoma Press, 1985); Isaac Chauncey Haight, Journal, holograph, Huntington Library, Pasadena, California.

where he was teaching school. They were baptized in the winter of 1838 39, he was ordained an elder and immediately began service as a missionary. In 1842, they moved to Nauvoo, from where he filled a mission to New York in 1843. In Nauvoo he served on the police force and was standing guard at the temple when, at 2 A.M., he learned of Joseph Smith's martyrdom. After the exodus across Iowa, he traveled to Salt Lake Valley in Daniel Spencer's hundred of the Big Company, arriving in the fall of 1847.

Isaac Chauncy Haight. Courtesy LDS Church Archives, copy photograph by J M. Heslop.

On the Southern Exploring Expedition he kept a daily journal that, though brief, proved invaluable in tracing the geography and progress of the exploration. He remained in charge of the party with the wagons in Little Salt Lake Valley and carefully studied the area's mineral and other resources while Parley and the mounted party were exploring the Virgin River country. He acted as official clerk at that time, because Campbell accompanied the Pratt party. On the homeward trip, he went ahead with Parley's group on horseback, leaving the men with the wagons to follow later.

Within weeks of his return from this arduous trip he was called to serve a mission in Great Britain, being absent from his family 1850–53. In the fall of 1853 he was called on the Iron Mission to manage the iron works near Cedar City. He became mayor of Cedar City, a member of the territorial legislature, and postmaster. More important, he became stake president in 1854 and in this capacity directed the settlements of Hamilton Fort five miles south of Cedar City as well as Toquerville and Rockville on the upper Virgin River. He traveled through the area preaching repentance during the reformation movement of 1857.

In 1857, his life turned upside down with the massacre of California-bound emigrants by Mormons and Indians at Mountain Meadow. As presiding authority in the stake, Haight was blamed. In 1859 he asked release as stake president because of persecution and went into hiding. He was excommunicated in 1870, but even in those unhappy years continued to serve the church and southern Utah. He assisted Jacob Hamblin in the Indian mission and in aiding the John Wesley Powell exploration of the Colorado River. He helped construct the road to Lees Ferry, and helped explore the Little Colorado River area for Mormon settlement. On March 3, 1874, his church membership was restored, but he went into hiding again that year when a warrant was issued for his arrest. He was, however, never tried for any part in the massacre.

In 1882, at the intercession of Erastus Snow he was allowed to return home and worked in the St. George Temple, but in 1885 was forced to leave again because of hostility. He moved to the Mormon colonies in Mexico, then back to Thatcher, Arizona, where he died September 8, 1886. His wives, besides Eliza Ann, included Mary Murray (m. May 16, 1849); Eliza Ann Price (m. October 10, 1853, ten children were born of this union); Anabella Sinclair Macfarlane (m. October 16, 1853); and Elizabeth Summers (m. January 24, 1856).

MADISON D. HAMBLETON, FIFTH TEN[154]

Leaving behind his wife and eight children to suffer through the bitter Sanpete winter of 1849–1850, Madison Hambleton was one of the five Sanpete men who joined the Southern Exploring Expedition just two weeks after arriving at Manti to establish the first Mormon settlement south of Utah Valley. With the other four Sanpete men he joined the expedition's Fifth Ten.

Hambleton was born in Erie County, New York, on November 2, 1811. He married Chelnecha Smith on January 7, 1835. They were baptized in October 1842 and their marriage sealed in the Nauvoo Temple December 20, 1845. She had borne eight children before the exploration of the southern part of the territory.

Madison Hambleton. Courtesy LDS Church Archives, copy photograph by J M. Heslop.

On the expedition, he rode with Parley's mounted party to explore the Virgin River region, but on the journey homeward remained with the snowbound wagons at Fillmore while Parley and others pushed

---

154. Black, *Members*; Utah census, 1850.

forward on horseback to reduce the drain on the company's provisions. While the wagon company struggled to advance through deep snow near the present site of Holden, Hambleton and two other Sanpete men, John Lowry, Jr., and Gardner Potter, determined to return home to Manti. Fashioning crude snowshoes and expecting to reach home in two days, they took a few biscuits and set out on what would be a grueling and near-fatal four-day ordeal. According to Lowry's later reminiscences, Hambleton narrowly escaped death from exhaustion.

The 1850 census lists Hambleton as a carpenter in Manti, where he remained until his death May 29, 1870. He had three more marriages: to Maria Jane Davidson, Burksetta Vebue Olsen, and Clarinda Green.

Isaac Burrus (or Burres) Hatch, Fifth Ten[155]

Isaac Hatch possessed a "mineral rod" he used several times on the Southern Exploring Expedition, with limited success. He was a member of the Fifth Ten. He remained with the wagon company in Parowan Valley while Pratt's mounted party explored the Virgin River region, but on the return journey, as a family man, was assigned to ride with the forward company, leaving the snowbound wagons to follow later.

Hatch was born February 14, 1823, in Providence, Bedford County, Pennsylvania. He was converted to Mormonism in 1840 and married Mary Jane Garlick on September 10, 1845, and her sister Hannah in 1846. By the time he was called on the exploring expedition he had a child by each of his wives.

Isaac Hatch. From Irvin C. Warnock, *Our Own Sevier* (Richfield: Sevier County Commissioners, 1966), 292.

The 1850 Utah census lists him as a farmer in Salt Lake County, but he died not much later, March 25, 1853.

Henry Heath, Third Ten[156]

Henry Heath was a young man and relatively recent convert to Mormonism when he joined the Southern Exploring Expedition of

155. Black, *Members*; Utah census, 1850.
156. Black, *Members*; Journal History, March 30, 1908; obituary, *Deseret News*, March 30, 1908; Utah census, 1850 and 1870.

1849. He was born November 22, 1828, in Hanley, Staffordshire, England, and was baptized eighteen years later, November 22, 1846. Coincidentally, it was on that same date, November 22, that he left his home and traveled to the home of John Brown in Cottonwood for the organization of the exploration.

On the expedition, Heath remained with the teams and wagons in Little Salt Lake Valley while Parley P. Pratt and others on horseback explored south to the Virgin River. As a single man, he also remained with the snow-bound wagons near Fillmore while Parley and half the party rode ahead to rejoin their families early. Describing that ordeal in the snow, his obituary in the *Deseret News* on

Henry Heath. From Frank Ellwood Esshom, *Pioneers and Prominent Men of Utah* (Salt Lake City: Western Epics, 1966), 94.

March 30, 1908, said, "Mr. Heath with others had to subsist on what rabbits they could kill, while they slept in holes dug in the hardened snow, which was four feet deep and sometimes five. . . .[He] often recalled going out with long poles which were strung with jack rabbits on the return journey to camp, this kill being the only guarantee that starvation would not overtake the camp that day."

The 1850 census lists him as a farmer in Salt Lake Valley, where, on February 18, 1851, he married Sarah Ann Bird. They were parents of twelve children. He was among six former expedition veterans and their families called to help colonize on the Virgin River, but the 1870 census listed him as a miner in Salt Lake Valley. He died in Salt Lake City April 4, 1908, at age eighty-one.

WILLIAM HENRIE, FOURTH TEN[157]

At age fifty, William Henrie was one of the older members of the Parley P. Pratt exploring expedition of 1849, and among the most experienced. He had been a scout and hunter with Brigham Young's Pioneer Company in 1847, and after arrival in Salt Lake Valley had joined Parley in exploring Utah, Cedar, and Tooele valleys.

---

157.   Black, *Members*; Callie Olsen Morley, "History of William and Myra Mayall Henrie: Pioneers of 1847 and 1848," typescript in possession of editors; Carter, *Our Pioneer Heritage*, 2:534–35; Jenson, *Bio. Enc.*, 4:707.

Henrie was born in Marietta, Greene County, Pennsylvania, September 11, 1799. After the death of his father he moved to Ohio, where he married Myra Mayall on November 16, 1823, settled on a large tract of land, established a horse ranch, and erected a sawmill and gristmill. Myra bore seven children in Ohio, five of whom lived to adulthood. He had previously been married to Mary Dade, who may have died soon after the marriage.

They learned of the Mormons from Pratt, were baptized July 17, 1842, sold out their holdings in Ohio and moved to Nauvoo. There they bought a farm from Joseph Smith and became his close friends. Family tradition holds that Joseph, on the way to his martyrdom in Carthage, borrowed one of Henrie's horses.

William Henrie. Courtesy LDS Church Archives, copy photograph by J M. Heslop.

Driven from Nauvoo, the Henries endured the wintertime struggle across Iowa in 1846 to Winter Quarters on the Missouri River. Brigham Young asked Henrie to act as bishop for families of Mormon Battalion members. Leaving Myra and the family to suffer another year at Winter Quarters, William joined the Pioneer Company to Salt Lake Valley, arriving July 22, 1847. He aided in settling the emigrants into the old fort and in April 1849 was a speaker at the old bowery in Salt Lake City. Called to join the Southern Exploring Expedition, Henrie provided an ox team and wagon, with which he remained in Parowan Valley while Parley and others explored the Virgin River country. He also remained with his wagon in deep snows near Fillmore as Parley and half the group rode ahead on horseback. Many oxen died during the struggle homeward; On March 17 on the Sevier River Henrie left his failing ox as a gift to hungry Indians.

Henrie settled in Bountiful where he successfully operated a sawmill. In 1865 he was called to establish the Mormon colony at Panaca on the Muddy River in Nevada. Now sixty-six years old and weary of pioneering, he declined the call. Myra and her grown sons went, however, and she became first Relief Society president in Panaca. In 1871 a survey determined the area was in Nevada, which tried to collect six years of back taxes. With Brigham Young's approval, Myra and her sons moved to Panguitch, where Myra taught school and became the first Relief Society president. The town of Henrieville in Kane County was named for the brothers, who ranched there.

William died December 18, 1883, in Bountiful, willing his remaining property to the church.

Sylvester Hewlitt (or Hulet), Fifth Ten[158]

Sylvester Hewlitt was one of the five men who had established the tiny settlement of Manti and just two weeks later joined the Parley P. Pratt exploration. With his team and wagon he remained in Parowan Valley while Pratt and others explored south to the Virgin River on horseback. The Journal History reported that Hewlitt and William Wadsworth on December 30 "went up into the mountains and found very rich iron ore in abundance, and also waterlime and gypsum. The mountains appeared rich with minerals." He also remained with the snowbound wagons at Fillmore, then, after an exhausting struggle through the snow to the Sevier River, left the expedition to return home to Sanpete Valley. He reached there in early March 1850, and on May 7 that year, left on a mission to the Hawaiian Islands.

A Sylvester Hulet, who may be the same man, was born in 1800, in Berkshire, Maine. He married (Mrs.) Christain Whitmer, probably early. No other information is available about that marriage. He married Catherine Stoker and they had a child April 17, 1857, in Springville. He died in 1883 in Manti.

John Daniel Holladay, Second Ten[159]

John D. Holladay was born in Marion County, Alabama, June 22, 1826, the son of John Holladay, first and longtime bishop of Holladay, Utah, to which he gave his name. The family joined the LDS Church in 1844 when John D. was eighteen; shortly after, he went to Nauvoo to work on the temple.

On the trek to Salt Lake Valley in 1848 the young man frequently tied his horse to the wagon being driven by Mahalia Ann Rebecca Mathews and climbed on the seat beside her. The courtship was successful; soon after arrival in the valley, they were married by the light of a campfire in Holladay.

Called to the Southern Exploring Expedition, young Holladay accompanied Parley P. Pratt on the horseback exploration of the Virgin River country. With a young wife waiting at home, he was also privileged to ride home early when the wagons were bogged down in the snow near Fillmore.

In 1851, Holladay was called to accompany Amasa Lyman and Charles C. Rich to establish a Mormon colony at San Bernardino, where

---

158.   Black, *Members*; International Genealogical Index; Journal History, dates indicated.
159.   Carter, *Our Pioneer Heritage*, 2:471–72; obituary, *Deseret News*, September 16, 1909.

he served as county sheriff and city marshal. When that settlement was abandoned at the outset of the Utah War in 1857, he established a farm in Santaquin, where he was presiding elder until a ward was organized. He served as captain of militia in the Black Hawk war, as a Utah County deputy sheriff, as a guard at the state penitentiary from 1876—80, and as an overseer during construction of the Utah Central Railroad. He was one of the first missionaries to the southern states after the Civil War.

His first wife, Mahalia, bore him twelve children, his second wife, Johannah Blake, seven. He died September 16, 1909.

John D. Holladay. Courtesy Daughters of Utah Pioneers, copy photograph by Nelson B Wadsworth.

CHARLES A. HOPKINS, FOURTH TEN[160]

Charles Hopkins was born February 20, 1810, in Burlington, New Jersey. He was converted to Mormonism in 1844 and moved to Nauvoo, where he received his temple endowments January 28, 1846, days before the Mormons were driven from that city. On the westward exodus he joined the Mormon Battalion and marched to San Diego before returning to join the body of the church in Salt Lake Valley.

Called to join the Parley P. Pratt exploration of southern Utah, he rode with Pratt to explore the Virgin River region. When the teams and wagons bogged down in the snow near Fillmore, he joined the mounted party that rode ahead.

Charles Hopkins. Courtesy LDS Church Archives, copy photograph by J M. Heslop.

160. Black, *Members*; Carter, *Our Pioneer Heritage*, 2:172–73; Utah census, 1860.

In 1851 he settled in Lehi, where he and others built a toll bridge across the Jordan River. On October 11, 1852, he married Mary Ann Webber Edds. He joined the Iron Mission in Cedar City 1855–59, then in 1860 established a farm in Fillmore, where he died October 12, 1863.

JOSEPH HORNE, CAPTAIN, THIRD TEN[161]

Joseph Horne was well known to Parley P. Pratt, having been one of his early converts. He was also well equipped to serve as captain of the Third Ten of Pratt's Southern Utah Expedition, having suffered through the persecutions in Missouri and Nauvoo and having been one of four men who explored Sanpete Valley to establish the first Mormon settlement south of Utah Valley. His part in the exploration of southern Utah was impressive enough that he was later twice called to pioneer settlements there.

Joseph Horne. Courtesy Daughters of Utah Pioneers, copy photograph by Nelson B Wadsworth.

Horne was born in London January 17, 1812. At age six he emigrated with his parents to Canada and settled in Toronto, known then as Little New York. There, he married Mary Isabella Hales, May 9, 1836. They were parents of fifteen children. In that year, Parley P. Pratt came as a Mormon missionary to Toronto and made a number of converts, including the young newlyweds and also John Taylor, later to become third president of the church. In 1837 Joseph Smith visited them in Toronto, and the following year they moved to Far West, Missouri.

From that point, their history became much like that of the church itself, suffering through the Missouri mobbings, driven to Quincy, Illinois, and helping build Nauvoo. In that city Horne engaged in the mercantile business until being driven out in February 1861 in the first company of Mormons to start west. Mary delivered their fourth child during the struggle across Iowa. After a winter at Winter Quarters, he brought his family to the Salt Lake Valley, serving as captain of the First Fifty in the Edward Hunter company and arriving October 6, 1847.

---

161. Bitton, *Guide*, 163; Black, *Members*; Esshom, *Pio. and Pro. Men*, 942; Joseph Horne, "Reminiscences and Diary, 1858–1861," LDS Church Archives; Jenson, *Bio. Enc.*, 1:806–7.

In August 1849, after Ute Chief Walker invited the Mormons to settle Sanpete Valley, Brigham Young sent Horne, W. W. Phelps, Dimick Huntington, and Ira Willes with Walker to explore the area. Phelps, Willes, and Horne climbed Mount Nebo and from its summit sketched the surrounding territory. They located the site of Manti for settlement, which followed within four months.

Horne was then called to accompany Pratt's exploration of central and southern Utah for settlement sites, and was elected captain of the Third Ten. As the owner and driver of one of the expedition's twelve wagons, he did not accompany Pratt's mounted party exploring the Virgin River basin, but stayed behind to explore the minerals and other resources of Parowan Valley. On the homeward journey he rode ahead with the advance company, arriving February 2.

That fall, he was called to accompany George A. Smith to develop the iron ore he and others had discovered. The first settlement was Parowan, where Horne and the wagon company had camped, and where he returned and built the first log cabin. Returning to Salt Lake Valley in 1854, he became a building supervisor on the temple block until 1858, when Brigham called him to take charge of a company of men to establish a cotton farm on the Virgin. In the meantime, in 1855 he married Mary Park Shepherd, who added ten children to his family. After two years of cotton farming, he was sent in 1861 and 1862 in charge of men and teams to bring emigrants from the Missouri river.

In later years he served on the Salt Lake City council, six years as justice of the peace, four years as keeper of the city pound, several years as city watermaster and school trustee. He served seventeen years on the Salt Lake Stake high council before being ordained a patriarch in 1890. He died in Salt Lake City on April 27, 1897.

DIMICK BAKER HUNTINGTON, INTERPRETER, FIFTH TEN[162]

With his knowledge of several Indian tongues and his hardiness and resourcefulness proven in his role as a rescuer in the Missouri persecutions and as a member of the Mormon Battalion, Dimick Huntington was one of the most valuable members of the Southern Exploring Expedition.

Born in Watertown, Jefferson County, New York, May 25, 1808, he married Fanny Maria Allen in 1830, by whom he had seven children. In 1835 they joined the LDS Church and moved to Kirtland, Ohio, and then to Far West, Missouri. The LDS Journal History on November 1, 1838, records that after the battle of Crooked River and Governor Lilburn Boggs's extermination order, Hyrum Smith instructed Huntington:

---

162. Bitton, *Guide*, 167; Black, *Members*; Jenson, *Bio. Enc.*, 4:748–49; Journal History, many entries.

"Gather all the Crooked River boys you can and take them out of the state, for, if found, they will be shot down like dogs." Huntington's account of the group's five-day flight across Missouri to Nauvoo, through snow and mud and without food, is a classic account of the suffering of those times.

In Nauvoo, Huntington became a coroner, constable, drum major in the Nauvoo Legion band, and body-guard for Joseph Smith. He was one of the men arrested for destroying the *Nauvoo Expositor*, and after Joseph and Hyrum Smith were killed as a conse-quence of that action he helped dress their bodies, bury them in the basement of the Nauvoo House and later rebury them at the Mansion House.

Dimick B. Huntington. From Frank Ellwood Esshom, *Pioneers and Prominent Men of Utah* (Salt Lake City: Western Epics, 1966), 71.

Following expulsion from Nauvoo, he joined the Mormon Battalion, spent the winter of 1846–1847 with the Sick Detachment at Pueblo, Colorado, and came on to Salt Lake Valley in July 1847. In the spring of 1849 he became one of the first settlers at Fort Provo, Utah Valley. On the Parley P. Pratt exploration of 1849–1850, he was usually at Parley's side acting as interpreter. Following the expedition he became Indian interpreter for Brigham Young and was ordained as patriarch to the Indians, who loved and respected him and called him "father." After the massacre of Captain Gunnison and his men on the Sevier River in 1853 he was sent to recover the party's papers and property and bury the remains. For years, "Dimick's Band," the fife and drum group he organized, was a principal feature of fourth and twenty-fourth of July celebrations in Salt Lake City.

His last words before his death February 1, 1879, were, "I am dying by inches, but I am not afraid to die, for I have been an honest man."

SCHUYLER JENNINGS, SECOND TEN[163]

Little is known of Schuyler Jennings, either before or after his par-ticipation in the Southern Exploring Expedition. He was born June 5, 1809, in Memphis, Tennessee, and married Polly Barnett. The date of his baptism and of coming to Salt Lake Valley could not be found.

---

163. Robert Lang Campbell, Journal, December 25 and December 26, 1849, LDS Church Archives; Fish, "The Southern Utah Expedition."

On the exploring expedition, his quick temper and threats of violence during the ordeal of crossing the mountains from the Sevier River to Little Salt Lake Valley resulted in a "furlough" and an early trip home.

After the expedition, Jennings settled in Utah Valley, and later established a farm in Levan, Juab County, where he died June 14, 1876.

DAN JONES, FIRST TEN[164]

Diminutive in stature but a powerful speaker, Dan Jones was one of the most effective missionaries and colorful characters in the early days of the LDS Church.

Born in Flintshire, Wales, August 4, 1811, he came to America in 1840 and soon began operating a steamer, the *Maid of Iowa*, on the Mississippi River. Here, in Nauvoo, he met Joseph Smith and early in 1843 joined the church. Joseph bought a half-interest in the *Maid of Iowa*, and Jones captained it as a ferry between Nauvoo and Montrose, Iowa.

Jones accompanied Joseph to Carthage Jail, spent the night with him and was assured by Joseph that "You will yet see Wales and fulfill

Dan Jones. Courtesy LDS Church Archives, copy photograph by J M. Heslop.

the mission appointed you before you die." Jones heard members of the militia plotting to kill Joseph, reported the plot to Governor Ford and, unsuccessfully, asked for protection. He was refused reentry to the jail and so was spared the attack that killed Joseph and his brother Hyrum. Shortly after, as Joseph promised, he left on a mission to his native Wales and there, with others, baptized some two thousand converts, including the ancestors of the future president of the church, David O. McKay. He brought 249 of his converts to Salt Lake Valley.

He married Jane Melling, who delivered a baby February 8, 1849; Elizabeth Lewis in 1849, who gave birth to seven children; and Mary Matilda Letrill.

Jones was called to the Southern Exploring Expedition in part because of the legend that there might be Welsh-speaking Indians in the area. On November 29, he received a blessing of health from Robert L.

---

164. Bitton, *Guide*, 185; Black, *Members*; Jenson, *Bio. Enc.*, 3:658–60.

Campbell, who promised him that, notwithstanding his injured lungs, "he would be able to roar like a lion in the congregations of this world in preaching this Gospel." He did, indeed, serve another mission to Wales, 1852–1856, this time bringing seven hundred converts back to Salt Lake Valley.

Following the expedition, Jones was called to join the infant colony at Manti, where he ran a threshing machine and was elected mayor. After his Wales mission, early in 1857, he began navigating the Great Salt Lake in the *Timely Gull,* a small boat built by Brigham Young. It was the first freight-carrying boat on the lake.

In the late 1850s Jones moved to Provo, where he died January 3, 1861.

ALEXANDER ABRAHAM LEMON, THIRD TEN[165]

Alexander Lemon. Andrew Jenson, *Latter-day Saint Biographical Encyclopedia,* vol. 1 (Salt Lake City, Utah: Western Epics, 1971), 435.

At age eighteen, Alexander Lemon was the youngest member of the Parley P. Pratt exploring company of 1849, but, even before his baptism as a Mormon, had already had the experience of driving an ox team across the plains.

Lemon was born in Tippecanoe County, Indiana, March 1, 1831. In 1846, his father's cousin told the family about the Book of Mormon. His father read it, believed, and rose from a sickbed to ride 250 miles to Nauvoo to learn more. The city had largely been evacuated by the fleeing Mormons, but the senior Lemon was baptized there. He returned to his family, sold his farm, and started west by way of Nauvoo. After spending the winter at Winter Quarters, they crossed the plains in the Perrigrine Sessions company of fifty. The father drove one ox team, sixteen-year-old Alexander another, and a sister drove sixteen head of loose cattle. Alexander was baptized in City Creek on July 1, 1848, by John Young and confirmed by Jedediah M. Grant.

---

165.   Black, *Members*; Jenson, *Bio. Enc.*, 1:435–36. Alexander Lemon, "A History and Genealogy of Alexander Abraham Lemon," typescript, LDS Church Archives.

Called to the Pratt exploring expedition, Lemon served in the Third Ten. He remained with the wagons in Little Salt Lake Valley while Parley's mounted party explored south to the Virgin River, and, as a single man, remained with the snowbound wagons near Fillmore.

In 1856 he was sent to strengthen the infant Mormon colony at Las Vegas, Nevada. When, in 1857, those settlers were called home to face the approach of Johnston's Army, Lemon returned with them and spent much of the following winter in Echo Canyon manning fortifications built to block the army's path.

In 1862 he married Ann Eubry and moved to Paradise, Cache County, where his wife bore three sons and six daughters. He was ordained a high priest in 1890, and died May 14, 1902..

JOHN LOWRY, JR., FIFTH TEN[166]

John Lowry, Jr., was one of the five men who joined the expedition in the newly established settlement at Manti. At age twenty-one he had moved there with his father, who became bishop of the Manti Ward shortly after its establishment. John, Jr., traveled farther on the Southern Exploring Expedition than any other member, completing a hazardous five-day journey from Scipio Valley to his home in Manti, returning to rejoin the expedition on the Sevier River with a message asking for any provisions and weapons the expedition could spare, finally taking the expedition's small cannon and some gunpowder back to Manti.

John Lowry. Courtesy LDS Church Archives, copy photograph by J M. Heslop.

John, Jr., was born on January 31, 1829, in Lewis County, Missouri. The family was baptized Mormons in 1833 and joined the body of the church in Jackson County, Missouri. They went through the Missouri persecutions and were driven to settle in Nauvoo. There John, Jr., worked on the temple and, at age fifteen, served in the Nauvoo Legion. They left Nauvoo in August 1846 for Winter Quarters, then went to Salt Lake Valley in the John Taylor company, arriving in September 1847.

John, Sr., was called to join the Sanpete pioneer settlement that reached the site of Manti in November. Two weeks later, Parley P. Pratt arrived with his exploring party, and John, Jr., was one of the five men

166. Anderson, "Sketch of the Life of John Lowry, Jr."; Jenson, *Bio. Enc.*, 4:623.

who volunteered to join them. His account of assisting two older men over the snow-choked mountains to Manti is a harrowing tale of starvation and near-death by freezing.

In Manti, where his father was the bishop, John, Jr., built homes for his first wife, Sarah Jane Brown, who ultimately bore him nine children, and for his second wife Mary Allen, who bore six. He was called in 1855 to join the Elk Mountain Mission to settle the Moab area, but Indians killed three members of that settlement, and it was abandoned. In 1856, either he or his father ignited the spark that touched off the Black Hawk War when he beat a Ute Indian in a dispute over a horse. During the war John, Jr., became an interpreter and carrier of messages between Brigham Young and the Indians. He won the confidence of the Ute chief Arapeen, who on one occasion saved his life when a message he delivered from Brigham angered the Indians to the point of killing him.

During his Manti years, he operated a gristmill and merchandise business, and served two terms in the Utah legislature. In 1906 he moved to Springville and established the Springville Canning Company. He was ordained a patriarch in 1911 and served in that capacity until his death November 7, 1915.

GEORGE BRINTON MATSON, SR., FIRST TEN[167]

George B. Matson was born October 26, 1827, in Centerville, New Castle County, Delaware, and was baptized June 20, 1843. He became a brick mason and helped build many of the early homes in Salt Lake City as well as the first State House in Fillmore.

Driven with the Saints from Nauvoo, he came to Salt Lake Valley in the A. O. Smoot company, arriving in September 1847. Called to join the Parley P. Pratt exploring expedition in 1849, he rode with Parley's mounted company to the Virgin River. On the homeward journey, as a single man he remained with the wagons while family men rode the strongest mules and horses to reach home earlier. Later he assisted in building the State House in Fillmore. In 1856 he

George B. Matson. Courtesy Daughters of Utah Pioneers, copy photograph by Nelson Wadsworth.

---

167.   Black, *Members*; Don Carlos Johnson, *A Brief History of Springville, Utah* (Springville: n.p., 1900).

joined the arduous and dangerous relief mission to rescue the Willie and Martin handcart companies from the blizzard-swept high country of Wyoming. In 1857 he helped build Camp Floyd, and in 1864 drove an ox team to the Missouri River to bring freight back to Salt Lake City.

He settled in Fountain Green in 1865, Moroni in 1866, and finally Springville in 1867, where he was elected city councilman. Beginning in 1898 he served a mission to Philadelphia. He died in Provo on Christmas Day 1912.

JOSEPH MATTHEWS, CAPTAIN, SECOND TEN[168]

Joseph Matthews, chosen captain of the Second Ten, came well prepared for that responsibility. He had served as captain of the Fourteenth Ten and as a scout and hunter with Brigham Young's Pioneer Company of 1847 and entered Salt Lake Valley on July 22 with the main body of pioneers. He won Brigham's confidence. Nearing the Rocky Mountains, Brigham one day gazed through his binoculars at a distant hill and remarked, "Do you see that antelope over there?" One man answered that he did, but Matthews responded, "No, and neither do you for there aren't any antelope over there." Brigham agreed: "Brother Matthews has to see a thing. He would not see that antelope just to please me. I find his reports and judgment are always good."

Matthews was born in Johnson County, North Carolina, January 29, 1809. He married Rhoda Carroll in 1832 and moved to Neshoba County, Mississippi, and there, in 1843, joined the LDS Church. In 1845 he moved with his wife and three children to Nauvoo, where he worked on the temple, and filled missions to the eastern states. In 1846, he was driven with the Saints from that city and struggled across Iowa to Winter Quarters on the Missouri River. Like most of the Pioneer Company, he left his little family there to join the trek to the Great Basin.

On the Southern Exploring Expedition, one of the men in Matthews's ten was Schuyler Jennings, whose quick temper won him an early trip home after the company reached Parowan Valley. As Jennings's captain, Matthews was assigned to accompany him, carrying letters to Brigham and to the explorers' families.

In 1851, Matthews was called to join Charles C. Rich and Amasa M. Lyman to establish a Mormon colony at San Bernardino. He remained there until the settlement was abandoned in 1857, then built a farm in Santaquin. His second wife, Polly Boss, was a midwife and frontier doctor. They became parents of eight children. He married a third wife, Martha Jane Potter, in 1865. Their union produced four children. After a mission to the southern states, he was called in 1880 to Arizona, where he died May 14, 1886.

---

168. Black, *Members*; Carter, *Our Pioneer Heritage*, 2:627–28; Jenson, *Bio Enc.*, 4:713.

WILLIAM MATTHEWS, SECOND TEN[169]

William Matthews was born in South Carolina in 1807 and was one of the converts who was a close associate with John Brown in the company that became known as the Mississippi Saints. In 1845, he and other southern converts worked on the Nauvoo Temple in the last stages of its construction. They then returned home to gather their families for the trek to the Rocky Mountains in 1846. Learning that Brigham Young's Pioneer Company would not cross the mountains that year, they wintered with members of the Mormon Battalion Sick Detachment at Pueblo, Colorado, then journeyed to Salt Lake Valley with or just behind the Pioneer Company in 1847.

William Mathews. Frank Ellwood Esshom, *Pioneers and Prominent Men of Utah* (Salt Lake City: Western Epics, 1966), 435.

Called to the Parley P. Pratt exploring expedition in 1849, he became captain of the Second Ten in Little Salt Lake Valley when Joseph Matthews, the original captain, was sent home with Schuyler Jennings after Jennings swore and threatened violence during the arduous mountain crossing from the Sevier River. Matthews remained with the wagons in Little Salt Lake Valley while Parley and a mounted party explored south to the Virgin. He also remained with the snowbound wagons near Fillmore.

After the expedition he and his family moved to Utah County. The 1850 census lists him as a farmer there. Little else is known about him.

GEORGE NEBEKER, THIRD TEN[170]

George Nebeker was a young man of twenty-two and a fairly new convert to Mormonism when he joined the Southern Exploring Expedition. But his life following the expedition was long and especially

169. Black, *Members*, lists several William Matthewses, only one of which possibly matches the William who accompanied Parley P. Pratt. He was born January 28, 1808, in Sanford, Monroe County, Mississippi, and died November 27, 1888, in Washington County, Utah. He married three times: to Elizabeth Adeline Henderson (eleven children), Elizabeth Eleanor Brown, and Sarah Ann Smith. He had lived in Nauvoo. The information given in the text comes from Fish, "The Southern Utah Expedition," whose main source is the Utah census of 1850.

170. Black, *Members*; Jenson, *Bio. Enc.*, 1:682–83; Whitney, *History of Utah*, 4:111–12; obituary, *Deseret News*, December 3, 1886.

productive, and he was one of the last surviving members of the expedition. Born at Stanton, New Castle County, Delaware, January 22, 1827, he joined the church in 1846 and suffered through the winter of 1846–47 at Winter Quarters. He arrived in Salt Lake Valley in September 1849. On the Pratt expedition, he stayed with the teams and wagons in Parowan Valley and, as a single man, also stayed with the snowbound wagons near Fillmore.

Shortly after his return, he married Elizabeth Dilworth, who bore him eleven children. In 1863 he married Maria Leonard, by whom he had six children.

Much of his life was spent in missionary service. He was called to the Elk Mountain Mission in 1855, an effort to colonize the Moab area

George Nebeker. Courtesy Daughters of Utah Pioneers, copy photograph by Nelson B Wadsworth.

on the Colorado River; it was cut short by the Indian killing of three of the missionaries. In 1856 he was called to colonize the Carson Valley in Nevada; that ended with the approach of the U.S. Army to occupy Utah. Other missions followed, the most notable being thirteen years spent building the church in the Hawaiian Islands, much of it as mission president. During that time he purchased for the church for $14,000 property on the eastern side of Oahu, where he established a sugar plantation and a gathering place for native converts. Brigham Young University Hawaii and the LDS Polynesian Cultural Center now occupy part of the site.

Nebeker's last major effort was building the Utah and Salt Lake Canal Company, which brought thousands of acres of land under cultivation in those two counties. He died December 1, 1886.

JONATHON TAYLOR PACKER, FIFTH TEN[171]

Jonathan Packer was born in Perry, Richland County, Ohio, July 26, 1817. He was baptized a Mormon in Ohio March 10, 1835, and moved to Missouri, where he married Sarah Ewell May 14, 1837. She bore a child in 1838 and died in Hancock, Illinois, in 1839 after suffering the wintertime expulsion of the Mormons from Missouri. In 1840, Packer married

---

171. Black, *Members*; Utah census, 1850 and 1870.

Angelina Avilda Chaplan in Nauvoo. They had nine children. He married two more wives, Christiana Petrene Sunby in 1857 (five children), and Helen Linquist in 1872.

On the Southern Exploring Expedition, he remained with his team and wagon in Parowan Valley while the mounted party explored the Virgin River region. As a family man with four children, he was assigned to the group that hurried home on horseback to conserve the provisions of the group remaining with the snowbound wagons near Fillmore.

The 1850 Utah census lists him as a farmer in Salt Lake City. Later, he established a farm in Box Elder County, and still later was called to help establish a Mormon colony on the Gila River in Arizona. He died there, in Safford, January 26 or 29, 1889.

WILLIAM WINES PHELPS, FIRST COUNSELOR[172]

From his conversion in 1831 to his death in 1872, W. W. Phelps contributed importantly and in various ways to the progress of the Mormon Church, both before and after his call as first counselor to Parley P. Pratt on the Southern Exploring Expedition.

Born February 17, 1792, in Hanover, Morris County, New Jersey, he married Sally Waterman April 28, 1815, and became a printer, newspaper editor, and candidate for lieutenant governor of New York. In his fortieth year, he learned of and read the Book of Mormon, was convinced of its truth, and sought out Joseph Smith in Kirtland, Ohio. After their meet-

W. W. Phelps. Courtesy LDS Church Archives, copy photograph by J M. Heslop.

ing, in June 1831, Joseph received a revelation, section 55 of the Doctrine and Covenants, instructing that Phelps was to preach and baptize, but, more specifically, that he was to be involved in selecting, writing, and printing books for the church. He was baptized shortly after.

Following instructions, Phelps became a printer in Independence, Missouri, and a member of the local church leadership there. He

---

172. Black, *Members*; Esshom, *Pio. and Pro. Men*, 1104; Cook, *The Revelations of the Prophet Joseph Smith;* Jenson, *Bio. Enc.*, 3:692–97; Journal History, many entries.

founded the monthly *Evening and Morning Star* in Jackson County, assisted Emma Smith in compiling and publishing the first Mormon book of hymns, and helped publish the Doctrine and Covenants. During that time he was also a major target of persecution, and wrote and delivered various petitions to civil authorities for relief, and offered himself as a sacrifice for the church.

Between 1825–36 in Kirtland and 1841–44 in Nauvoo he acted as scribe and speech writer for Joseph Smith. He was an influence in the meeting that rejected Sydney Rigdon and accepted Brigham Young as leader of the church after the martyrdom of Joseph Smith. He wrote the lyrics of many well-known Mormon hymns. Section 55 of the Doctrine and Covenants is addressed to Phelps. Joseph Smith wrote, "While we were preparing for our journey to Missouri, William W. Phelps and his family arrived among us—'to do the will of the Lord,' he said: so I inquired of the Lord concerning him and received [section 55]."

Following the exodus from Nauvoo to the Great Basin, he secured the press and type for the area's first newspaper, the *Deseret News*, stayed active in governmental matters, taught school, was a member of the first board of regents of what became the University of Utah, helped draft the territory's first constitution, and was seven times elected to the legislature. He published the *Deseret Almanac* from 1851 to 1857 and associated with the Deseret Horticultural Society, the Deseret Theological Institute, and other civic and church activities. In 1859 and 1864 he served as chaplain in the Utah legislature and for several years acted as a notary public.

Greek, Latin, Hebrew, the classics, world history, geography, and the law were all part of his training as well as topographical engineering, the latter of which served well for the expedition of 1849. In August 1849, guided by Ute Chief Walker, who had urged Brigham Young to establish a Mormon settlement in Sanpete Valley, Phelps led a group including Joseph Horne, Ira Willes, and D. B. Huntington to explore the area. On that occasion he climbed Mount Nebo and from its summit made a drawing showing the Sanpete Valley and the surrounding country. Shortly after, he was called to join Parley P. Pratt to explore much of the rest of Utah. On the journey he made astronomical observations of latitude and longitude and frequently was sent ahead to break trail through the snow. He rode with the mounted company to explore the Virgin River region and with the party that left the snowbound wagons near Fillmore and rode ahead.

In addition to his first wife, Stella Waterman, whom he married in 1815 (eleven children), Phelps married Laura Stowell, Elizabeth Dunn, Mary Jones, Sarah Betsy Gleason, and Harriet Schreder. He died March 7, 1872, at his home in Salt Lake City.

GARDNER G. POTTER, FIFTH TEN[173]

Gardner Potter was one of the five men who joined the Southern Expedition just two weeks after he and others had arrived in Sanpete Valley to establish a settlement at Manti. Susan Easton Black's *Early LDS Membership* records his birth as 1820, with a marriage to Emily Allen, undated, and one to Eveline Maria in December 1844. Her study has him arriving in Salt Lake valley in December 1848.

On the exploring expedition, he rode with Parley P. Pratt's mounted exploration of the Virgin River basin, but on the homeward journey remained with the wagons snowbound near Fillmore. After struggling with the wagons as far as the Sevier River, he with John

Gardner G. Potter. Frank Ellwood Esshom, *Pioneers and Prominent Men of Utah* (Salt Lake City: Western Epics, 1966), 173.

Lowry and Madison Hambleton struck out for their homes in Sanpete Valley, crossing the mountains on crudely improvised snowshoes in a harrowing five-day journey that almost cost their lives.

Following the expedition, Potter settled in Springville, where he died March 14, 1897.

PARLEY PARKER PRATT, PRESIDENT[174]

At age forty-two, Parley P. Pratt was well prepared to lead a strenuous and hazardous exploration to Southern Utah. His loyalty to Brigham Young had been sorely tried on the Mormon trek westward. Between Nauvoo and Winter Quarters Brigham lashed out at Parley and others by letter and in person. In his *Autobiography* (pp. 306–7) Parley wrote, "The president then reproved us and chastened us severely for several things. . . . He said there was manifestly a spirit of dissension and of insubordination manifested in our movements. I could not realize this at the time, and protested that in my own heart, so far as I was concerned, I had no such

173. Black, *Members*; Utah census, 1850.
174. Bitton, *Guide*, 282; Black, *Members*; Cook, *The Revelations of the Prophet Joseph Smith*; Esshom, *Pio. and Pro. Men*, 1113; Jenson, *Bio. Enc.*, 1:83–85; Whitney, *History of Utah*, 4:73–79. Much of this information comes from Pratt, *Autobiography*. Numerous other books chronicle the achievements of Pratt: for a complete list, look under the subject Parley P. Pratt in the database at the LDS Church Historical Department.

motive. . . . However, the sequence soon proved that it was the true Spirit which reproved and chastened us. . . . And here I would observe that, although my own motives were pure, so far as I could know in my own heart, yet I thank God for this timely chastisement; I profited by it, and it caused me to be more watchful and careful ever after."

This experience perhaps explains Pratt's leadership style on the Southern Exploring Expedition of 1849. He assembled a company of extraordinary men of diverse ages, temperaments, and talents. He kneaded them into a group that rose above dire challenges, although he sometimes worried about the attitudes of the men. He himself tackled the hardest tasks, even when he was desperately ill.

Parley P. Pratt. Courtesy LDS Church Archives, copy photograph by J M. Heslop.

This commitment began when, in 1830, he found in the infant Church of Jesus Christ of Latter-day Saints the simplicity and authority he deemed important to the true church. He had been born April 12, 1807, in Burlington, Oswego County, New York, and in 1827 had married Thankful Halsey. Although they owned a thriving farm, through his scripture study Parley felt "constrained," as he put it, to become a traveling preacher, and embarked on the first of many travels he would make in the name of religion. While thus engaged he was introduced to the Book of Mormon, was converted, sought to meet Joseph Smith and, in his absence, was baptized by Joseph's brother Hyrum.

During his lifetime, Parley went on numerous missions for the church: to the American Indians in Missouri, to Illinois, to Canada, to New York, to the eastern states, to England, to California, to Chile to open missionary work in South America, to the Pacific Islands, to Virginia, and to Arkansas.

He participated in Zion's Camp, a semi-military body that tried to rescue Mormons in Missouri from mob violence; it failed, except in tempering its members for the trek west to come. He became a member of the Quorum of Twelve Apostles in 1835, spent time in prison with Joseph Smith in 1838, and edited the *Latter-day Saints Millennial Star* in England, as he served as president of that mission. He also served two more missions there. He was twice a delegate to Washington for unsuccessful bids

for statehood, and helped form the constitution for the provisional government of the Territory of Deseret. He wrote numerous Mormon tracts
and responses to attacks. He wrote hymns and essays. He published the
first book of Mormon poetry. His missionary tracts helped solidify
Mormon doctrine; the first of these was "Voice of Warning," which had
twenty-four editions in English and was also published in Danish, Dutch,
French, German, Icelandic, Spanish, and Swedish before 1900.

After the Pioneer Company reached Salt Lake valley in July 1847,
Parley explored Utah Valley and areas around Utah and Salt Lakes. He
was sent to explore an entrance into the Salt Lake Valley that would be
better than the arduous route over Big and Little Mountains and down
Emigration Canyon. He recommended a route down what would become
Parleys Canyon. When that recommendation was rejected, he undertook
in the summer of 1849 a private venture to build a toll road for the
California-bound gold-seekers then streaming into Salt Lake Valley.

Returning to the city that November he was called to gather a fifty-
man company to explore the length of Utah and recommend places for
settlement. As on all his missions, the call meant leaving a large family.
His first wife, Thankful, had died in 1837, and his second, Mary Ann Frost
(m. 1837) was still in New England. But left in the Salt Lake Valley to
await his return from the exploration were wives Elizabeth Brotherton
(m. 1843); Mary Wood (m. 1844) and two children; Sarah Huston (m.
1845) and one child; Phoebe Sopher (m. 1846); Martha Monks (m.
1847), who bore a child the day Parley returned, January 30; and Ann
Agatha Walker and one child. He later married Keziah Downs (m. 1853)
and Eleanor J. McComb (m. 1855), whose jealous former husband murdered him on May 13, 1857, in Van Buren, Crawford County, Arkansas,
where he is buried.

THOMAS E. RICKS, FOURTH TEN[175]

When Thomas Ricks joined the Southern Exploring Expedition,
twenty-one years of age and less than five years a Mormon, he was limping
from a permanently crippled leg and only recently recovered from
wounds inflicted in an Indian attack. But he did his part and went on to a
heroic life of service, sacrifice, and pioneering, including founding of the
academy that became the college that now bears his name.

Ricks was born July 21, 1828, in Christian County, Kentucky, and,
with his family, was baptized February 4, 1845. Though limping on a leg
permanently shortened after a horseback accident at age sixteen, he

---

175.   Bitton, *Guide*, 296; Black, *Members*; Thomas Davis, Autobiography, MSSA, 2543, Utah
       Historical Society, 20–25. Esshom, *Pio. and Pro. Men*, 1187; Jenson, *Bio. Enc.*,
       1:455–61; Thomas E. Ricks, "History of Thomas E. Ricks," Mormon Biographical
       Sketches Collection, LDS Church Archives.

worked on the Nauvoo Temple, acted as a teamster for Charles C. Rich's family during the freezing, mud-plagued exodus across Iowa to Winter Quarters, and started for the Rockies in Heber C. Kimball's company in the spring of 1848. On the way, at the Elk Horn River, he suffered three bullet wounds in the back during a skirmish with oxen-stealing Indians. Thought to be dying, he was blessed by Kimball and others. He lived, but was bedridden for months. The company reached Salt Lake Valley September 24, 1848.

In the fall of 1849 he went back along the trail with an eight-ox team to assist a company of emigrants under Ezra T. Benson and George A. Smith. Meeting them at Independence Rock

Thomas Ricks. Courtesy LDS Church Archives, copy photograph by J M. Heslop.

on the Sweetwater, they returned to the valley October 23—and just a month later Ricks left on the Parley P. Pratt expedition. As a teamster on that journey, he remained with the teams and wagons in Parowan Valley while Parley's mounted company explored the Virgin River country, and also remained with the snowbound wagons near Fillmore on the return journey.

In the spring of 1856 he was called to an Indian mission to build a settlement at Las Vegas, and in the fall that year was called to help rescue the starving Martin handcart company from the blizzard-swept high plains of Wyoming. In 1858 he was called to help bring back settlers from the Indian-plagued colony on the Salmon River, and returned in time to evacuate Salt Lake City against the approach of Johnston's Army in the so-called Utah War.

In 1859 he located in Cache Valley, where from 1851 to 1863 he served as sheriff. Twice, in 1863 and 1866, he captained ox team companies to bring emigrants from Council Bluffs. One of the emigrants in 1853, Thomas Davis, wrote in his reminiscences that Ricks was a teamster who could "pop the big whip good and loud." During the 1870s and early 1880s Ricks contracted to grade road bases for railroads through Idaho and Montana. In 1882 he was called to lead the settlement of the upper Snake River country, establishing the town of Rexburg and other communities there. He served as first bishop and first stake president in the area, built the first gristmill, the first ferry across the North Fork of the Snake, the first sawmill, the first mercantile store, and in 1888 founded the Church Academy at Rexburg that eventually became Ricks College.

He married Tabitha Hendricks in 1852/1853 (twelve children), Tamar Loader in 1857 (seven children), Elizabeth Jane Shupe in 1857 (ten children), and Ruth Caroline Dilly in 1863 (five children), and was twice arrested for polygamy but not convicted. He died at his Rexburg home September 28, 1901.

ROBERT M. SMITH, SECOND TEN[176]

Robert M. Smith, born in South Carolina in 1804, became part of the "Mississippi Saints" who started west in 1846 but wintered at Fort Pueblo, Colorado, before coming to Salt Lake Valley with or just behind Brigham Young's Pioneer Company in July 1847.

Called to the Southern Exploring Expedition, Smith rode with Parley P. Pratt's mounted company to explore the Virgin River country and also accompanied Pratt and others who arrived home on horseback in February 1850.

In 1851 Smith was called to join the company led by Charles C. Rich and Amasa Lyman to establish a Mormon colony at San Bernardino. The Journal History records that on July 5, 1851, at the mouth of Cajon Pass, in the first conference of the church in southern California, "Brother Charles C. Rich nominated William Crosby to be acting bishop of this branch of the Church. Bishop Crosby then nominated Robert M. Smith and Albert Collins as his counselors." In subsequent conferences, on April 6, 1852, and April 8, 1855, Smith and the others were sustained in the same positions. But the Journal History on March 16, 1856, recorded that at a conference of the San Bernardino Branch, Robert M. Smith was cut off from the church for "unchristianlike conduct." His subsequent whereabouts and date of death were not found.

BENJAMIN FRANKLIN STEWART, THIRD TEN[177]

Benjamin Stewart (also Stuart) was a member of Brigham Young's Pioneer Company of 1847, though he didn't arrive in Salt Lake Valley with Brigham. Instead, he was one of seven men left to build a ferry on the Platte River to assist the large body of emigrants coming later that year. He arrived in the valley with them September 27, 1847.

Stewart was born October 22, 1817, in Jackson Township, Monroe County, Ohio. He was baptized a Mormon on February 20, 1844, and ordained an elder the same day.

---

176. Carter, *Our Pioneer Heritage*, 2:462; Journal History, dates indicated.
177. Jenson, *Bio. Enc.*, 2:717–18, 4:719; Journal History, dates indicated; obituary, *Deseret News*, June 30, 1885.

On the Southern Exploring Expedition he rode with Parley P. Pratt on the mounted exploration of the Virgn River country, and joined other married men with families to ride home ahead.

He married three times: Polly Richardson in 1837 (ten children), Elizabeth Jane Davis in 1851 (ten children), Rachel Hunter Davis in 1851 (one child).

In 1851 he helped settle Payson, where he built a sawmill and nail factory. He served there as counselor in the bishopric and was elected to two terms as mayor. There, the Journal History on July 24, 1856, records, he gave a toast to "Pioneers—Orbs around whom many bright constellations of young ladies revolve, like the planets around the great luminary." In a different vein, according

Benjamin Stewart. Andrew Jenson, *Latter-day Saint Biographical Encyclopedia,* vol. 2 (Salt Lake City: Western Epics, 1971), 717.

to the Journal History on March 18, 1859, Stewart originated and signed a petition to Territorial Judge John Cradlebaugh protesting the stationing of U.S. troops as bailiffs and sheriffs in the Provo courthouse where they intimidated jurors and witnesses, "a circumstanced unparreled [*sic*] in the history of our great republic, and if not checked will have a deleterious effect on the judicial bench of this nation."

In 1862, he helped establish the town of Benjamin, Utah County, which was given his name in fulfillment, his obituary states, of a prophecy in his patriarchal blessing given in 1847 by Patriarch John Smith. In 1871 he was appointed to preside over the Benjamin Branch, a position he held until his death by lightning on June 22, 1885. He had two wives and twenty-two children.

NATHAN TANNER, SECOND TEN[178]

At the time of his death in 1910, Nathan Tanner had been a member of the LDS Church for seventy-nine years, longer, it was thought at the time, than any other person. Almost certainly he was the last surviving member of

---

178. Bitton, *Guide,* 351–52 (an account of the expedition attributed to Nathan Tanner is exactly the same as that of John Brown; they must have shared information); Black, *Members;* Jenson, *Bio. Enc.,* 4:691–92; Nathan Tanner, "Incidents in the Life of Nathan Tanner," LDS Church Archives; obituary, *Deseret News,* December 19, 1910.

Zion's Camp, a paramilitary march of Mormons from Kirtland, Ohio, to western Missouri to succor Saints being persecuted there. While the effort failed, it served to weed out the weak in faith and to temper the rest for the trials to come. Tanner was one of the tempered.

Born May 14, 1815, in Greenwich, Washington County, New York, Tanner was baptized a Mormon September 20, 1831. Three years later, at age nineteen, he joined Zion's Camp. In 1836, he served a mission to the eastern states where he met and married Rachel Winter Smith. They witnessed the spiritual manifestations reported at the dedication of the Kirtland Temple, suffered financial losses in

Nathan Tanner. Courtesy LDS Church Archives, copy photograph by J M. Heslop.

the banking disaster, were driven, in turn, from Ohio, Missouri, and finally Nauvoo. They arrived in Salt Lake Valley in the Amasa Lyman company in September 1848.

On the Southern Exploring Expedition, Tanner rode with Pratt on the mounted exploration of the Virgin River region and, as a family man, rode ahead to reach home while wagons were snowbound near Fillmore.

He was a freighter between Salt Lake City and Los Angeles and ran both a store and a farm. He served several missions and made several trips across the plains to bring convert companies to Salt Lake Valley. By five wives—Rachel Winter (m. 1836), Mary Rosina Baker (m. 1847), Perris or Pansy Tippets (m. 1849), Sarah Littley (m. 1857), and Mary Augusta Benbow (m. 1863), he had eighteen children, most of whom survived him when he died December 17, 1910, at age ninety-five.

SETH BENJAMIN TANNER, THIRD TEN[179]

Seth Tanner was born March 6, 1828, in Bolton, Warren County, New York, and was twenty-one years old when he joined the Southern Exploring Expedition. On that journey he remained with the teams and wagons in Parowan Valley while Parley's mounted company explored south to the Virgin. He also remained with the snowbound wagons near Fillmore and finally reached home in late March 1850.

---

179. Fish, "The Southern Utah Expedition."

Following the expedition he was sent to colonize Washington County, where at Pine Valley in 1858 he married Charlotte Levi. In October 1876 he married Anna Marie Jensen. At some point he moved to Taylor, Arizona, where he died December 5, 1918.

Stephen Taylor, Fifth Ten[180]

Stephen Taylor had been a member of the LDS Church only eighteen months when he joined Parley P. Pratt's exploration to southern Utah. He was born in Wiltshire, England, April 11, 1808, and was baptized April 19, 1948.

During the expedition, Taylor remained with the teams and wagons in Parowan Valley. Though no record was found of his marriage, he apparently was a family man because he rode home with the advance party of horsemen from Pahvant Valley. He wandered away from the group and was found in dire circumstances when the rescue team rode back with provisions.

The 1870 Utah census lists a Stephen Taylor as a blacksmith in Morgan County, Utah. The Journal History on September 25, 1870, names a Stephen Taylor as president of the Cheltenham, England, mission district, and on October 9, 1870, reports his attendance at a conference in London. Whether this is one man or two and which, if either, is the veteran of the Southern Exploring Expedition could not be determined.

William Perkins Vance, First Ten[181]

William Vance, a member of Brigham Young's Pioneer Company, arrived in Salt Lake Valley July 22, 1847, two days before Brigham. Born October 20, 1822, in Jackson County, Tennessee, he had joined the LDS Church in 1842 and had

William P. Vance. *Our Pioneer Heritage,* vol. 2 (Salt Lake City: Daughters of Utah Pioneers, 1959), 546.

---

180. Black, *Members*; Journal History, dates indicated.
181. Black, *Members*; Jenson, *Bio. Enc.*, 4:721.

lived for a time in Joseph Smith's Nauvoo home. In 1844 he served a mission to his home state of Tennessee.

On the Southern Exploring Expedition he remained with the teams and wagons and explored the Little Salt Lake Valley and surrounding mountains while Parley Pratt and his mounted company explored the Virgin River country. He also remained with the snowbound wagons near Fillmore.

In 1851, Vance accompanied George A. Smith's pioneering company to settle in Parowan and develop the iron ore Vance and others had discovered. He served a mission to the eastern United States and on his return settled in Summit County where he became the county's first judge. In 1858 he was a member of the company that settled Las Vegas, moved to St. George in 1884 and to Lund, Nevada, in 1902, where he died December 5, 1914.

He married Ann Hudson Richardson in 1865 and her daughter by an earlier marriage, Hannah Richardson, in 1874. He and Hannah were parents of seven children.

WILLIAM SHIN WADSWORTH, FIRST TEN[182]

William Wadsworth (also known as Wardsworth or Wordsworth) was a member of Brigham Young's Pioneer Company, entering Salt Lake Valley July 22, 1847. On that journey he was remembered for his hard work in building bridges and clearing roads.

He was born March 5, 1810, in Woodstorm, Salem County, New Jersey, baptized in 1841 by George Adams in Philadelphia, and ordained a seventy in 1846. After arrival in Salt Lake Valley he assisted in exploring the surrounding country, and was called to the Parley P. Pratt Southern Exploring Expedition in 1849. On that expedition he stayed with the teams and wagons in Little Salt Lake Valley while Parley and others rode horseback to explore the Virgin River region. Having three children at home, he rode with the

William Wordsworth (or Wadsworth). Frank Ellwood Esshom, *Pioneers and Prominent Men of Utah* (Salt Lake City: Western Epics, 1966), 65.

---

182.   Black, *Members*; Carter, *Our Pioneer Heritage*, 2:547; Jenson, *Bio. Enc.*, 4:722.

mounted party that left the snowbound wagons near Fillmore to reach home the end of January.

William Shin married Ann Fogg, Nancy Ann Vance (six children), Martha Strepes, and Nellie Griffith. He settled in Springville, where he established a farm and also fished in Utah Lake. He was elected as an alderman and mayor of Springville, and died there January 18, 1888.

CHAUNCEY WALKER WEST, FIRST TEN[183]

Twenty-two years old when he joined Parley P. Pratt's Southern Expedition, Chauncey West was already experienced in the responsibilities and trials facing early Mormons. Born February 6, 1827, in Erie County, Pennsylvania, he joined the church at age sixteen and promptly began service as a traveling elder. He was ordained a seventy at the unusually young age of eighteen. And at age twenty, after his father, mother, and brother had died at Winter Quarters, he took charge of the family and brought them safely to Salt Lake Valley, arriving in the John Taylor company in September 1847.

Chauncey W. West. Frank Ellwood Esshom, *Pioneers and Prominent Men of Utah* (Salt Lake City: Western Epics, 1966), 125.

His service on the exploring expedition was also remarkable. He stayed with the teams and wagons in Parowan Valley and on the way home, rode with the mounted party that left in order to conserve the dwindling provisions. Fifty miles short of civilization, that group faced starvation, so Pratt and West rode two days and much of the night, "extremely hungry and feet badly frozen" as Pratt reported, to reach the settlement at Provo and send back a rescue party that saved the others.

West's subsequent life was no less extraordinary. In 1852 he and thirty-six others left on missions to Asia, where West served three years in Ceylon and India. During that period he experienced remarkable evidence of the power of prayer, including healing of smallpox, stilling of waves during a shipwreck, and a dream-warning to leave a ship that was subsequently lost on the return voyage.

---

183.   Bitton, *Guide*, 375–76; Black, *Members*; Esshom, *Pio. and Pro. Men.*, 1230; Jenson, *Bio. Enc.*, 1:749–54.

He was called as bishop of the Ogden First Ward, moved to that city, and was soon called as presiding bishop over Weber County. He was elected to the House of Representatives, named a colonel in the Weber Military District, and in 1858 was made a brigadier general in the Nauvoo Legion for distinguished service in the Utah War. In 1863 he served as president of the European mission, traveling and preaching through England and much of Europe.

While accomplishing so much, he also found time to marry ten wives: Mary Hoagland in 1846 (five children), Sarah Elizabeth Covington in 1855 (eight children), Martha Joiner in 1856 (five children), Jeanett Nichol Gibson in 1857, Adeline Amanda Wright in 1857 (seven children), Angeline Shurtliff in 1860, Mary Ann Covington in 1864, Susan Hannah Covington in 1867, and Louisa Musgrave in 1868.

He built canals and wagon roads, sawmills, a livery stable, mercantile business, a hotel, meat market, a blacksmith and wagon shop, and a tannery, boot and shoe, and saddle and harness business. His final business enterprise was disastrous. With Ezra T. Benson and Lorin Farr he contracted to grade rail bed west of Ogden for the Union Pacific Railroad. During the intense competition between Union Pacific and Central Pacific, nearly two hundred miles of road bed were laid side by side at enormous extra cost. Farr and his associates were promised that their costs would be repaid, but they never were. While in San Francisco trying to get the promise fulfilled, West became ill and died January 6, 1870, at age forty-three.

CHRISTOPHER WILLIAMS, FIFTH TEN[184]

At age sixty, Christopher Williams was one of the oldest members of the Parley P. Pratt exploring expedition. At the time of his call he was a bishop, having been ordained bishop of the Salt Lake Third Ward February 22, 1849, five months after entering Salt Lake Valley in the Orson Pratt company. He served as a bishop until 1856.

Christopher Williams. Frank Ellwood Esshom, *Pioneers and Prominent Men of Utah* (Salt Lake City: Western Epics, 1966),178.

---

184. Black, *Members*; Esshom, *Pio. and Pro. Men*, 1249; Jenson, *Bio. Enc.*, 4:[?].

On the Southern Utah Expedition he remained with the oxen and wagons in Parowan Valley and also stayed with the wagons on the arduous trip home. He was, along with William Henrie and Samuel Gould, doubtless one of the "old men who stay in camp melt snow for cattle," according to Campbell's March 10 journal entry.

Although Fish in his thesis reports Williams as being married seven times, Black mentions three marriages, one of which is obviously a duplicate. His wives were Milicent VanOstrand and Jacobina Wells Patton. Three children are recorded. Williams lived out the rest of his life as a farmer and carpenter in Salt Lake City, where he died December 31, 1873.

WILLIAM SIDNEY SMITH WILLIS (OR WILLES), FOURTH TEN[185]

William Willis was a member of the Mormon Battalion, and according to some accounts actually was first to discover gold at Sutter's Mill, keeping it quiet until after James Marshall announced he had found some. It is said Willis made the first scales on which gold was weighed in California. Later in life, he made jewelry for his daughters from some of the gold he brought back to Salt Lake Valley.

Willis was born March 18, 1819, in Jefferson County, New York. According to the *LDS Biographical Encyclopedia*, Willis and his brother were baptized July 16, 1846, by Parley P. Pratt. Four days later, the Mormon Battalion, including the two brothers, left Council Bluffs for the march to Santa Fe and subsequently California. Why the brothers were with the Saints and apparently members of the battalion before being baptized is not clear.

On the Southern Exploring Expedition, Willis remained with the wagons in Parowan Valley and also with the snowbound wagons near Fillmore while half the company hurried home.

In 1852 he married Alzina L. Lott, with Brigham Young performing the ceremony. They moved to Lehi, where Willis built the first cabin with a wood floor. He is credited with bringing the first bees to the Lehi area. In 1855 he was commissioned a captain in the Lehi post of the Utah Militia and was part of the militiamen who defended Echo Canyon against approach of Johnston's Army in 1857–1858. In 1858 he was captain of a company sent to assist Mormon settlers on the Salmon River. In 1862 he was made a president of the 678th Quorum of Seventy, and in 1863 left on a three-year mission to England. While on his return he captained an emigrant company that arrived in Salt Lake Valley November 29, 1865.

Willis was considered a master mechanic, able to fashion any kind of device needed to perform a needed task. Lacking a spirit level, for

---

185. Black, *Members*; Jenson, *Bio. Enc.*, 3:566–68; Journal History, November 10, 1846.

example, he cut a groove in a piece of wood and filled it with water to survey the Spring Creek ditch in Lehi. But while working at a sawmill in American Fork Canyon he was caught in the saw and died February 3, 1871.

ALEXANDER WRIGHT, THIRD TEN[186]

Alexander Wright, a Scotsman, was one of the first missionaries who preached Mormonism in his native land, serving there from 1839 to 1842. He was born in Marnoch Parish, Banffshire, Scotland, January 27, 1804/05. In 1835 he emigrated from Scotland, was converted to Mormonism, was baptized the following year, and emigrated to Kirtland.

Following his mission to Scotland, he joined with the Saints in Nauvoo, where he married Hannah Butterfield, who died during the birth of their first child. He suffered the exodus from Nauvoo across Iowa to Winter Quarters and crossed the plains in 1847, driving a team for John Taylor, and arriving in Salt Lake Valley in September.

Alexander Wright. Courtesy LDS Church Archives, copy photograph by J M. Heslop.

On the Parley P. Pratt exploring expedition, he rode with Parley on the exploration of the Virgin River region, but on the homeward trip, as a single man, remained with the snowbound wagons near Fillmore while family men rode home.

In January 1851, he married Hannah Leigh. They lived in Salt Lake City until 1856, when they were called to colonize the Virgin River country he had explored. They were among the first settlers of the town of Virgin, where he married Hannah Walters. He died there August 3, 1876.

---

186.   Black, *Members*; Jenson, *Bio. Enc.*, 3:571–72; Utah census, 1870.

Robert Campbell's Ute Dictionary

UTE
INDIAN WORDS
WITH THEIR MEANINGS IN ENGLISH

Ash'enty.	I want.	Kish	be still. S
Ābbat	Large.	Kick'āmush,	more
An'ka	Red:	Kamush'	another
Annāniah,	What you call it.	Kī'ba	Mountain
Āt	Good.	Kāv'owuts	a colt
Annebin	How many.	Kut'ōshy	done.
Āp	Day or hour.	Kunōk'ship,	burnt
Ā'dick	Stop.	Kishōp'	Lasso
Ash'py,	to ride.	Kōkweep'	charcoal
Āt'pāgā	a trout.	Kābuah	you're a fool
Bā'ragy	to wash	Kāranoop'	saddle
Empā'gā	to talk	Kāda,	stay, sit down
Em	you	Kārawim,	a seat
Ephikō	to morrow	Kutā'uā	Powder
Ēsh'ump	you lie	Kāmpunk	Item
Ē'tēsk	long ago	Kān'ābits	Poor
Ē'irut	like this or that.	Kuse	Pants
Ē'wun	tired.	Kāt'suge	a Hat
Ēlilā	to drink	Kap,	sing.
Ē'bā	here	Koāk	sharp
Ep'wā	sleep	Kān'up	willow
Ē'betā	wood	Ku'tōni	spit
Humpā	what	Kār'agit	miss the mark
Huk'abā	when	Keow	yesterday
Hā'rān	many	Kātū'ritch	warm
Inch	thisthat it	Kōkue	to shoot
Ī'pits	Boy	Koue	to steal
Īdz	Bow	Moo	hands
In'its	move out of the way	Moowa	nose
Kāts	no	Mowūshuk	other side
Kootch	Buffalo	Mīntso	beard

Mānikish	to make.	Nāmpāu,	foot
Mūggi'	give	Niat	Wind
Mihe	whats up, what you doing, where going		
Mitopige,	moon,	Nangits	Girl

249

Māvā	over	Nanpats	moccasin
~~Mā~~	~~is it right~~	~~Nawuk~~	~~give~~
Mābā,	off	Nauhākā	to hear
Mā'ūpā	a whip S	Nāgi	cough
Mārā	this one, or that:	Nōkō'mē	crooked
Moobuk	fall down	Nōi	to pack
Moorē	Girl	Ne'āgā	thats what
Morōkiue	squaw		I call it
Mābā	short distance	Obān'unk	Goose
Moorits	Mule	Ōōpe	bone
Mānōnā	whole	Ōkige	Rifle
Mē	away	Ōnshump	enough
Mūra	father	Ōimbāngā	wagon
Nān'asooz	a few	Onup	egg
Nāvūsh	nothing	Ōkump	dust, dirt
Niwipe	snow	OO	arow
Newapi	"	Ō Ōkwēge	old Bear
Nārriint	powerful	Ōpit	Timber
Nātāwap	trade	Ōakārum	thats it
Narrawitch	gamble	Ōwap	grass
Ninne	I, myself,	Pēgi	coming
Nārrukura	fight	Penunkō	soon
Nāguts	Mt. sheep	Piāput	large
Nāmp	walk	Pātēā	heavy
Nāmige	Sister	Pāōra	rain
Nānāpige	old	Pawinch	Beaver
Nāncobin	ear	Pāwunk	fish hawk

Pānguits	fish	Patish'ua	eyelashes
Piēka	call, like Hullo, come here		
Pa	water	Pannawanup	arrow point
Pungo	horse	Pāmbus	a son
Pē'ung	heart	Pariup	to scratch
Pikua	to go	Parraway	to walk
Pumka	look	Pacheut	mouse
Pishāna	to tell	Pēwākwa	ragged
Pishauya	hunt	Quitsimbungo	cow
Piuki	dead	Queet	snipe
Pichy	milk	Quashoo	shirt
Punkaroo	run	Qiunniken	target
Pan'nokilch	cup	Quantia	Eagle
Pakneet	to blow	Quando	'yonder
Piskup	Paint	Quanto	other side
Pí'na	sweet	Queep	smoke
Pabitit	older Brother	Queean	Bear
Pūēan	eye	Queetadan	to wound
Pishāga,	understand,	Quidgeway	to live

Pātēn	blood vein				Sēgātshaby	close by
Pap	blood	Soonk	pipe		Shādy	Dog
Pē'muts	love	Sātea	cold,		Shinaub	God
Pēconka	sick,				Shuki	to whistle
Pānt	long				Shumī	remember
Pūa	skin	Shoopky	cold,		Skabin	to cut
Pō	read	Shēga	duck,		Sēgish	spear
Pārēā	Elk	Sūa	fool,		Sı	catch it,
Pē'age	Mother,	Sēkīge	Brother,		Shēgo	finger
Panguts	don't go so fast,				Shoop	house
Pēna	feather				Sūkige	Younger Brother
Pē'ābā	Lake,	Tami	me,		Timbio	Bullet

Tāmes	sinew				Tōānow	alike
Tāmbāgup	Bridle,				Tāpinunk	on top
Tēā	B.T. Deer				Tāpunkety	to kick
Tēcup,	eatables	Tōnā	strike,		Tawa	teeth
Tē'litch	little				Taminum	a tree, they smoke
Tūē ge	very				Tāmba	under lip.
Tupēkua	to be out of anything.				Tamba	up
Toy	enough said				Tāmpunougip	flint
Tōmūn	year.	Totina	scalp,		Tamope	milk
Towun	night.	Tābēbin	throw		Tōbēpit	short
Tabi	sun				Tōmkuntā	strait
Timp	Rock	Tāngā,	kick,		Tehig	Duck
Tishump	you lie all the time,				Swaga	White
Tēge	hungry				Tāmiaka	give it to me
Tutsin	head,	Tsi,	catch it,		Tāteog,	small Rabbit
Terriby	to throw away,				Tabiaka	sunset
Tieōba	to eat,	Tasha	Day.		Tamun	Summer
Tinsinā	hard,				Umpio,	don't really know
Tātā	father	Weetch,	knife,		Wēū	awl
Tōats	young,				Waunowgip,	Gun caps
T ō'ōb	Rattlesnake				Wāugets	Antelope
Tānup	man S	Wēbita	down,		Wimp	Pine
Tāsipawa	hair S				Yāckā	hand it here
Tackibit	Winter S				Yop	fat or hollow
Tō'ōmi	do,	Yobaga,	afraid,		Yoge S	Wolf
Tack	vest,	Yumbā	Salt Valley,		Yoap,	Valley
Timuge	file,				Yeakwē	killed by frost
Timbuēā	Rifle				Youtowap	Door.
Tapitshy	hunt				Oowa	yes
Tapitch	string					
Tigaboo	friend					

Robert Campbell's Emigrant Guides

GUIDE FROM GREAT SALT LAKE CITY TO SAMPITCH
PROMINENT POINTS AND REMARKS
FEBRUARY 1850*

Prominent Points and Remarks	Distance from point to point	From G. S. L. City	From Sampitch Settlement
	miles	miles	miles
Great Salt Lake City, Lat. 40 deg, 45 sec. 44 min. Long 111 deg, 26 min. 34 sec. Altitude 4300 feet.			130¾
Kanyon Creek. Bridge over, in Big Field	4¼	4½	126½
Mill Creek. Bridge over at Gardner's Mill in Big Field. Mile further you take to the left where the road strikes out from the Big Field	2½	6¾	124
Cottonwood Creek crossing	2	8¾	122
Farther Cottonwood Creek crossing	4	12¾	118
Forks of road—take the right	1¼	14	116¾
Dry Creek, no water, some fuel, feed plenty	3½	17½	113¼
Willow Creek, soft and swampy, good feed and water, no fuel	2¾	20¼	110½
Hollow, steep ascent, good road	1½	21¾	109
Hot Springs by wayside to the right—one of them 136 deg. F.T	1½	23	107¾
Road turns left, ascend Kanyon, steep for 300 yards	1½	24½	106¼
Summit of dividing ridge between S.L. and Utah valleys. Good view of S.L. and Utah lakes and valleys. Turn to the left few hundred yards, then descend long hill into Utah valley.	½	25	105¾
Dry Creek, Little good water, (Nov. 26)	6¼	31¼	99½
American Fork [illegible] ft wide [illegible] in. deep	3¼	34½	96¼
'Swamp creek, muddy and soft for 100 yards	3¾	38¼	92½
Pond by wayside to the right	¾	39	91¾
Provo River, 34 yds wide, 18 in. deep, timber plenty, Utah Fort on the south bank, an enclosure made by 57 log houses, on 1½ acre of ground, Within 1 mile you cross a branch of the Provo and a large irrigation furrow.	7	46	84¾
Two (soft) springs. Swampy	4½	50½	80¼
Slough, caused by spring few yards east running out of the mountain. Bad crossing	1¼	51¾	79

*   Robert Campbell, Southern Exploring Expedition Papers, 1849–1850, LDS Church Archives

Spring Creek, 19 yards wide, 10 in. deep; rocky bottom.	¾	52½	78¼
Hobble Creek, 28 ft wide, 2 ft. deep. Plenty cottonwood fuel and willows and feed. From this point you bear southwest.	1	53½	77¼
Spanish Fork, 14 yards wide, 14 in. deep. ; Cottonwood, willows and feed plentiful.	6	59½	71¼
Low swamp continues for ¾ mile. By bearing to the left you get through without any difficulty.	3	62½	68¼
Peteetnet Creek. 9 ft. wide, 17 in. deep. Fuel and feed abundant	2¼	64¾	66
Ap Creek, 6 yards wide, 1 foot deep.	3¼	68	62¾
Branch of Summit Creek, 3 ft. wide, 10 in. deep; 200 yds further, Summit creek, 30 ft wide, 1 ft. deep. Fine feed, water and fuel.	2¾	70¾	60
Rocky Spot. Here you descend into Yohab [Juab] Valley	2¾	73½	57
Pang'un Spring by wayside to the right. This spring is bottomless. within ¼ mile, 3 other springs left of road.	4½	78	52¾
Warm Spring creek. Water will do to cook with; but little fuel	¾	78¾	52
Watadge Creek flows in several small branches; muddy crossing. Willows and feed abundant	3¼	82	48¾
Forks of road [where the road made by the Sanpete settlers leaves the road made by the California-bound Jefferson Hunt wagon train]	3¾	85¾	45
Mouth of Onnappah [Salt Creek] Kanyon. the creek is 4 yards wide, 1 foot deep. but little timber in the Kanyon, tho plenty for fuel. some steep crossings & short turns.	5	90¾	40
Ninth Crossing of creek, leave the main Kanyon now, which turns up left. There is a Salt rock up the main branch of the Kanyon 300 yards before you cross & 2 miles further up 2 Salt Springs, from which is gathered beautiful fine white Salt Rocks, clear Salt, without alloy	4½	95¼	35½
Summit of ascent from Kanyon. Travel over level land for 2 miles then gently descend into Sandpitch valley	3	98¼	32½
Pleasant creek 3 ft wide, 12 in deep, tight of road, cedars to the left; sage and feed plentiful	4½	102¼	28
Springs &Slough, right of road, feed, sage &greasewood	8	110¾	20
Sandpitch creek, willows along banks	1¾	112½	18¼
Sandpitch Creek, crossing, 25 feet wide, 1½ feet Deep, Willows, sage, greasewood &feed	1¾	114¼	16½
Timpa creek 12 feet Wide, 18 in deep; few cedars &cotton wood, plenty feed	9¼	123½	7
Mound creek 2 ft wide, 6 in deep	2	125½	5¼
City creek, Sandpitch Settlement 14 ft wide 18 in deep	5¼	130¾	

GUIDE FROM G.S.L. CITY TO SANTA CLARA, TRIBUTARY OF THE RIO VIRGIN FEBRUARY 1850 PROMINENT POINTS AND REMARKS	Distance from point to point	From G. S. L. City
Great Salt Lake City, Lat 40° 45' 44" Long 111° 26' 34". Altitude 4300 Feet.	miles	miles
Kanyon Creek, Bridge over, in Big Field	4¼	4¼
Mill Creek, Bridge over, ar Gardners Mill in Big Field	2½	6¾
Cottonwood creek, crossing	2	8¾
Further Cottonwood Creek crossing	4	12¾
Forks of road take the right	1¼	14
Dry Creek, no water, some fuel, feed plenty	3½	17½
Willow creek, soft &swampy, Good feed &water, no fuel	2¾	20¼
Hollow, steep ascent, good road	1¼	21¾
Hot Springs by wayside to the right, one of them 135° F.T.	1¼	23
Road turns left ascend kanyon, steep or 300 yard	1½	24½
Summit of dividing ridge between GSLake and Utah vallies, turn to the left few hundred yards, then descend long hill into Utah Valley.	½	25
Dry Creek, little good water (26th Novr)	6¼	31¼
American Fork [illegible] ft. wide [illegible] in. deep	3¼	34½
Swamp creek, muddy &soft for 100 yards	3¾	38¼
Pond by wayside to right	¾	39
Provo 34 yards wide 18 in deep, timber plenty, Utah Fort on south bank made by 57 log houses on 1½ acres of ground, within a mile cross branch of Provo, large irrigation furrow	7	46
Two springs, swampy	4½	50½
Slough, caused by spring, few yards East, running out of the Mountain. Bad crossing	1¼	51¾
Spring creek, 19 yds wide, 10 in deep, Rocky bottom	¾	52½
Hobble creek 28 ft wide 2 ft deep. Plenty willows &feed. From this point you bear South West	1	53½
Spanish Fork 14 yards wide 14 in deep cotton wood willows &feed plentiful	6	59½
Low swamp continues for ¾ mile, by bearing to the left go thro without any difficulty	3	62½
Peteatneet creek 9 feet Wide 17 in deep fuel &feed	2¼	64¾
Ap creek 6 yards Wide 1 foot deep	3¼	68

Branch of Summit creek 3 ft wide 10 in deep 200 yards further, Summit creek 30 ft Wide 1 foot deep, fine feed, water &fuel	2¾	70¾
Rocky Spot—here you descend into Yohab [Juab] valley	2¾	73½
Pang'un Spring, by wayside to the right. This Spring is bottomless within ¼ mile 3 other Springs left of road	4½	78
Warm Spring creek, Water will do to cook with, little fuel	¾	78¾
Watadge creek, flows in several small branches, muddy crossing, willows and feed abundant	3¼	82
Fork of Road [where settlers' road to Sanpete leaves road made by Jefferson Hunt's wagon party] From here to Slough Creek bottom, avoided the road in consequence of deep snow. Distances may not by exactly as in the road	3¾	85¾
Mouth of Onnappah Kanyon creek [Salt Creek at site of Nephi], flows in 2 branches	4	89¾
Slough Crck bottom, feed &water plentiful, water brackish some Sage &greasewood, Travel near the bottom to the crossing	13	102¾
Slough Creek crossing 3 yds Wide 16 in deep, miry crossing some cedars n side of the hills	4	106¾
Sevier crossing 30 yds Wide 2 feet deep, Willows &feed on banks about 1 mile before crossing where you first strike river extensive bottom and feed	9¼	116
Small Stream, left of road. From Sevier avoided the road &went round on the west side of the valley	12	128
Summit of dividing ridge, about gradual and smooth descent, feed &cedars plenty on mountain sides	4	132
Spring Stream, 2 yds wide, 4 in deep, cedars &feed Plentiful, many springs to the left about ¾ mile further another spring stream	9¼	141¼
Thorn Plum creek 2 yds Wide 6 in deep steep descent sage &feed.	2¾	143½
Rock Creek, 14 ft wide 14 in deep, fuel &feed (Jany 1850) nearly 3 ft snow, could not find road so distances may be shorter or longer	6¼	149½
Prairie creek willows and good feed 3 ft Wide	10	159½
Rush creek Plenty feed last water for 29½ miles	4¼	163¾
Turn right &ascend hill ½ mile further, track leading left to Cedar Hollow encampment	5½	169¼
Wagon track coming up from encampment where there is feed &fuel	3¼	172½
Sage Ridge grove of cedar ¾ mile to the right	2	174½
Ascend Hill leaving large valley, Go over hills or ridges for 1 mile covered with sage, cedars &feed	4	178½
Rocky Bluff Pass ¼ mile along East Foot	6	184½
Rocky Hill, descent steep	5	189½
Cedar Creek, to the left; willows; near this, road winds round East foot of hill you now pass near &partly thro' a bottom 2 or 3 miles long of tall grass	3¾	193¼

Willow Stream, muddy, plentiful feed, sage, and cedar, fuel	5¼	198
Ascend Mountain, steep; here again uncertain of being on Captn Hunts track, snow so deep	3	201½
Sage Creek 3 ft wide plenty fuel, feed off 1 or 2 miles	14½	215¾
Beaver Creek 6 yds wide 8 in deep, Willows. Bottom densely covered with feed. Before reaching this creek within ¾ mile you cross 2 small streams one having very steep banks	5	220¾
Margin of valley bottom, ascend gradually thro' sage 5 miles then wind around short turns among the cedars; steep sideling ascent over Mountain	¾	221½
Descend mountain, steep, Plenty feed &fuel	7½	229
Ascend rocky sideling, steep hill, 1 mile over this hill to the South East foot into a Kanyon that soon opens out into the neck of the Little Salt Lake Valley	3½	232½
Spring, south end of grass plot 120 yds left of road, fuel scant; 2½ miles on road comes in from left made by Southern Exploring Expedition of 49 and 50, sent out by the State of Deseret Many Springs by wayside, especially to the left farther on.	7	239½
Red creek 10 ft wide, Willows and drift wood fuel, feed towards mountain	10	249½
Center creek [site of Parowan] 4 yds Wide 6 in. deep Plenty timber &feed	4½	254
South creek 8 ft. Wide 6 in deep Plenty Timber &feed	6	260
Springs on brow of hill right of road Feed &sage	5	265
Muddy creek, overflows all over. [Coal Creek where it sinks in Cedar Valley northwest of Cedar City] Plenty cotton woods, feed towards mountains. Road turns west	12	277
Warm and Cold Springs Good mountain feed and cedars	7	284
Said to be a small Willow Spring by taking fork of road to left [illegible] distant	14	298
Small creek, near mouth of Kanyon, beautiful feed for few milles up Kanyon cedars	11	309
Stream of Water coming from Spring in grassy bottom [Mountain Meadow] last water flowing north	10	319
About ten miles farther will bring you over the rim of the Great Basin some steep sideling descents to a small run of water where the main track descends and goes round east foot of hill, but where a few wagons have gone over the hill. Considerable Green Grass on hill Jan 7, 50. Six miles farther brings you to the narrow bottomed, well timbered stream [Magotsu Creek]	16	335
Santa Clara, along which traveled to where Road leaves it [near Shivwits] some steep crossings Willows in the way, where road cut thro dense willow patches, but little feed along Santa Clara	20	355

BIBLIOGRAPHY

Books and Periodical

Allen, James B. "The Evolution of County Boundaries in Utah." *Utah Historical Quarterly* 23 (July 1955): 261–78.

Antrei, Albert C. T., ed. *The Other Forty-Niners: A Topical History of Sanpete County.* Salt Lake City: Western Epics, 1982.

Arrington, Leonard J. *Brigham Young: American Moses.* Chicago: University of Illinois Press, 1986.

————. *Great Basin Kingdom.* Lincoln: University of Nebraska Press, 1958.

Arrington, Leonard J., and Davis Bitton. *The Mormon Experience: A History of the Latter-day Saints.* New York: Alfred A. Knopf, 1979.

Arrington, Leonard J., Feramorz Y. Fox, and Dean L. May. *Building the City of God: Community and Cooperation among the Mormons.* Salt Lake City: Deseret Book Co., 1976.

Bailey, Paul. *Walkara, Hawk of the Mountains.* Los Angeles: Westernlore Press, 1954.

Bitton, Davis. *Guide to Mormon Diaries and Autobiographies.* Provo, Utah: Brigham Young University Press, 1977.

Black, Susan Easton. *Membership of the Church of Jesus Christ of Latter-day Saints.* 50 vols. Provo, Utah: Brigham Young University Press, 1977. Reprint, Provo: Utah: Brigham Young University Studies Center, 1984.

Book of Mormon. Salt Lake City: Church of Jesus Christ of Latter-day Saints, 1981.

Brooks, George R., ed. *The Southwest Expedition of Jedediah S. Smith: His Personal Account of the Journey to California, 1825–27.* Glendale: Arthur H. Clark Co., 1977.

Brooks, Juanita. *The Mountain Meadows Massacre.* Norman: University of Oklahoma Press, 1985.

Brown, James S. *Life of a Pioneer.* Salt Lake City: n.p., 1900

Brown, John. *Autobiography of John Brown, 1820–1896.* Salt Lake City: Stevens and Wallis, 1941.

Carter, Kate B., comp. *Our Pioneer Heritage.* 20 vols. Salt Lake City: Daughters of Utah Pioneers, 1959.

Chronic, Halka. *Roadside Geology of Utah.* Missoula: Mountain Press Publishing Co., 1990.

Cline, Gloria Griffen. *Exploring the Great Basin.* Norman: University of Oklahoma Press, 1963.

Cook, Lyndon W. *The Revelations of the Prophet Joseph Smith.* Salt Lake City: Deseret Book Co., 1985.

Cooley, Everett L. "Utah's Capitols." *Utah Historical Quarterly* 27 (July 1959) 259–73.

Crampton, C. Gregory. "Utah's Spanish Trail." *Utah Historical Quarterly* 47 (fall 1979): 361–83.

Crampton, C. Gregory, and Steven K. Madsen. *In Search of the Spanish Trail.* 1952. Reprint, Salt Lake City: Gibbs Smith Publishing Co., 1994.

Dalton, Luella Adams, ed. *History of Iron County Mission and Parowan.* Provo, Utah: Brigham Young University Press, 1973.

Doctrine and Covenants of the Church of Jesus Christ of Latter-day Saints. Salt Lake City: Church of Jesus Christ of Latter-day Saints, 1981.

Dutton, Captain Clarence E. *The Physical Geology of the Grand Canyon District.* Washington, D.C.: U.S. Geological Survey, 1880–81, 1882.

Esshom, Frank. *Pioneers and Prominent Men of Utah.* Salt Lake City: Utah Pioneers Book Publishing Co., 1913.

Fowler, Catherine S., and Don D. Fowler. "Notes on the History of the Southern Paiutes and Western Shoshonis." *Utah Historical Quarterly* 39 (spring 1971): 95–113.

Frémont, John Charles. *The Exploring Expedition to the Rocky Mountains.* 1845. Reprint, Washington, D.C.: Smithsonian Institution Press, 1988.

————. *Report of the Exploring Expedition to the Rocky Mountains in the Year 1842 and to Oregon and North California in the Years 1843–44.* 28th Cong. (1845), 2d sess., House Exec. Doc. 166.

Hafen, LeRoy R., and Ann W. Hafen. *Frémont's Fourth Expedition: A Documentary Account of the Disaster of 1848–49 with Diaries, Letters, and Reports by Participants in the Tragedy.* Glendale: Arthur H. Clark Co., 1960.

————. *Journals of the Forty-Niners: Salt Lake to Los Angeles.* Far West and Rockies Series, vol. 2. Glendale: Arthur H. Clark Co., 1954.

————, eds. *Old Spanish Trail: Santa Fe to Los Angeles.* Far West and Rockies Series, vol. 1. Glendale: Arthur H. Clark Co., 1954.

Hunter, Milton R. *Brigham Young the Colonizer.* Salt Lake City: Deseret News Press, 1940.

Inventory of the County Archives of Utah, no. 25. Ogden, Utah: Utah Historical Records Survey, 1940.

Iron County Centennial, 1851–1951. Salt Lake City: Daughters of Utah Pioneers, 1951.

Jackson, Donald Dean, and Mary Lee Spence, eds. *The Expeditions of John Charles Frémont.* 3 vols. Urbana: University of Illinois Press, 1970.

Jenson, Andrew. *Church Chronology.* Salt Lake City: Deseret News Press, 1914.

————. *Encyclopedic History of the Church of Jesus Christ of Latter-day Saints.* 4 vols. Salt Lake City: Deseret News Press, 1941.

————. *Latter-day Saint Biographical Encyclopedia.* 4 vols. Salt Lake City: Deseret News Press, 1920. Reprint, Salt Lake City: Western Epics, 1971.

Johnson, Don Carlos. *A Brief History of Springville, Utah.* Springville: n.p., 1900.

Johnson, G. Wesley, and David L. Schirer. *Between the Cottonwoods: Murray City in Transition.* Salt Lake City: Timpanogos Research Associates, 1992.

Jones, Daniel W. *Forty Years among the Indians.* Salt Lake City: Juvenile Instructor, 1890. Reprint, Salt Lake City: Bookcraft, 1960.

Judd, Neil A. *Archaeological Investigations at Paragonah, Utah.* Washington, D.C.: Smithsonian Institution, 1919.

Larson, Andrew Karl. *I Was Called to Dixie.* Salt Lake City: Deseret News Press, 1961.

————. *The Red Hills of November.* Salt Lake City: Deseret News Press, 1957.

Lee, John D. "Journal of the Iron County Mission." *Utah Historical Quarterly* 20 (July 1952): 253–82.

Lever, W. H. *History of Sanpete and Emery Counties, Utah.* Ogden, Utah: W. H. Lever, 1898.

Ludlow, Daniel H., ed. *Encyclopedia of Mormonism.* 5 vols. 1987. Reprint, New York: Macmillan Publishing Co., 1992.

McCune, Alice Paxman. *History of Juab County, 1847–1947.* Salt Lake City: Daughters of Utah Pioneers, 1947.

Ogden, Peter Skene. "Ogden's Journal of His Expedition to Utah, 1825." *Utah Historical Quarterly* 20 (April 1952): 159–86.

Peattie, Donald Culross. *A Natural History of Western Trees.* Boston: Houghton Mifflin Co., 1953.

Poll, Richard, Thomas Alexander, Eugene Campbell, and David E. Miller. *Utah's History.* Provo, Utah: Brigham Young University Press, 1978.

Pratt, Orson. "Interesting Items . . . from the Private Journal of Orson Pratt." *Millenial Star,* February 15, 1850.

Pratt, Parley P. (son), ed. *Autobiography of Parley P. Pratt.* 1938. Reprint, Salt Lake City: Deseret Book Co., 1985.

Remy, Jules. *A Journey to Great Salt Lake City.* 2 vols. New York: AMS Press, 1861.

Roberts, B. H. *A Comprehensive History of the Church of Jesus Christ of Latter-day Saints.* 6 vols. Salt Lake City: Deseret News Press, 1930.

Roylance, Ward J. *Utah: A Guide to the State.* Salt Lake City: Utah Arts Council, 1982.

Schindler, Harold. *Orrin Porter Rockwell: Man of God, Son of Thunder.* Salt Lake City: University of Utah Press, 1966.

Smart, Donna T., ed. *Mormon Midwife: The 1846–1888 Diaries of Patty Bartlett Sessions.* Life Writings of Frontier Women, ed. Maureen Ursenbach Beecher, vol. 2. Logan: Utah State University Press, 1997.

Smith, George D., ed. *An Intimate Chronicle: The Journals of William Clayton.* Salt Lake City: Signature Books, 1995.

Smith, Joseph. *History of the Church of Jesus Christ of Latter-day Saints.* 7 vols. and index. Salt Lake City: Deseret News Press, 1932–1970.

Sonne, Conway B. *World of Wakara.* San Antonio: Naylor Co., 1962.

Stanley, Reva. *A Biography of Parley P. Pratt: The Archer of Paradise.* Caldwell, Idaho: Caxton Printers, 1937.

Steward, Julian H. *Basin-Plateau Aboriginal Sociopolitical Groups.* Bureau of American Ethnology Bulletin 120. Washington, D.C.: U.S. Government Printing Office, 1938.

Stokes, William Lee. *Geology of Utah.* Salt Lake City: Utah Museum of Natural History and Utah Geological and Mineral Survey, 1986.

Stringham, Guy. "The Pioneer Roadometer." *Utah Historical Quarterly* 42 (summer 1974): 258–72.

Van Cott, John W. *Utah Place Names.* Salt Lake City: University of Utah Press, 1990.

Warner, Ted. J., ed. *The Dominguez-Escalante Journal.* Provo, Utah: Brigham Young University Press, 1976.

Whitney, Orson F. *History of Utah.* 4 vols. Salt Lake City: George Q. Cannon & Sons Co., 1892.

Winkler, Albert. "The Circleville Massacre: A Brutal Incident in Utah's Black Hawk War." *Utah Historical Quarterly* 55 (winter 1987): 18–19.

Wright, Norman Edward. "The Mormon Pioneer Odometers." *BYU Studies* 37 (1997–1998): 83–115.

Young, Brigham. *Discourses of Brigham Young.* 13 vols. Selected and arranged by John A. Widtsoe. Salt Lake City: Deseret Book Company, 1925.

Manuscripts and Unpublished Material

Anderson, Olive. "Sketch of the Life of John Lowry Jr., 1829–1915." Typescript. Manuscript Division, University of Utah Library, Salt Lake City, Utah.

Armstrong, John Christopher. Diary. Typescript, four leaves. Archives of the Historical Department, Church of Jesus Christ of Latter-day Saints, Salt Lake City, Utah, hereafter called LDS Church Archives.

Ashworth, Ardelle Harmon. "Stories Found in Appleton Milo Harmon's Journal," manuscript in her possession, Provo, Utah.

Bleak, James Godson. "Annals of the Southern Utah Mission." Church Historian's Office. Copied by Utah Writers Project, WPA, 1941.

Brown, John. Reminiscences and Journals. Typescript. LDS Church Archives. Also on microfilm.

Campbell, Robert Lang. Journal. Holograph. LDS Church Archives.

————. Southern Exploring Expedition Papers, 1849–1850. LDS Church Archives.

Thomas Davis. Autobiography. MSSA 2543, Utah Historical Society, 20–25.

"Diagram of the 6th Standard Parallel and Exteriors in the Territory of Utah, Surveyed by Joseph Gorlinski, U.S. Dep Sur: Under His Contract No 13 Dated January 11th, 1871." Bureau of Land Management, Salt Lake City.

Fish, Rick J. "The Southern Utah Expedition of Parley P. Pratt 1849–1850." Master's thesis, Brigham Young University, Provo, Utah, 1992.

Geneva Steel Company. Brochure. N.p., undated.

Haight, Isaac Chauncey. Journal. Holograph. Huntington Library, Pasadena, California.

Joseph Horne. "Reminiscences and Diary, 1858–1861." LDS Church Archives.

Jenson, Andrew, comp. "Sanpete Stake Historical Record." Manuscript. LDS Church Historian's Library, Salt Lake City, Utah.

Jolley, Marcia A. "History of Pioneers John Christopher Armstrong and Mary Kirkbridge Armstrong." Mormon Biographical Sketches Collection. Microfilm. LDS Church Archives.

Journal History of the Church of Jesus Christ of Latter-day Saints. Chronological collection of clippings and other information, typescript and microfilm. LDS Church Archives.

King, Volney. "Twenty Five Years in Millard County." Typescript. Territorial Capitol Museum, Fillmore, Utah, 1910.

Lemon, Abraham. "A History and Genealogy of Alexander Abraham Lemon." Typescript. LDS Church Archives.

"Map of an Exploring Expedition to the Rocky Mountains in the Year 1842 and Oregon & North California in the Years 1843–44 by Brevet Capt. J. C. Frémont of the Corps of Topographical Engineers," Bancroft Library, Berkeley, California..

Morley, Callie Olsen. "History of William and Myra Mayall Henrie: Pioneers of 1847 and 1848." Typescript in possession of editors. Also in LDS Church Archives.

Pratt, Parley P. Report of the Southern Exploring Expedition Submitted to the Legislative Council of Deseret, February 5, 1850. Holograph. LDS Church Archives.

Ricks, Thomas E. "History of Thomas E. Ricks." Mormon Biographical Sketches Collection. LDS Church Archives.

Tanner, Nathan. "Incidents in the Life of Nathan Tanner." LDS Church Archives.

Utah census, 1850, 1860, 1870. LDS Church Historical Library.

Index